Praise for Kate Mulgrew's

BORN WITH TEETH

Chosen as an Amazon Best Book of the Month

"A vivaciously lyrical memoir, revealing Mulgrew as a character more fascinating than any she's played."

—Natalie Beach, *O, The Oprah Magazine*

"Mulgrew swaggers endearingly across its pages, her 'able and hardy constitution' ever on display as she powers through the many challenges—both personal and professional—that life has tossed her way. Eloquent and impassioned, *Born with Teeth* reaches beyond the standard Hollywood memoir to something more affecting and enduring....Beautifully written.... Throughout, she narrates with the grandeur of a stage diva holding court. 'Actresses. What a bunch of sad saps we are,' she intones. 'Madly in love with the child. Madly in love with the craft. Trying desperately to forge an alliance with the two, and constantly failing.' Mulgrew can be proud that this memoir, her defining monologue, proves otherwise."

—Nora Krug, *Washington Post*

"A powerful, beautifully written piece of work."

—Heidi Stevens, *Chicago Tribune*

"The story behind the actress is more dramatic than anything she's played on screen....Mulgrew pulls back the curtain on her own life with an honesty that's raw and refreshing."

—National Public Radio

"Resistance is futile. You will fall in love with this wonderful memoir. You will read it, as I did, all in one sitting. You will press it into the hands of friends, saying, 'You must read this now.' You already know Kate Mulgrew as an actress of fierce intelligence and blinding charisma. *Born with Teeth* is exactly what you might expect and more: the story of Mulgrew's brilliant and unconventional life, told with elegance and humor, and underpinned by that same intelligence that underpins each and every one of her performances."

—Joanna Rakoff, author of *My Salinger Year*

"Mulgrew has a big story to tell—several stories, actually—and she tells it with a straightforward lyricism that made me think immediately of Patti Smith's *Just Kids* and Frank McCourt's *Angela's Ashes*. It's that good."

—Joanna Connors, *Cleveland Plain Dealer*

"Stunningly candid about everything from the search for her daughter to aging in Hollywood, the actress…brings it *all* in her arresting new memoir."   —Mary Green, *People*

"Gorgeous.…Deeply personal, and shockingly revealing."

—Kevin Fallon, *Daily Beast*

"I was blindsided by the fierce intensity, intelligence, and grace of this memoir. *Born with Teeth* is gorgeously written, breathtakingly honest, and impossible to put down."

—Augusten Burroughs, author of *Running with Scissors*

"The perfectly titled *Born with Teeth* is a moving, artful memoir. Kate Mulgrew is a fierce and brilliant talent, both on the stage and on the page, and I'm filled with admiration for this wonderful book."   —Haven Kimmel, author of *A Girl Named Zippy*

"It seems unfair that such a talented actress is also such a talented writer."   —Gwen Ihnat, *The Onion A.V. Club*

"Candid, jaunty...and written with a marvelous flair for anecdote and detail."

—Joe McGovern, *Entertainment Weekly*

"Mulgrew's voice is engaging and funny.... Reading about her life, which contains real trauma as well as success, is like being told stories by a good friend over drinks. She takes you behind the scenes onstage and off, and it's a fascinating journey."

—Jenn Northington, *Book Riot*

"From the start, Mulgrew's voice jumps off the page, her prose bold, informal, and at times effervescent as she cracks open her eccentric and ebullient world.... *Born with Teeth* jumps spectacularly from tale to trial, each approached with abandon and honesty. Reading it feels like joining a friend on a spontaneous adventure that extends to another day, another party, another trip, leaving you breathless and unable to do anything but follow."

—Christine Thomas, *Miami Herald*

"In this superb and beautifully written memoir of life, love, and laughter interspersed with devastating crashes into darkness, Mulgrew keeps us looking for the rainbow. Honest, gritty, and hilarious, *Born with Teeth* leaves us thinking how nice it would be to call Kate Mulgrew a friend."

—Malachy McCourt, author of
A Monk Swimming

"*Born with Teeth* goes far deeper than the everyday life and struggles of an emerging actress.... Throughout, Mulgrew is brazenly honest. She is a woman filled with passion. She falls in and out of love, she makes mistakes, she goes after what she wants and builds her career, and if that makes her controversial, then so be it. She reveals this all without shame, and while her tone may be familiar, the character behind it is a brave one."

—Chelsea Langford, *Kirkus Reviews*

"She has formidable literary skill herself, as she makes clear from the first page of her book (I defy anyone not to fall for her from the first lines)." —Cahir O'Doherty, *Irish Voice*

"Mulgrew's enjoyable narrative is compelling as she portrays her decades of acting work, personal triumphs and heartbreaks, and her mesmerizing life." —Sally Bryant, *Library Journal*

"Richly descriptive and relatable, *Born with Teeth* will make you a fan of Mulgrew." —Marisa Spyker, *Coastal Living*

"Engaging." —Colette Bancroft, *Tampa Bay Tribune*

"Breathtakingly honest." —Viv Groskop, *The Telegraph* (UK)

"If you've seen Kate Mulgrew holding down the bridge of the USS *Voyager* as Captain Kathryn Janeway on *Star Trek: Voyager,* or watched her controlling Litchfield Penitentiary as Galina (Red) Reznikov on *Orange Is the New Black,* you'll know that she is, to use her own words, 'one tough cookie.' But if you read her powerful new memoir, *Born with Teeth,* you'll discover that cookie has bittersweet frosting.
—Richard Ouzounian, *Toronto Star*

BORN
WITH
TEETH

A MEMOIR

KATE MULGREW

BACK BAY BOOKS
LITTLE, BROWN AND COMPANY
New York • Boston • London

Back Bay Books / Little, Brown and Company
Hachette Book Group
1290 Avenue of the Americas, New York, NY 10104
littlebrown.com

Originally published in hardcover by Little, Brown and Company,
April 2015
First Back Bay trade paperback edition, January 2016

Back Bay Books is an imprint of Little, Brown and Company, a division
of Hachette Book Group, Inc. The Little, Brown name and logo are
trademarks of Hachette Book Group, Inc.

Certain names and identifying characteristics have been changed.

The quotation on page xiii is from *The Rubaiyat of Omar Khayyam*,
translated by Edward FitzGerald.

The publisher is not responsible for websites (or their content) that are
not owned by the publisher.

The Hachette Speakers Bureau provides a wide range of authors for
speaking events. To find out more, go to www.hachettespeakersbureau.com
or call (866) 376-6591.

ISBN 978-0-316-33431-0 (HC) / 978-0-316-33929-2 (LP) /
978-0-316-33432-7 (PB)
LCCN 2015930445

10 9 8 7 6 5

LSC-C

Printed in the United States of America

For Beth,
who always met me there

Contents

Photographs

The Bird of Time has but a little way
To fly—and lo! The Bird is on the Wing.

—Omar Khayyam, Rubai 7
(from my mother's secret box of sayings)

BORN
WITH
TEETH

Langworthy Avenue

I started out in a green house with a red door in a small town, where mysteries abounded. Immediately after issuing me into the world, my mother took me to this house and put me in a shoebox, which she placed on the dining room table so that one and all might come and gaze upon my perfect miniature beauty. Hands like starfish, to hear her tell it, grave but ravishing cornflower-blue eyes, and, most remarkable of all, a set of baby teeth. Two pearls on top and two, nonpareil, on the bottom. Shakespeare, my mother said, would have a field day. The neighborhood ladies were not impressed and stood there in silent judgment with arms crossed over pregnant stomachs. It wasn't good form to crow about your child's beauty, especially considering the vast numbers of children that populated those

Irish-German households. My mother, however, was undaunted and maintained her frantic vigil until she convinced herself that I, her first daughter, was growing even tinier than I had been at birth. Alarmed, she rushed me to the hospital and demanded that I be incubated. Dr. Sharp, her obstetrician, shook his head but to no avail. And so it was that in that strange aquarium of light and warmth, my mother's face pressed against the glass, I developed a constitution that could only ever be described as able and hardy.

My father observed my growing appetite for solid food with ill-concealed contempt. "Jesus. H. Christ," he would mutter as I shoved yet another fistful of banana pudding into my mouth, "I'm going to the Lux Club for a belt." Of course, the Lux Club at happy hour was thick with young Catholic fathers looking for a quick reprieve before heading home to their harried wives and hordes of screaming children. These strapping Irish boys would then stumble home to find the madhouse magically transformed into an oasis of quiet, children tucked in, dishes done, the lovely young wife lying achingly still in the bed. He might whisper "Shhh" if she started to turn and then, oh so quickly, the nightgown was up over her thighs and the deed was done in a lightning flash so that neither he nor she could ever remember with nostalgia the actual moment in which any of their children was conceived.

My father was not surprised when Dr. Sharp visited and announced that I would need a special crib, one with bars on all sides as well as over the top because would you believe it, said the good doctor, but this kid has no sense of pain. Mother was delighted by the novelty of this condition and stood stoically by as my baby teeth were pulled, quickly and without incident, so as to prevent my eating them. I was too young to wink with intention, but I like to think I caught my father's eye as he pulled on his overcoat and invoked yet again the name of his secret friend, Jesus. H. Christ.

Babies appeared with maddening regularity. The bassinette, to my horror, was constantly emptied of one baby and filled with another. This was a sleight of hand I simply could not grasp, and yet I was told sternly that this was my younger brother Joe and to always rely on my older brother, Tom, and to hold this newest one gently and quietly because she was just an infant and her name was Maggie. I was given a bottle and told to feed this baby while the other kids went streaking out the front door to the Odd Lot across the street, where all the neighborhood children were at play. Screams of pleasure and abandon pierced the living room where I sat in an armchair holding my baby sister, who seemed to me quite leaden, swathed, as she was, in thick cotton blankets. My resentment blossomed into rage when it dawned on me that I was not to be allowed my freedom that afternoon, that I was, in fact, being held prisoner by this lump of obligation called a sister and that not only had my siblings abandoned me but my mother had, as well.

With growing fury, I rose and carried the baby into the kitchen, where I placed her on the countertop. I then took the bottle, unscrewed the lid, and poured the milk into the sink. At four years of age, I was sturdy and capable, or so my mother clearly thought, besetting me with duties far beyond my ken. My mother would pay for this injustice, and she would come to appreciate that I not only needed but deserved to play with the other kids, at dusk, in the Odd Lot. With hatred and precision I turned the faucet on, and when the water ran cold, I filled the bottle up. I gathered Maggie and the bottle in my arms and trudged back to the armchair, where, without hesitation, I fed my little sister the bottle of ice-cold water that would kill her.

When my mother at last came home and retrieved her baby, I struggled to tell her that it was I who had dealt the deathblow, which was why Maggie now lay in her crib silent and inert. I desperately wanted to confess to this homicide and clear my conscience, but my mother would have none of it and shooed me out the door to join my friends in what was left of the day's play.

The next morning, I crept into the nursery and on tiptoe peered closely at my sister. Maggie gazed at me with mild eyes and gurgled as only very sentient babies do. At that moment, I heard peals of laughter emanating from the basement and raced out of the room and down the stairs. The sound of my mother's laughter was the sound I lived for, because it was absolute, and good. I found her doubled over, clutching her sides, tears streaming down her cheeks as she pointed helplessly at the walls. Months before, my mother had painted the walls of the basement with murals depicting popular fairy tales and nursery rhymes: "The Three Little Pigs," "Little Red Riding Hood," "Mary Had a Little Lamb," "Jack and the Beanstalk," and, of course, "Sleeping Beauty." The murals were very clever because my mother had been an artist before she had married my father and become an indentured servant, however glorified.

"Look, Kitten, look!" she cried, pulling me by the hand until I was just inches from the Three Little Pigs. Only then did I realize that a P-51 Mustang bomber had been painted to indicate the imminent annihilation of not only the Three Little Pigs, but when I looked to the opposite wall I saw that Little Red Riding Hood had a missile suspended directly over her head and that Jack was clinging with particular fervor to the beanstalk as bomber after bomber dove from beneath my mother's fluffy clouds, threatening to destroy the idyllic landscape. Some wicked-looking soldiers had been painted peering out from behind a barn, one of whom, wearing a helmet, held a rifle to the little lamb's head, and yet another leered at Little Red Riding Hood, all of which seemed to delight my mother and kept her, as she herself would say, in veritable stitches.

When my father came home after his daily nip at the Lux Club, my mother gave him the cold shoulder and said, "Boy, are you in trouble." He grinned sheepishly, which I thought an inappropriate response to my mother's obvious displeasure. We were put to bed early that night, but when I was sure my brothers and sister were fast asleep I stole out of my little bed and worked my way stealthily down the stairs. I discovered my parents in the basement, their shapes only partly visible in the dimly lit room, but it was clear that they were holding on to each other and that their faces were very close together and that my father was grinning, and my mother was laughing until suddenly, and for no reason at all, they pressed their faces together and stayed like that for a long, long time.

Desire and disillusion created the chiaroscuro of my parents' early marriage. Just a year earlier my mother had danced with Jack Kennedy at the Inaugural Ball and, despite her advanced pregnancy, the president had pulled her close and, smiling, whispered in her ear, "You missed your chance, Jik."

But Catholic girls from good families don't miss chances; they dodge bullets and slowly relinquish their dreams. They go to Mass and wait for a miracle and aren't terribly surprised when it arrives in the shape of a handsome young man with modest ambition, dry wit, and honorable intentions. In gratitude for this miracle, the young woman will curb her passions with a sharp discipline, she will pack her bags with nothing of the trousseau she had been promised, she will leave a world of fortune and entitlement, and she will travel a very long way to a remote city in Iowa, where she will be met at the train by her mother-in-law, an elegant woman dressed in a chartreuse silk suit, who will extend her hand and say, "I would prefer it if you called me Mrs. Mulgrew."

In Dubuque, Iowa, the green house with the red door was unconventional. Inside lived a woman who came from the East, a striking young woman with auburn hair, freckles, and a ready laugh, who was often seen in the company of her very good-looking and charming husband, and though they were christened Joan Virginia and Thomas James, they were known as Jiki and Ace, and they knew how to drink, how to dance, how to talk, and how to stir up the devil.

My father, intense and tightly wound, was a presence strongly felt. He wanted things to happen, and he desperately wanted things to happen that would please his prize of a wife. Above all, he wanted her to love him. He opened the front door at seven p.m. one Friday night to find all four of us children stark naked and screaming with delight as we jumped, one by one, down the laundry chute, bottoms splintered and foreheads bruised as we crash-landed onto an ever-growing pile of dirty clothes. In the adjoining room, he watched quietly as my mother mixed her paints and regarded her canvas with complete concentration, oblivious to the chaos surrounding her.

"How about a drink, Jik?" he asked, and she turned, slightly exasperated, and said, "Sounds like heaven."

We were left with the neighbor girl then, Kathleen McGrane, a formidable creature who came from a family of giants. Everyone knows that giants enjoy tormenting Lilliputians, but my parents were deaf to our pleas as they bundled themselves into heavy coats and drove away, not once looking back. They drove far into the countryside on a frostbitten winter's night until they found an isolated tavern, a neon sign beckoning in the darkness. The door swung open, and the place greeted them in silence, these good-looking, high-spirited travelers from town.

These people were country folk, and they didn't like anything too fancy, too smart, or too different. My parents were decidedly different, and this was instantly acknowledged when my mother, instead of sliding properly into a booth, slipped onto a barstool and, turning to the fellow next to her, said, "What are you drinking to cut the ice?"

The fellow at first blushed, then, startled by his own insecurity, grew suddenly bold and ordered the bartender to get the "little lady" a drink, which she immediately accepted, and when she raised her glass to clink with his, the man threw back his head and laughed. In very short order, there were many drinks and many clinks and the jukebox lit up and the country-man wanted my mother to dance and so she did but she didn't like his style, which was rough and overreaching, and that was when she called out for my father to save her, but when my father, laughing, intervened, the rough man turned purple and, before there was even a second's grace, fists were flying, chairs were overturned, and it was a real down-and-dirty, place-your-bets bar fight. My father was the victor and my little mother, cheeks blazing and blood racing, bundled him into the car and took the wheel, peeling out of that parking lot like there was no tomorrow.

Once home, my mother ministered to my father's wounds, medication in the form of many whiskeys was taken and so too, in the end, was the nurse, who found my father's black eye and bloody nose absolutely irresistible.

On a Sunday morning two weeks later, the house was curiously still. My father lay in bed much later than usual. I was in the kitchen doing what I did best, foraging for food. The boys were outside raising hell and my mother seemed to be hiding. I did not find her in the basement, at her painting, or in the backyard at the clothesline or in the living room, reading her book. I slowly climbed the stairs to the second floor, thinking

I might discover her stealing a quiet moment for a bath, but the bathroom was empty. Suddenly, I heard a soft noise, one with which I was unfamiliar but that nonetheless sent a chill through me and made me stand very, very still, as if frozen in place. From where I stood, I could see into my parents' bedroom, and in the half-light I could make out my mother's form, bending over Maggie's crib. But my mother was not touching the baby; instead she had one hand over her mouth and the other extended above her, as if reaching for someone. I heard a mangled groan and saw my father as he approached my mother, who suddenly turned and looked at him as if she didn't know him, frantically waving her arm at him as if warning him to stay away. That's when I saw the most confusing thing of all: my father stepped quickly to my mother and, pinning her arms to her sides, turned her away from the crib and, bending down, put his free hand on my little sister's neck. His head dropped for a moment, and then he straightened, gathered my mother in his arms, and carried her out of the room.

Maggie disappeared from the house and we were told nothing. Little children could not grasp the notion of death. Nevertheless, at the age of four I felt my mother's growing distance and I became her constant shadow, sometimes even demanding that she put me in her lap, and so she would, whereupon I would take her hand and place it deliberately over my own so that I could play with her slender wristwatch and imagine that I was, if only for a moment, in charge of my mother's happiness. The crib was removed from the master bedroom, and all of Maggie's clothing was stored in a bin, which my father sealed and put away in the attic. A week later, he came across my mother in the laundry room, where she had long ago organized individual cubbies in which to place each child's clothes. Each cubby had a name colorfully painted on it, to identify the owner. My father watched as my mother, leaning over a bin, extracted one article of clothing after another, which she carefully folded and refolded and then placed in the cubby painted with the name MAGGIE.

She looked at him, smiled, and went back to her work.

Some weeks later, my father and my grandmother decided to send my mother on a cruise. My father bought my mother new dresses and a new coat, not only to accommodate her fifth pregnancy but because she had become so thin, having subsisted for weeks on a diet of cigarettes and coffee. I can't remember whether she kissed me good-bye or not, but it didn't matter because I knew I would be spending many days alone in my room, watching the other kids playing in the Odd Lot, secure in the knowledge that it was I, and I alone, who had killed my sister Maggie that fateful day when I had forced the ice water into her lungs.

I had tried to tell my mother, but she wouldn't listen. And now it was too late.

Derby Grange

To atone for his sins, and the regularity with which he committed them, my father drove into the countryside one Sunday afternoon when I was six years old and did something marvelous. He bought a house. Certainly, it was a gift for his wife, who had tired of town life and longed for solitude, surrounded, as she was, by an ever-deepening pool of offspring. To add to the first three, my father had committed two new sins, whom they called Laura and Tessie and who had arrived so quickly and unceremoniously it was as if they were pulled out of a hat. Perhaps that was my father's intention: a magic trick so dazzling that my mother would be forced to shake off her sadness and leave the memory of Maggie behind.

As it turned out, we left everything we'd known behind and traveled what seemed great distances, across highways, through valleys, and onto curious and foreign gravel roads until suddenly we came upon a place so vast and beautiful as to appear unreal. We were very little — Tom, Joe, Laura, Tess, and me —

but even very small children know paradise when they see it, and this was paradise. The driveway led up to a big brick house with a wide front porch that opened onto a sweeping lawn studded with magnificent trees. There were cornfields to the right as far as the eye could see and, to the left, a shadowy glen that we would learn turned into a secret timberland, and beyond that timberland, a ribbon of creek wound its way over hills and through valleys of untamed farmland.

The house had been built in the 1850s, Italianate in design, with high ceilings and clean, stately lines. It contained surprises of every kind, awe-inspiring novelties such as a maid's room and a stairway for servants, wooden shutters that closed over floor-to-ceiling windows, a basement cool and deep, full of dark corners and secret caves.

Upstairs, there were five bedrooms and a long, curved stairway with a smooth mahogany banister that served as the main artery to the downstairs, in which every room had a distinct purpose. The "good" living room eventually evolved into a formal living room, but in the beginning it is where we all slept, camp-style, in sleeping bags on the floor. There was a comfortable middle room that we dubbed the "TV room" because the single television set we owned but were never allowed to watch was put in there to serve as a reminder of a dream that might come true if only we behaved like perfect children, along with the stereo set, all of Mother's books, a complete set of *Encyclopaedia Britannica*, and my father's prize photograph of a Sioux Indian chief who had swallowed a bumblebee. The dining room, airy and graceful, had windows on all sides, and almost every room boasted a fireplace, which, to us, was unspeakably thrilling. The main kitchen led into the summer kitchen, which was tenuously attached to the house, and then, beyond the back door and very close to the big house, was another, smaller house, which we immediately christened the Ghost House, and beyond this a chicken coop, an apple orchard, and a red barn with a silo.

This modest estate was called Derby Grange. My father had stumbled across the place on one of his Sunday drives, had been invited in for a drink, and left four hours and twenty-one thousand dollars later the proud owner of not only the house but also the forty acres of land that surrounded it. Because of this unexpected and astounding gift, I instantly and unconditionally forgave my father all of his sins and, in fact, decided that it was the one place on earth capacious and beautiful enough to accommodate all of my siblings, despite their shortcomings.

During the day Tom, Joe, and I attended the one-room schoolhouse down the road called, appropriately, the Derby Grange School. In it, six grades of children matriculated in short rows consisting of no more than five chairs each. Ellen Birch, tall and peculiar, stared at us with unblinking black eyes from her lonely solo seat in the fifth grade. In the back, there was an outhouse, inglorious and filthy, and, for recess, a small yard with a swing set. A dirt ditch marked the school boundary. Mrs. Hartley was the teacher for all six grades, a jolly woman whom my brother Tom wooed with large jars of mayonnaise spiked with ketchup. He got straight As. I, however, did not, because next to me sat the infamous Peggy Hickey, who was forever whispering nonsense in my ear but who nonetheless brought a lunch box to school so full of delightful things that I couldn't help but respond to her incessant questions and even managed to overlook the fact that she allegedly wore a diaper instead of underpants, so desperate was I for a nibble of anything that resembled real food.

At home, my little mother went about the business of making Derby Grange her own, but maybe because she herself was so petite and because she smoked incessantly and drank endless cups of coffee, dinner was always a disappointment. The fanfare that preceded the event, however, was executed with élan every night.

If it was chicken and rice, we were going to Seville! If it was overcooked meatloaf and undersized mashed potatoes, it nonetheless came from a Craig Claiborne recipe, so pretend you're eating at the 21 Club in New York! And if it was fish sticks, tepid brown pellets served on a cookie sheet every Friday night, she'd sigh and say, "I didn't make the rules." So much anticipation, and so little actual food. We never saw bread or fruit or sweets of any kind, and one small chicken divided among five starving children did not the trick do. We were always hungry, so much so that Mother tempered our appetites with criticism. "Joe, you look like a tiny truck driver hunched over the wheel — sit up!" "Kitten, keep eating like that and you'll blow up like a balloon!" "Laura, for God's sake get out from under the table — what are you *doing* down there? Very odd child." And then, infuriatingly, "Tom, would you like to take Mrs. Hartley another jar of mayonnaise? She loves your secret concoction, doesn't she?" Followed by complicit chuckles between mother and son and accompanied by the sound of five little mouths voraciously sucking on chicken wings the size of paper clips.

We discovered other ways to subdue our hunger. My mother was never one for conventional boundaries, and so we were free to do as we liked every day after school and on weekends. We hiked for miles, we swam in Gronau's Creek, we played every conceivable kind of game our imaginations could contrive, such as seeing who could hold on longest to the electric cattle fence at Breitbachs' farm, who could jump from the hayloft into Willie Breitbach's arms without looking, who could spear the most frogs and, encouraged by my brother Tom the great wordsmith, take them home to Mother and say, "Look, Mom, a whole jar of little bastards!" We had fights with cow pies and fights with snowballs and fights to the finish. We had contests to see who could hold their breath long enough to faint, at which point we would run over and pummel the semiconscious person's chest, shouting, "Live, you must live!"

We organized freak shows over which my brother Tom presided, calling us into the neighbor kid's bedroom to observe, for only a nickel, the little guy's minute erection. We were often gone for hours, and when we would finally return home, exhausted, thirsty, and complaining of starvation, my mother would glance up from her book and say, "You should be grateful. You were born in wedlock, you're an American citizen, and you live on dry land. Now go back outside and play."

In the early years of their marriage, my father was infatuated with my mother and upon occasion was inspired to wax lyrical about his love for her. In the dead of night, we would all be awakened, hurried into winter coats and boots, and made to stand outside in the front yard in a straight line, where Dad, pointing toward Mother's bedroom window, would begin his testimonial. "In that room lies an extraordinary woman, a remarkable woman, a beautiful woman. She is the woman I love. And she is your mother." We needed to bear witness to his devotion until the bitter end, at which time, white with cold, we were sent off to our beds with a fond if brusque dismissal, leaving our father still standing there, face upturned toward her light.

One afternoon, while my father was at work, I heard my mother's voice from upstairs, calling to me: "Katy Kitten Kat Mulgrew, get up these stairs, quickly!" I ran up the stairs and saw my mother standing in the bathroom just off the landing. She beckoned me to come in and indicated that I should close the door behind me. Then, pointing to the toilet basin, she said: "I need you to bear witness." The bright crimson toilet bowl was full of strange clumps of dark brown debris. Mother stood over the basin and, making the Sign of the Cross, said, "I baptize you in the name of the Father, and of the Son, and of the Holy

Ghost. Amen." She flushed the toilet. "I'm going to lie down for a minute, Kitten," my mother said, "I'm having a sinking spell."

Soon enough, however, another little face peered out from within the bassinette. My parents named him Sam, and he was a quiet baby, towheaded and serious. We older kids never paid much attention to who was in the bassinette, since obviously such a creature could make little if any contribution to the tribal elders, an elite group consisting of Tom and me with the occasional bone thrown to Joe, whose volatility often had us elders on tenterhooks.

In the second grade, I fell in love with a plump-cheeked, bespectacled boy named George, whose quiet, serious demeanor intrigued me. So entranced was I by his eyeglasses, and the fact that not only adults but evidently little kids could wear them, that I didn't see Peggy Hickey pumping hard on the swing and flying toward me like a bat out of hell, and before I knew it I was out for the count, blood streaming from my forehead.

My mother, upon being notified, asked if someone would walk me home, and when I arrived, she applied a Band-Aid to the wound and told me to lie down and take a nap. She had a friend over for lunch, and this woman, the mother of sixteen children, took one look at me and said, "Joan, this girl needs stitches and she needs them now!" Whereupon we set off on an adventure that resulted in twelve stitches sewn laboriously into my brow and a nice doctor who said to my mother, "Your daughter's lucky—another inch and she'd be missing an eye." When we got into the car to drive home, she pulled out of the hospital parking lot and said, "I think that doctor was a bit of a flirt, don't you?"

In the third grade, we had a new teacher called Mrs. Rideras. She was tall with pitch-black hair and a nice, if slightly severe, manner. She was no Mrs. Hartley, that's for sure, as my brother quickly learned when he attempted to dazzle her with his culinary masterpiece. "Pink mayonnaise? Oh no, Tommy, I don't think so." Mrs. Rideras sat at her desk, instead of strolling among us as Mrs. Hartley used to do, and she had insisted that a phone be installed in the classroom in case of emergencies.

One day the phone rang, and Mrs. Rideras picked it up. "Derby Grange schoolhouse, this is Mrs. Rideras." Twenty-five faces looked up expectantly, each hoping that it was an emergency requiring his or her immediate dismissal from school. At first, we were perplexed by Mrs. Rideras's silence—weren't phone calls supposed to work both ways? She held the phone rigidly to her ear and then, reacting as if someone had actually hit her, Mrs. Rideras winced, her eyes filled with tears, and, after what seemed an eternity, she whispered, "I see. Yes, I see." She put the phone down and, turning to the class, said, "Go home, children. The president of the United States has been shot, and you must all go home."

Assuming a solemnity we neither understood nor truly felt, we all left the schoolhouse and made our respective ways home. There were no cars and no buses. Everyone walked. Our house was a quarter of a mile down the road, and we walked toward it slowly, sensing that what awaited us would not be good. When we arrived at the stone gates, we were surprised to see the driveway filled with cars. We entered through the back door and slipped into the kitchen unnoticed. From there, we could observe what was happening in the living room. The scene was disturbing. My father was the Dubuque County Democratic chairman, and it was not unusual to see him in the company of his political cronies, but it was extremely rare, and very unsettling, to see so many men gathered together in a confined space, watching the television in the middle of a weekday. They stood in absolute silence, their faces riveted to the screen. The room was thick with cigarette smoke.

I crept past them, through the kitchen and dining room, and it was then that I saw my mother. She was alone, perched at the top of the stairs. One hand was under her chin, elbow on knee, and the other grasped a banister rail.

Her hair was unkempt, and she was wearing a soiled apron that only slightly concealed the omnipresent pregnancy, but what struck me most was the look in her eye when I called up to her. It was a look I had seen once before and would see only once again in years to come, and it was a look that so frightened me, I actually could not move toward her.

Blank, vacant, empty eyes looked not at me but past me, and I knew my mother was lost in a memory I could never understand, nor ever be allowed to share. Some ancient sadness behind her eyes made me feel utterly helpless and alone. She wasn't my mother in that moment; she was someone else entirely, a stranger to whom my existence mattered not at all.

My mother attended the president's funeral and returned a week later, just in time to have her eighth baby. This time, she stayed in the hospital longer than she had with any of her other deliveries, but what was most troubling was the appearance of a young farm girl at the back door one afternoon, a plain straw-haired girl who carried a suitcase and said her name was Dora Lamb and could she please come in. My father escorted this girl into the kitchen and introduced her as "a mother's helper." She was to live in the maid's room and, evidently, she was going to "help" our mother.

When my mother came home, we all gathered in the front yard to greet her. Dad helped her out of the car and, smiling, she walked toward us carrying a pink bundle in one arm and a shopping bag in the other. She turned to Dora Lamb, transferred the pink bundle to her arms, and said, "Her name is Jenny. Good luck." Then she went into the house, all of us trailing behind her like ducklings, and when she reached the

TV room, she took off her coat, reached into the shopping bag, and withdrew what looked like a large jar of preserves.

She then proceeded to pull an ottoman over to the fireplace, and, in one deft move, she jumped onto it, kissed the jar, and placed it with two hands dead center on the mantelpiece. "I think I'd like a drink!" she called to my father, and sailed into the kitchen. We all ran to the fireplace, mad with curiosity, and, climbing onto whatever pieces of furniture we could find, examined the mysterious jar. It was filled with amber liquid in which were floating my mother's ovaries, which, just before she'd gone under, she had instructed Dr. Sharp to "pickle."

On the ride home, she had taken out one of her felt pens and, on a broad strip of medical tape she had stolen from the operating room in which her hysterectomy had been performed, she had written in bold black ink: FROM WHENCE YOU SPRANG.

My parents decided that the Derby Grange schoolhouse was somehow insufficient to meet our intellectual needs, and so we were transferred to the local Catholic grammar school, which was called, disturbingly, Resurrection. A flat and unprepossessing building, it sat amid acres of farmland and had little to recommend it, from my point of view, other than a small woman named Sister Benedict, who taught the fifth grade and who first recognized in me the poet I longed to become. She was a plain woman with a severe overbite and kind, beautiful brown eyes. The sisters often attended Mass with the parishioners, and one Sunday I was keenly aware of Sister Benedict's watchful eyes on my family. My father knelt at one end of the pew and next to him, in various states of regrettable posture, were Tom, Joe, Laura, Tess, Sam, Jenny, myself, and, finally, Mother, who was not kneeling at all but instead sat on the bench with legs crossed, a thermos of coffee open beside her, and in her hands a book entitled *The Ethics of Spinoza*. The next day at school, Sister Benedict stopped me in the hall and said, "Your mother's a very interesting person, isn't she? Maybe you'd like to invite her to the poetry contest next week. She seems like the kind of person who might enjoy that."

Home I went, full of happy anticipation. When I told my mother that not only had I been writing poetry on the sly but that it appeared my poems were of exceptional quality because Sister Benedict had chosen me, out of the entire fifth grade, to compete in the Resurrection School Annual Poetry Contest that was to be held the following week. "Not only that, Mom," I said, "but she wants you to come and hear me recite my poems."

My mother cocked her head and, looking at me curiously, said, "I think have something for you, Kitty Kat girl." I followed her up the front stairs to her bedroom, where she kept a collection of her favorite books in a corner bookshelf near the window. She pulled out a slim volume with a blue-and-white cover and handed it to me. "This is a terrific poem about World War One by the writer Alice Duer Miller, and it's called *The White Cliffs*. I think when you've finished reading your original poems, you should surprise the nuns and just sail right into this one and see what happens. Fun, don't you think?"

My mother's idea of fun was a fifty-page poem about an American girl and an English aristocrat who meet in London on the eve of World War I and fall in love. We follow the young woman's narrative through romance, marriage, childbirth, war, the death of her husband, and, finally, into her middle age, at which point she stands overlooking the White Cliffs of Dover and says:

I am American bred
I have seen much to hate here — much to forgive,
But in a world where England is finished and dead,
I do not wish to live.

On the afternoon of the poetry contest, we were all led into the school auditorium (which doubled as the cafeteria) and told to take our seats as designated. The nuns and priests and a few of the ladies who worked the lunch shift sat on one side of the room, and the entire rest of the school body sat on the other. We, the poets, were given seats of honor in the very front row. The program began, and I sat stiffly through what I considered several really boring readings of very bad poems until, at last, my name was called. I walked to the podium with my sheaf of poems in hand and looked out over the crowd: kids of all ages and sizes, girls in ill-fitting uniforms and boys sporting John Deere caps, most of whom were making inappropriate sounds and fidgeting wildly in their metal chairs. On the other side of the room, the nuns and priests regarded me in austere silence. Suddenly, something at the back of the room caught my eye, and in a moment of tremendous relief and joy, I recognized my mother in her ubiquitous gray sweater, a red kerchief tied around her hair, leaning casually against the door. She acknowledged me with a small smile and a covert rolling of her hand, which I had been trained to understand meant, *Get on with it!*

After I read my five original poems, I eagerly awaited the response of my audience, but there was none. Sister Benedict clapped once or twice out of Christian charity, but other than that, it was dead quiet. At that moment, I pulled *The White Cliffs* from my blazer pocket and, taking a deep breath and without explanation, began to read. I didn't stop until I had read the whole thing. When I was finished, I looked up and realized, with a pang, that my mother was no longer standing in the back of the room. She had moved closer and now stood next to the row of nuns, and she was clapping. The nuns were applauding, too, but something else was happening that I found even more disconcerting—most of the nuns had tears streaming down their cheeks! Sister Mary Elizabeth was laughing and crying simultaneously, and Sister Benedict was standing, clapping delightedly, and beaming with pride.

On the way home, my mother was silent. This did not bode well, I knew, and although I was devastated, I turned my back to her and, feigning indifference, stared out the window as we drove past Gronau's Creek and started up the long gravel road toward home. Just as we were about to drive through the stone gates, my mother suddenly switched off the ignition and turned to face me. "You know, Kitten, I watched you today, and it dawned on me that you can either be a mediocre poet or a great actress. Now, which do you think you'd rather be?" I didn't know what to say to her then, but as it turned out no words were necessary. The following night, I found *The Complete Works of William Shakespeare* tucked under my pillow and a note from my mother, which read: "Find what you love and the rest will follow."

I threw myself into all things dramatic, joined the community playhouse, applied to summer acting programs, and read everything I could get my hands on. With seven children between the ages of thirteen and three, the house was in a constant state of turmoil, and I learned to escape by shutting myself in my room and burying myself in books. This was a trick my mother had taught me and one that she herself had mastered to perfection. Regardless of what was happening, and on pain of death, we were not allowed to disturb her afternoon nap. Like clockwork, she would run up the stairs at two o'clock, book in hand, and spend an hour reading or sleeping.

Increasingly, though, my mother would shut herself in her room for two, even three, days at a time. She had migraine headaches, and they were so severe (she explained, when I stood by her bedside holding a wet cloth and a glass of ginger ale) that when she had them she went temporarily blind and became violently sick. The most effective antidote to these headaches was adventure. Her best friend, Jean Kennedy Smith, would call, and before we knew it, Mother was out the door and on her way to New York or Paris or London. My father did not try to stop her, but it was clear he resented these interruptions. She had to beg him for pocket money, which infuriated and embarrassed her. Often, someone else drove her to the airport.

When my mother was away, the atmosphere in the house changed. It was hard to put a finger on it: colder, emptier, less safe. My father, never one to join us for dinner, now appeared only after we were in bed, and it was evident from the way he slammed the back door and barked "Goddammit!" that he'd stopped at the Coach House and had a few belts with his pals. Often, he would pour himself a nightcap and listen to Ella Fitzgerald on the stereo. The smoke from his Pall Malls drifted up to my room.

Sometimes, I would lie in my bed and imagine him down there, sitting on the couch with his glass of scotch, listening to the blues. I wondered what he was thinking about as he sat there, hour after hour, lost in thought. I loved my father—loved his gallantry, his grace, his Irish good looks—but his quicksilver moods frightened me, and I was always slightly on my guard. Beware, something inside me always whispered. Watch out.

There came a night when the house was too still. It was dark, the moon was full, and I felt afraid. So I went downstairs and turned the knob to the TV room door, and there, illuminated by the moon, lay my father and Dora Lamb, in silhouette, on the couch. He had been lying on top of her and when he saw me cried "Jesus Christ!" and, jumping up, started after me. I was fast, but he was faster. He stood at my bedroom door, one arm blocking my way and the other extended toward me, as if in greeting. I noted with surprise that he was still holding his glass of scotch and felt contempt for my father's need to carry that glass of scotch with him as he ran upstairs to confront his twelve-year-old daughter and to plead for her understanding. He said "Kitten" then, as if that would change the game. "Kitten" had been his idea, and how like him to find a nickname that felt like a kiss every time I heard it. But I didn't want that kiss now, and in fact, the very thought that my father might step into my room terrified me, and so I said, "Don't come in here, Dad, I'm warning you. Don't come in."

"Kitten, you don't understand, it means nothing. A stupid, silly mistake and it means absolutely nothing because nothing happened. You know how much I love your mother—"

I stopped him right there. "Okay, Dad, that's enough. I need to go to bed now."

He looked at me—a soft look, a pleading look, a look that didn't belong to him—and said, "I promise you, sweetheart, this will never happen again, and it's something your mother doesn't need to know about. No point. Understood?"

"Sure, Dad, whatever you say, but now I really want to go to bed."

He looked at his scotch, as if discovering it for the first time, and then, backing away, said, "Love you, sugar." He was still standing there when I closed the door and locked it.

A few days later, my mother returned from her trip, took one look at me, and said, "Let's go to your room." It didn't take much for me to betray my father. Maybe she stroked my hair, although that's unlikely, maybe she gave me a present, maybe she even suggested an afternoon at the movies, but within minutes she had the whole story.

As I stumbled through the memory, fighting tears, she smiled at me and said, "Slow down, honey, and don't forget the details, details are crucial," and curled up on my bed like a child being read a bedtime story. When I was finished, she sighed as if she was sorry the story had ended but that it had been, nonetheless, a dish well served and, kissing me lightly on the top of my head, started downstairs. It was time to make dinner.

The next morning, I hurried into the kitchen and found my mother standing over the stove, making eggs. I looked expectantly at her, or perhaps beseechingly, but she just smiled and turned back to her cooking. It was then I heard my father coming down the stairs. He walked into the kitchen, smelling of Old Spice and strikingly handsome in a seersucker suit with a yellow-and-pink paisley tie, his thick black hair still wet from the shower. Mother looked up at him and asked, "Would you like some breakfast, Tom, or are your lips too parched too eat?" Incredibly, then, she turned and winked at me. In a flash, my father grabbed the chair next to me and, just as he was about to pick it up, my mother put her hand on his arm and, looking directly into my father's eyes, said, "I don't think so, Tom."

Without a word, my father walked out of the kitchen, got into his car, and started the ignition. He was my ride to school, there was no other way, and so I gathered my book bag and, screwing up my courage, started after him. But in the five seconds it took me to pass through the kitchen and open the back door, my father had performed yet another magic trick, this one more stunning than all the rest. He had vanished into thin air.

Tessie

After a particularly disheartening day in my freshman year of high school, in which my arrogance had once again stirred up the insecurity of my classmates and driven them to acts of ill-concealed hostility, I came home and announced to my mother that I found high school a complete waste of time, that I was going to apply for early graduation, that I had my heart set on the London Academy of Music and Dramatic Art and that nothing was going to deter me. "Very good!" my mother responded, slapping the kitchen table for emphasis. "But you'll need to get a job to cover expenses. And I couldn't agree with you more about high school. A wasteland of mediocrity. Besides which, I've always said that all boys between the ages of fifteen and twenty-five should be incarcerated."

Once I had redirected my focus, there was no time to waste. I got two jobs in quick succession: after school, I flipped burgers at Pete's Coffee Shop, and on weekends I served cocktails at the Holiday Inn. It didn't seem to faze anybody that I was underage, least of all my employer, whose only complaint was that I wore my skirt to just above my knee, rather than to the preferred panty line. I worked hard, made good tips, raced to rehearsal at the University of Dubuque, where I was a member of the Player's Club, won the lead in almost every school play, and spent my free time applying to summer acting programs.

There were boys, too, of course. All kinds. Amazing the elasticity of time when romance must be squeezed into the schedule. There was the captain of the football team, tall, good-looking, and Irish, who deceived me and broke my heart; there was the charismatic psychopath at the university who, after I slapped him for standing me up, pleaded for another chance and drove me deep into the country, where he threatened me with a crowbar and left me in the middle of a pasture, miles from nowhere.

There were the men I encountered at home, some of them friends of my father, some of them acquaintances who had just stopped by for a beer and a laugh, most of them drinkers and all of them old enough to know better, but none of them disciplined enough to resist the impulse to flirt with a precocious sixteen-year-old girl. Curiously, this neither alarmed nor dismayed my parents. "A certain je ne sais quoi," my mother said, to which my father responded, looking me dead in the eye, "Trouble."

"Trouble," in my father's vernacular, referred to anything sexual in nature. It was delicious trouble, mischievous trouble, the kind of trouble everyone longed to get into and, at Derby Grange, frequently did. There were bonfires in the front yard, conclaves in the kitchen, and a piano in the dining room, and seated at that piano was a woman whose fingers danced over the keys, long black hair falling over her tired, pretty face.

Sometimes, my father would pass through the dining room on his way to the bar and, resting a hand on her shoulder, would say, "That's the way to do it, sugar," and her eyes would light up with laughter and longing. Nancy Gilbert, we all knew, was in love with our father, but we didn't hold that against her. She had a sad, sweet manner that softened the chaos around her, and she lifted my father's mood.

My life was so full and so busy that I actually needed an assistant, but since such a notion was inconceivable I settled for the second-best option, which was a slave. An in-family slave, one who would both serve and adore, was what I wanted, and I found her in the person of my younger sister Tess. Six years my junior, she was known as the Creature, was splendidly limber, and had almond-shaped green eyes and an olive complexion, long, slender fingers, and a complicit smile. She was the perfect slave, and I was a beneficent slave driver. I allowed her free access to my room, I provided her with cigarettes, candy, and any junk food I could get my hands on, I occasionally permitted her to take a nap with me, and in exchange for all this, I expected my bed to be made, my dirty clothes to be thrown into the closet, my coffee fetched, my dialogue rehearsed (however haltingly), and an absolute and utter show of devotion and fidelity. This was our pact, and we sealed it, again and again, by playing a game in the front yard called Robe. I would let Tessie get into my long pink velour robe (which she coveted), and as she took her place at one end of the yard, I would take mine at the other. At the count of three, I would shout, "Tessie!" and she would shout, "Katie!" and we would fly toward each other until we met, and then I would take her hands and, lifting her off the ground, swing her around and around and around, screaming, "I simply *adore you!*"

Alternatively, we would lie in the grass and gaze heavenward, reciting our favorite quote from the New Testament. The goal was to deliver it in as many accents as possible within a prescribed period of time. Jesus, near death, is fed up with the thief on his right and says to the thief on his left: "You will be with me in Paradise."

My ambition knew no bounds, and I worked tirelessly toward my goal, which was to get out. I yearned to become a real actress. I lived at home, but I was already separating myself from the family. My siblings crossed my line of vision on my way out the door, to rehearsal, to the coffee shop, or into my boyfriend's car, but I seldom engaged with them. I was on a mission. Tessie alone witnessed my frustration, my anxiety, and my unrelenting longing to be free. She sat on the bed and helped me pack for Europe when I was invited to participate in the final audition process for acceptance into the London Academy of Music and Dramatic Art, and she was there when I came home, in defeat, devastated and mortified. Too young, they had said.

My father was furious with me for having ignored his telegram insisting that I return home immediately. In London, I had been introduced to Hal Bagot, the youngest member of the House of Lords, and he had invited me to his parents' home in Kent for a long weekend. Hal had no idea that I was only sixteen, but his mother, Lady Bagot, was a woman of great sensitivity, and when I appeared in the library wearing pink bell-bottoms and a black angora turtleneck, my long hair pulled back with a black velvet ribbon, she took my hand and said, "Oh, my, what an absolutely charming little American girl!" That night, at a formal dinner, I was seated far away from Hal, next to a much older man in a deep-blue uniform elaborately decorated with medals. "Now, my dear girl," he said, turning to me, "do as I do, and all shall be well. Always remember, work from the outside in, follow Lady Bagot's example, and you'll be splendid." Dinner was followed by a movie and then by dancing in the ballroom, and the following day I was put in a small open car and told that we would be following the hunt but not riding in it.

Lady Bagot had put me in the Rose Room, where my bath was drawn by a maid who laid my pajamas on the bed and placed my hairbrush on a small white cloth next to the bed.

Hal was eager to get me back to London, but I told him that my father would come after him with a shotgun if I didn't get on the next plane home.

Instead, my father gave me a punishment calculated to teach me a lesson I would never forget. Dad insisted that I attend the local women's college in Dubuque for at least a semester because, as he put it, "You're in such a goddamn hurry, you'll break your neck right out of the gate." Strangely, it didn't really matter; nothing mattered but reaching my goal. I set myself on a course and didn't look back.

My slave was always around, but I didn't always require her services. I wanted to be alone, to daydream about my escape and the world that awaited me: the work, the glory, and the promise just beyond that front yard. Once or twice, I passed Tess in the kitchen, and it struck me that she looked tired, even mournful, sitting at the kitchen table with her head in her hands. That's not like her, I'd say to myself. I'll ask her if something's bothering her when I get home.

But she was always asleep when I got home, or it would simply slip my mind. Sometimes, she complained of headaches, but this she would do sotto voce because it was an unspoken rule in our house that children didn't get sick, that hypochondria was unacceptable and would not be tolerated. We understood this and toughed it out most of the time, although there had been some close calls over the years.

There was the time that Joe fell on the ice and punctured his thigh, at which point Mother told him to put some salve on it and go to bed. When he woke up, the wound had become infected, and his leg looked like someone had wound a purple ribbon around it, a sign of imminent septicemia. They made it to the emergency room just in time. On another occasion Tom, from fifty yards away, threw a dart at Joe and hit him in the back of the neck, and when Joe staggered into the house howling for Mother, she reached up, plucked the dart from his neck, and said, "Don't be a baby. Put some salve on it and go back outside." And I would have to live forever with the memory of the mortifying incident of my faux pneumonia. I was having trouble breathing—does it matter why?—and evidently the medical staff agreed because I was put into the hospital under an oxygen tent, and when I looked up from my bed, I saw my mother leaning against the doorway, and the look on her face said it all: *I hope you're enjoying this, Sarah Bernhardt, because it's going to be all over in the morning.*

Outsiders regarded my mother's inability to cope with sickness as a kind of sickness itself, but then, no one understood my mother like I did, and very few were privy to her history, which explained everything. My maternal grandmother had died in childbirth when my mother was just three years old, whereupon my grandfather quickly remarried a woman named Alfreda, who was beautiful, glacial, and utterly self-absorbed. My mother was sent to a convent boarding school where she met a plump little girl by the name of Jean Kennedy.

This little girl became her best friend and saved my mother's life by taking her home for Christmas holidays in Boston and long summer vacations in Hyannis. They were wonderful to my mother, the Kennedys, but even their glorious largesse could not make up for what my mother secretly yearned for: a mother of her own.

To that end, my mother approached me one day and asked me to sit and have a cup of coffee with her in the kitchen. "How old are you now, Kitten?" my mother asked, as if we were second cousins who had come across each other at a family picnic.

I sighed heavily and said, "I am fifteen years old, Mother."

She tapped my hand lightly with her fingers and, looking out the window, said, "You know, I've missed having a mother. It's a gaping hole. I think having a mother is one of the great things in life—one of the only things that can save you. I'm always looking for my mother and, frankly, Kitten, it's becoming exhausting, so I thought I'd ask you if *you* would be my mother. You just have that way about you. You're not really what anyone would call a typical daughter, but I think you have exactly what it takes to be a mother. Don't you think it's a good idea?"

I was flattered, I was appalled, and accustomed as I was to her eccentricities, I was rendered temporarily speechless when suddenly, as if God had taken a moment out of His busy day to check in, the phone rang. I picked it up and, looking at Mother, whispered, "It's Father O'Rourke." She jumped up, made the *not home* gesture (a quick slash across the neck with the right hand), and pantomimed that I should hang up.

"Jeez, Mother, what's going on?" I asked. "Are you and Father O'Rourke having a fight?" Kevin O'Rourke was the head of the archdiocese, a big, strapping Irish priest with a penchant for power, palaver, and seduction.

A long, long pause, then my mother spoke: "That's something else you're going to have to handle, if you're going to be my mother."

I shook my head in disbelief. My mother laughed. A short laugh, devoid of mirth, followed by a keening sigh. Oh, I said to myself as my heart sank, my mother's in trouble. Big trouble.

Father O'Rourke had many names, which made him seem very important. To the community, he was Father Kevin, over drinks with my parents in the front yard he was Dave, and when Mother and I were alone together, and she needed to talk, he was Star.

"He thinks he's a big star, Kitten," Mother said, staring out the kitchen window, "so that will be our code for him from now on.

Star!" We laughed, thinking of all the wonderful, devious ways we could make fun of him using our secret name. My mother again looked out the window. "I could kill him," she whispered, and then, looking at me, said, "I must be out of my mind."

The kitchen table served not only as a confessional but as a theater. It was where everyone's mood was on display. Food was the one common interest that both united and betrayed. It told the truth of who we were while we were eating it, and the process, though loud and unruly, was always honest. We needed to eat as expeditiously and efficiently as possible, in order to get the maximum bang for our buck. At breakfast one morning, it was puzzling to see that Tess was not eating and that she had actually pushed her plate aside and was, once again, holding her head in her hands.

"Eat your eggs, Tessie, or I'll give them to Sam!" Mother threatened from where she stood behind the counter.

Twelve-year-old Tessie looked up, took her hands from her face, and said, "I have a headache, Mom, I told you."

A pause, and then Mother said, "If you keep crossing your eyes like that, they'll stay that way, so stop it."

But Tessie couldn't stop it, neither the crossed eyes nor the headaches that attended them. Exasperated, my mother said, "Okay, I'm going to take you to the doctor and then we'll settle this nonsense once and for all."

Mother and Tess didn't come home that night, and neither did my father, and the next day we were told that they had taken Tess to the Mayo Clinic in Minnesota.

It seemed a very long time before we finally saw Dad's car coming down the gravel road, and I have little recollection of what Tess looked like or what was said, but that was the moment when we all understood that something irreparable had happened and that Tessie would never be the same again. My mother came into my room that night, climbed onto my bed, and said, "Your sister has what they call a butterfly tumor—it's spread throughout the brain. It's inoperable, so your father and I have decided to keep her here at home." She looked so weary. I wanted to comfort my mother, but I didn't know how—those vacant eyes weren't looking at me; they were looking past me. Sitting there on my bed, she seemed to have left the room and disappeared into another world altogether.

The house became quieter, more subdued. Tessie tried to go back to school, but the headaches got the better of her, reading and writing became increasingly difficult, and, when her balance was compromised and the kids at school made fun of her accidental pratfalls, my parents decided it was best to let her stay at home. She was taken to Mayo a few times for cobalt treatments, but those, too, were ultimately discontinued, and instead, my mother was given a two-year supply of morphine and told to take her daughter home. Tessie tied one of Dad's red handkerchiefs around her balding head, and that became her signature style, a concession to modesty and vanity both.

Although no longer able to perform her duties, Tessie was still my slave, and this gave me certain privileges. One night I crept into where she'd set up camp, in the old maid's room, and sat next to her on the bed. It was late, and moonlight was pouring in through the window. Even at night, she wore her kerchief, but now she pulled it off, exposing her bald head, and whispered, "Why me, Kate? Why do I have to die? It's not fair. I'm the good one in the family." Tears started down her cheeks, and in order to hide my own, I pulled her to me and held her, not knowing what to say or how, only sure that whatever I said would have to be the truth, because that was our pact. "You're right, sweetheart, it's not fair and it doesn't make any sense, because you *are* the good one in the family. You're the best one in the family, and everyone knows it." I don't know if this comforted her, but soon she fell asleep, and I stayed with her for a long time that night, holding her hand and memorizing it. To this day, etched in my memory, are those beautiful hands—long, slender, elegant fingers, perfect nails, and her skin, so warm.

I had been accepted at New York University, into a new theater program that would allow me to earn my academic credits while studying almost full-time uptown at the Stella Adler Studio of Acting. It was the beginning of my adult life. It was the beginning of my life as an actress. It was the beginning of a journey that, by necessity, meant the end of my girlhood.

The night came when I was to leave. It was an evening flight because Dubuque was a small town and the regional puddle jumper only flew twice a day to Chicago. My suitcases stood by the front door. Had I said good-bye to everyone? Was it my mother in the car outside, or was it my father? All a mystery now, the details that marked that leave-taking. All but this: Just as I reached for my suitcase, I heard a noise, and when I looked up, I saw Tessie sitting at the top of the stairs. Her little red kerchief was slightly askew, and she was crying softly. I had to strain to hear her say, "I don't want you to go, Kate. I'm scared. I'm going to miss you so much."

I looked at my little sister sitting there, and even though it was impossible to say good-bye, impossible to think of what lay ahead, and impossible to understand how desire and despair can conspire to lead to a moment such as this, I knew I had no choice. Tess knew, too, and in the twinkling of an eye—like a whisper, like a dream—she flew up the stairs and was gone.

Actress

The traffic, the pavement, the patterns, the lights. I was home, and I knew it. In a taxi hurtling across the Triborough Bridge, the cabbie and I traded barbs and bon mots as if this was just another day and I was just another fare headed downtown to Washington Square. I jumped out of the taxi on the corner of Fifth Avenue and Eleventh Street, grabbed my bags, and swung through the revolving doors of the Samuel Rubin International Residence Hall, where life would begin.

It was understood that I would be taking my academic courses downtown and studying acting uptown, but from the very beginning this arrangement did not suit me. Too much distance between what I craved and what kept me from it. The academics suffered from the get-go, but it was a different story altogether once I got off the subway on Fiftieth Street and Seventh Avenue and entered the doors to the Stella Adler Studio of Acting, situated in the north side of the City Center Building. On the floor that shaped me as an actress, there were three rooms, and in the largest of these rooms there was a throne, and upon this throne sat a queen.

Stella Adler regarded herself as royalty, and so, as a consequence, did we. She was a tall woman of indeterminate age, blond hair masterfully coiffed so as to look at once unstudied and very chic, ropes of pearls draped around a long neck, a white silk blouse (the collar of which was perpetually ringed with makeup) revealing a full bosom, and a face unlike any I had ever seen. It was rubber; it was marble; it was sadness; it was joy—it was anything she wanted it to be, and she wielded those sudden transformations like a weapon. Stella did not suffer fools—not lightly, not briefly, not ever.

Students were dismissed for wearing blue jeans, for chewing gum, for looking bored, and woe betide the person whose insecurity masqueraded as arrogance. "You have somewhere you'd rather be?" she once asked a young man who was holding an unlit cigarette in his hand. He smiled seductively. Then she struck a match, and when he put the cigarette to his lips, she instead touched the flame to his hand. The young man didn't flinch. She blew out the match. The room was dead quiet.

"Get out," she said to the young man, "and don't come back. You're in the banker's way!"

The "banker's way" meant that you were not fit for acting, not able to channel passion, not sensitive to the subtleties of human nature. In other words, you were a creature of the material world and therefore neither welcomed nor suited to this life, where money was regarded with disdain and personal sacrifice was the order of the day. By Stella's decree, our mettle was tempered in her classroom, and those who lacked the spine simply disappeared.

Stella was not sympathetic. "Who's ready?" were the words that opened the day. Heart in my throat, I raised my hand and took the stage. To show Stella that I was a fearless contender and here to stay, I chose Maggie's opening monologue from *Cat on a Hot Tin Roof.* Perhaps three lines escaped my lips before she called out, "Stop!" Then she rose to her full, imperious height and, approaching me, asked, "Where are you from, sweetheart?"

"Dubuque, Iowa, Miss Adler."

Pause. "Well, that's not your fault." Laughter. "And don't call me Miss Adler, my name is Stella. Tennessee Williams understood the meaning and the power in that name, and in every line he wrote." She took ahold of my ponytail and shook it. "Maggie the Cat is fighting for her life. Her *life!* She isn't sweet, she isn't cute — she's dangerous, and she's on fire. No Iowa in Maggie, and by the time you find out who she is, why she is, and what she is, there won't be any Iowa left in you, either." She dropped my ponytail and took my chin in her hand. "Bring it back next week and get out of the Midwest, I never want to see it in you again."

I had my small band of comrades-in-arms at the acting studio, but ours was an uncertain intimacy, one in which we viewed one another as fellow survivors on a life raft. When we weren't sharing a common bowl of lentil soup at the hole-in-the-wall across from the studio, I would take my meals in the mess hall at Samuel Rubin. With a book propped in front of my face, I could observe the room at leisure. Who were these young women and what were they studying at New York University, what great passion inspired them, what greatness did they hope to achieve? I observed, and I learned. The vast majority of the girls living in this dormitory were upper middle class, Jewish, and good-looking. They all had a common interest and one that absorbed their every thought: men. In particular, young men pursuing pre-med or pre-law degrees. It was a marriage market, full of chatter, perfectly manicured nails, and Louis Vuitton bags of every shape and size, all placed smack in the middle of tables that were, of course, devoid of food.

I watched all of this from the vantage point of my hiding place, in which I was made all the more invisible by virtue of my books, my plate of fried chicken, and my freckles. Freckles were not widely on display, and so I was caught off guard one night when my eye fell on a face that was full of them. She sat a few tables away from me, lost in a manual of some kind, a cloud of black hair framing a face that I recognized, on some primitive level.

When the crowd had thinned out and she and I were pretty much alone in the room, I lifted my hand in greeting and called out, "You're Irish, aren't you?"

She looked up, bright blue eyes full of mischief, and said, "You guessed it. You too, huh?"

We both laughed, and then I proposed the most natural thing in the world. "Drink?"

She smiled and gathered her books. "I thought you'd never ask."

Her name was Beth Kehoe, she was from the South Side of Chicago, the oldest of five in an Irish-Catholic family, and she wanted to become a doctor. We spent the entire night comparing notes until, hesitant but hopeful, she asked me to recite something for her. A monologue, she said, or a poem. We were in my cramped room on the fourth floor of the dormitory, and all I had easily at hand was my constant companion, *The White Cliffs*. She adored it, and wanted more, so from memory I performed my monologue from *Cat on a Hot Tin Roof*. It was now past midnight and we both had early class in the morning, but it was clear that we didn't want it to end. When we had serendipitously caught each other's eye in that dormitory cafeteria, we had struck gold, and we knew it. Here was a spirit that quickened, a curiosity that shone, and a heart that sympathized. We were two Celts lost in Jerusalem.

Uptown, the stakes were high. Stella wanted more from me, and I wanted nothing more than to deliver. There was no time for anything else and little need for courses in modern philosophy or English lit when I spent my days under the tutelage of a woman who freely quoted Goethe and Rilke, a mentor who, in the course of an afternoon, could open our imaginations to the life and times of Harold Clurman and the Group Theatre, what it meant to be the daughter of the great Jacob Adler, and how she had transformed the Stanislavski method into a style of acting that was inimitably her own. We didn't have to ask how; she told us. "I found Stanislavski in Paris and I sat at his feet and I listened, until I understood."

At the end of the year, I decided not to return to NYU but to engage full-time in the acting conservatory. I conveniently failed to share this information with my father, knowing that this would only confirm his worst suspicion, that I was indeed out of the gate and galloping headlong toward a broken neck. But choosing between my father and Stella represented the proverbial fork in the road. Where my father feared disappointment, Stella embraced it. "Use it," she advised. "Williams was disappointed, Turgenev was disappointed, Odets was disappointed! Do you think you can understand what epic is without being disappointed?"

Stella lifted me up and filled me with the desire to throw away all the baggage I didn't need, to become the actress I was meant to be. To that end, I took an apartment uptown on West Seventy-Sixth Street, which I shared with a few friends, and to pay the rent I got a job waiting tables at the Friar Tuck, on Third Avenue. Stella did not seem in the least concerned that I had dropped out of school. "You're in the only school you'll ever need!" she declared, and I believed her. Still, I was impatient to work at the craft, dying to get out there and strut my stuff. This, however, did not fly with Stella. She had an inflexible rule that you could not work professionally while you were still in training, and the full course of training was two and a half years.

* * *

I broke this rule when I stole into the offices of Hesseltine, Baker Associates one sweltering summer's day on my way to work. I had done some research on Stark Hesseltine, had learned he was one of the most highly regarded theatrical agents in the business, that he loved the opera, and that he had a weekend house in East Hampton.

I handed the receptionist my picture and résumé and said, "Mr. Hesseltine may not remember me, but we met at a party in East Hampton, and he told me to come by and see him in the city when I had a chance."

The woman looked at me skeptically, then, placing my picture on a tall, sloping pile of similar pictures, she pressed a button on the phone and said, "Stark, there's a young lady here who says she met you in the Hamptons and that you asked her to come by." Pause. "What's your name, dear?"

"Kate Mulgrew," I answered, fighting back the first palpable surges of terror. She put the phone down and indicated that I should take a seat.

Forty-five minutes later, a tall, courtly, and formidable-looking Stark Hesseltine strode into the waiting area, took one look at me, and said the words that separated him from every other theatrical agent in New York: "Miss Mulgrew, why don't you follow me? And while you're walking, you can rehearse your little story about our fateful meeting in East Hampton. The rest of the office will be all ears."

Half an hour later, after I'd treated the office staff to Maggie the Cat as well as the abridged version of my life, Stark walked me to the door and said, "Go buy yourself a pretty dress and some new shoes. We'll schedule a photo shoot, and I'll have a contract ready for your signature next week." I stood there, incredulous. "And one more thing, young lady," he said, opening the door to let me out. "Don't ever lie to me again."

I didn't have to. Within just a few weeks, I was in serious contention for the role of Emily in *Our Town* at the American Shakespeare Theatre in Stratford, Connecticut. Michael Kahn, the artistic director, had put me through my paces and demanded nothing less than three auditions.

Clearly, he was hesitant about taking a chance on an unknown who he wasn't sure could deliver. After the third audition, wearing a synthetic wig I'd bought on the cheap in the Fashion District, and a long white dress I'd found at a flea market, I got down on my knees and looked into Michael Kahn's shrewd brown eyes.

"Mr. Kahn," I said, "if you give me this chance, you won't be sorry. I'm ready for this and I promise that I will not let you down."

The man was not unkind, but neither was he stupid. He said, "I'll let you know by Friday."

The following day, which was Thursday, I'd agreed to meet my grandfather for lunch at the Russian Tea Room. Frank Kiernan, my mother's father, was a dapper man, some might even say elegant. I liked him for his vitality and sense of fun, but I measured myself when I was with him. After all, this was the man who had let go of his little girl's hand, and so I knew him capable of selfishness, and I didn't ask for or seek his love. When we parted at the end of a very lively and pleasant lunch, he plucked an anemone from the table vase and pulled it through the buttonhole of my new jacket. "For luck," he said, kissing me on the cheek.

In a building not far from the Russian Tea Room, I took the elevator to the eighth floor, where Shirley Rich kept her offices. Shirley Rich was a casting director of some repute, and she had arranged an appointment for me to meet with the creator and head writer of a new soap opera called *Ryan's Hope*. I walked into the anteroom and was immediately escorted into Shirley's office, where a statuesque woman with sparkling brown eyes and a cap of chestnut hair stood up to greet me.

"I'm Claire Labine," she said, taking my hand, "and *where* did you get that anemone?"

When I told her my grandfather had given it to me as a token of good luck, she threw back her head and laughed, delighted. She asked me about my background, and with every detail I shared about my Irish-Catholic upbringing, she would look quickly at Shirley, then back at me, and then she would briefly close her eyes, as if processing the information and storing it somewhere.

They were looking for "the girl," she told me, the central character in a story that involved an Irish-Catholic family whose patriarch owns a pub in New York City. Da and Ma had come over from the Old Country and begun their life afresh, producing four children, all of whom contributed to the drama, dreams, and high jinks of life in an Irish bar, but none more so than Mary Ryan herself, who, Claire assured me, would bear all of the trademarks of a heroine. She would be smart, brave, funny, strong, and fiercely loyal. The serial would be unlike anything ever before done on daytime television. It would grapple with politics, ideas, family dynamics, religion, power, and, of course, romance. It was Claire's baby, and she meant to cast it to perfection, bringing new faces and fresh talent to the screen. Leaning forward, she asked me if I would agree to a test at ABC studios, and the sooner the better.

At twenty I had not yet formed a coat of armor. Incapable of guile, I relied on a kind of brazen honesty, which I suppose I thought would protect me or guide me or, at the very least, set me apart. And so I told Claire that I was being considered for the part of Emily in *Our Town* and that if I got the role it would be my first choice, no question about it.

Her face fell, but she pressed on, "Will you at least agree to the test? You haven't signed a contract yet, have you?"

Any actress, young or old, knows better than to close a door before she knows what's behind it. I agreed to test.

The world that I walked into the next day was unlike anything I had ever seen: bright lights glared from every angle, three massive cameras on wheels were operated by men in dark clothing, a sofa, chair, and coffee table were situated in the middle of the stage, and far beyond that was a long, tinted window behind which I perceived shadows moving. This, I learned, was the control room, where only the producers and directors were allowed. A disembodied voice instructed us to begin the scene on a countdown of five, four, three, two, one, at which moment the stage manager gestured with his right hand and, pointing at me, mouthed, *Go!* My christening felt nothing short of wonderfully natural. I felt confident, unthreatened, and even a little cavalier. When it was over, I thanked the actor who had done the scene with me, asked if I could leave, and waved in the direction of the control room, where I knew Claire Labine and a panel of experts sat in judgment. This did not concern me at all—if anything, it excited me. I walked out the studio door and took myself to lunch.

The fifth-floor walk-up where I lived on York Avenue looked like something out of an Elmore Leonard novel, spare, dusty, and bleak. It was composed of two tiny rooms, a kitchen that doubled as a bathroom, and a bedroom that had just enough space for a single bed, a dresser, and a lamp. Everything creaked, including the two old ladies who lived across the way. Invariably, when I put the key in the lock, their door would open, and one or the other, gray head bobbing, would inquire about my day, the weather, the landlord, and the grave injustice of having to scale five floors at their age. I never saw them either coming or going, so I could only conclude that they subsisted on canned goods and whatever leftovers I put in a takeout bag and hung on their doorknob.

Inside, I prepared to bathe by first dismantling the dining table, which was a plank of wood that rested on top of the bathtub. Just as I turned the faucet on, the phone rang in the bedroom. I turned the water off and made a beeline for the bedroom, picked up the phone, and heard my agent's voice on the other end.

"Kate, Stark here. Are you sitting down?" I sat very gently on the bed. "Well, my dear," he continued, "you're about to become a very busy young actress. You will be playing Emily Webb in *Our Town* at night, and during the day you will be taping *Ryan's Hope* in New York. Claire Labine demanded that ABC provide you with a car service. Said something about this casting being a deal breaker. You're off to the races, young lady. I think we should celebrate, don't you? Let me take you to the opera tonight, *La Bohème* is playing at the Met."

I was no longer sitting on the bed but had fallen to the floor on my knees, and when I hung up the phone, I stayed there for a long time and finally, looking heavenward, whispered, "It doesn't get any better than this, does it?"

Stella stood in the middle of the classroom, sipping from a tiny shot glass of vodka. There had been a party celebrating someone's birthday, but now it was getting late, and Stella and I were alone. Despite rising terror, I told her the unvarnished truth. "I don't feel I have any choice but to take my chances, Stella. I know it would be best if I completed the program, but even you have to admit that this is an extraordinary opportunity. I hope you'll give me your blessing."

My magnificent teacher drew herself up to her full height and, simultaneously lifting an eyebrow and lowering her gaze to meet mine, said this: "I fear for you, Kate. It will be so easy for you to take your eye off the prize and skate into Hollywood. And, believe me, Hollywood will beckon."

"But, Stella," I interrupted her, "you know that my first love is and always will be the theater, and while it's true I'll be doing a soap opera, I'll be cutting my teeth on Thornton Wilder. What could possibly be better than that?"

Those eyes, the color of the sea, stormy and tough, turned a sudden cool blue, and once again she took my chin in her hand and said, "Darling, there are endless temptations, but only the work will lift you up. Never forget that."

Rehearsals for *Our Town* began in earnest. Michael Kahn was exacting and utterly professional. At no time did he suggest that I was a rookie and should be handled with kid gloves. Instead, he threw me into the games arena the first day, where I found myself playing alongside some of the best. Eileen Heckart, an inveterate smoker and knitter, always wore a wry smile on her face as if to say, *It's only a play, kids—lighten up.* Everyone adored her. As Mrs. Gibbs, she stood in perfect counterpoise to the mysterious and beautiful Geraldine Fitzgerald, an unusual and inspired choice for the role of Mrs. Webb. She was quintessentially Irish, which is to say she was at once shy and stern, wise and vulnerable. Richard Backus played George, and I was devastated to learn that he had a wife and two children—it seemed somehow unnatural and lacking in taste, as if it were his professional duty not only to play the part beautifully but to fall madly in love with me while doing so. This disappointment was ameliorated by the presence of Fred Gwynne, the tall and marvelous actor playing the central role of the Stage Manager. This, above all others, was the friendship that caught fire—I took delight in his unbridled sense of mischief, and he took an unfatherly delight in sharing it with me.

Managing the business of life was another matter entirely. I moved like a vagabond, abandoning the fifth-floor walk-up on York in favor of a young man's apartment on West Seventy-Sixth Street. Arthur Karp was the production stage manager for *Our Town*, a lovely, carrot-topped guy with a maturity and generosity beyond his years. I think he liked me. He certainly never asked for anything in return.

A long weekend came up, during which I was released from all professional obligations, and I took the opportunity to fly home. There, I found my mother and my sister sequestered in the back of the house, in what was once my mother's studio but which now contained a narrow bed for my mother and, for my sister, a hospital bed overlooking the apple orchard. Not that Tessie could appreciate the view. The tumor, strategic from the beginning, had waged a slow, insidious, and relentless war. It had taken my sister's hazel-green eyes and forced them inward, so that now there was nothing left to look into but two ghoulish membranes. It took, too, her beautiful, lithe body and all of her grace. She lay there blind, paralyzed, and nearly deaf—nearly, I say, because she was adamant that the window remain open at all times. The birds sang in the orchard, and she strained to hear their music.

There was a small bathroom next to the studio and, as I passed it on my way into Tessie's room, a familiar face looked up from the sink. Nancy Gilbert looked at me and smiled. When she had learned of my sister's diagnosis, and understood what it was my mother would have to endure, Nancy had kissed my father lightly on the lips and, without explanation, moved quietly into the back of the house. There she had been ever since, at my sister's side, a tender, vigilant nurse and a devoted friend to my mother, who warned Nancy that if my father ever came into Tessie's room drunk, she'd kill him.

When I walked into the room, the first thing I noticed was the absence of the kerchief or any other concessions to vanity.

Tessie, by now living almost entirely on a diet of morphine and Ovaltine, lay in her bed, head unnaturally tilted backward, a cigarette in her hand. She could no longer speak, and so, in lieu of this faculty, she had devised a system of communication using her hand and her cigarette, which she used as a writing baton. She composed all of her questions and answers by drawing them in the air with her "baton." I kissed her and, leaning close, told her everything about my current life. I sensed the beginning of a smile, but perhaps this was wishful thinking, the longing for absolution. I put the cigarette to her lips and let her draw on it, exhaling the feeblest of vapors. How like my mother to have accommodated this last pleasure. While Tessie smoked, I studied her face, noting with relief that the birds were indeed singing in the orchard, when suddenly my brother cleared his throat and, catching my eye, tapped his watch. I struggled hard against tears so that I could embrace Tessie without upsetting her — the thought of this was unbearable — and when I took her head in my hands, I felt her lips move against my cheek. Pulling away, I understood that she wanted to say something to me, and I watched carefully as she lifted her baton in the air and began to write. Painstaking, they were, these last words, and harrowing to witness. Incredulous, I realized what she had spelled out for me. Something that once upon a time had been a great joke between us, part of our shared love of the irreverent.

The cigarette, in invisible script, had written: YOU WILL BE WITH ME IN PARADISE.

Coming of Age

Mother used an expression I didn't like very much; it seemed too cavalier in the face of anguish. But she had a point. *And the beat goes on* suited the reality of what happens when we part from someone we may never see again, get on a plane, and in short order resume life as if nothing had changed.

In New York, something unexpected was unfolding. Overnight, *Ryan's Hope* had become a huge success, and the character of Mary Ryan in particular attracted a diverse and sweeping viewership. Women of every stripe tuned in to see what Mary would do next. They loved her because she was an independent spirit, unafraid to speak her mind, passionate, impetuous, and brave. Seldom lauded for her beauty, Mary Ryan had something else to offer, something women could grab ahold of and understand. She had a powerful sense of self, and this proved more magnetic and more relatable than any other single quality. Almost immediately following the show's debut, I was recognized on the streets of New York. Whole gaggles of girls would call out "Mary Ryan!" and when I would turn and wave or blow a kiss, they would shriek and burst into applause. It was curious to me then, as now, the power of the performer over an audience when, in fact, the gift itself springs from the writer's pen. Claire Labine had poured her heart and most of her own unique qualities into the character of Mary Ryan, and she had done so with lyricism and authenticity. In many ways, Claire was Mary Ryan, and Mary Ryan was, in many ways, me. This synthesis, rare enough under the best of creative circumstances, proved even rarer as our personal friendship deepened into a sympathy that would survive, and surmount, many trials.

But in Stratford, trouble was brewing on the banks of the Housatonic River. In the middle of rehearsal one afternoon, I looked out into the theater and saw a stranger approaching Michael Kahn. There was nothing particularly prepossessing about this young man, but even as he strode down the aisle, something in me sat up. At the break, Michael introduced him to the company as the newly arrived directorial intern, whose job it was to assist the director and to learn from him. His name was David Bernstein, and he would be with us for the duration of the summer season. Black eyes, black hair, black mustache, a fringed suede jacket, black boots.

In no time at all, his lanky indifference and calculated elusiveness drove me to distraction. I was undone and done for.

Grayce Grant, an older member of the company, had taken me under her wing. A character actress of about fifty with small blue eyes, a broad nose, and a head of tight ash-blond curls, she confessed to me that her husband of many years had recently left her (and, by implication, their five children) for a younger woman. She was livid over this betrayal, and I often wondered who was looking after her children, as I don't recall having met a single one of them.

Grayce had rented an old farmhouse in Putney Woods, just outside of Stratford, and asked me if I would like to join her there. The house contained three bedrooms, and people came and went as the season demanded. After work, we often gathered around the small kitchen table for cocktails, which consisted of a giant bottle of very cheap Pinot Grigio and a plate of Grayce's preferred hors d'oeuvres, Triscuits topped with small shards of Muenster cheese.

One night, I walked into the kitchen and was surprised to find Grayce and David Bernstein in a curious *tableau vivant*. Grayce, in suspended animation, leaned forward in her chair, as if eagerly awaiting a response. In contrast, David looked as if he had brought his chair with him and sat with long legs comfortably crossed, slightly turned away as if in distaste, dangling a bottle of beer between index finger and thumb.

"Oh, Kate, guess what?" Grayce cried, when she saw that it was me and not Tom Everett, another Putney Woods tenant, who worked backstage and slunk around the house in a permanent state of gloom. "Tom has to leave—his girlfriend is threatening to dump him—and so when I told David about the available room, he asked if he could take it! Isn't that terrific?"

I looked at David, assessing the odds, and said, "I don't know, Grayce, does David think it's terrific?" The cool, hooded eyes, the hint of a smirk, and our new tenant was on his feet, suddenly needing to meet his friend Arthur Karp for a drink. "Say hi to Arthur for me," I said to David as he pulled car keys from his pocket. After his car was safely through the gates, I bounded up the stairs two at a time and hit the landing with a short, ebullient jig.

It was late July, and while the heat was intolerable in New York, it was pleasantly oppressive in Connecticut. I had established an efficient and satisfying routine, taping *Ryan's Hope* every day in the city and then being driven to Stratford to perform onstage at night.

Weekends were spent in Connecticut to accommodate the five-performance schedule. My life was busy, fulfilling, and very, very good. I recognized this period as one of unfettered happiness and found joy in everything. Every meal, every scene, every dip in the ocean, every curtain call, was an ode to exuberance.

This sense of abandon was modified by the arrival of my sister Jenny. Tessie's sickness had taken a toll on everyone, not least the youngest children, or as we referred to them, the Smalls. Jenny and Sam were closest in age to Tessie, and the burden of living with their sister and having to witness her suffering firsthand must have caused them considerable agony. Mother and I agreed that it would be a good idea for the baby of the family to come and stay with me, at least until the summer was over. Details were not discussed; it was simply understood that Jenny was coming and that I was to look after her.

Jenny's company in no way cramped my style—if anything, it enhanced it. At eleven, she was everything actors love: funny, full of life, and madly curious, she was a little freckle-faced dynamo with wide blue eyes, a button nose, long brown pigtails, and an inherent sense of mischief. Everyone embraced her as a kind of mascot, and when she wasn't standing in the wings mouthing my lines while I was onstage looking at the moon with George, she was in my dressing room, chatting up the other actresses, fingers in every pot, her newfound entitlement complete. She soon became a familiar presence at the beach, at the bar of the Blue Goose Grill, and in every corner of the house in Putney Woods.

Impossible to know where she might have been hiding one unseasonably chilly night when David Bernstein offered to build a fire, and I, bending down beside him, fully intending to assist the effort, instead found our hands touching over the fire and felt that first absurd, uncomfortable gurgle of laughter, followed by the meeting of the eyes, at once riveting and intense, then the second of calculation sent gleefully to hell when mouths came together in a kiss so sublime, so longed for, that if my hair had caught fire at that moment, I'd have snuffed it out and carried on.

David released me from the kiss and at the same time from any ancillary obligation that might attend such a kiss. He disappeared into thin air, or so it seemed to me. He wasn't at the theater; he wasn't at the house; he was nowhere to be found. Finally, in desperation, I employed Grayce as my spy and asked her to do the necessary reconnaissance. She found me waiting in the wings, about to make my entrance into the graveyard scene, and, using a resonant stage whisper so as not to disappoint the first two rows, said, "David went to Florida to visit his son. His son's name is Seth. Adorable, no?" And then, slipping into character, took her place onstage among the throng of mourners attending Emily Webb's funeral.

This information, though by no means promising, nonetheless allowed me ample space in which to live life as I liked to live it, with a modicum of restraint and plenty of abandon. My little sister, a constant appendage, kept my feet on the ground, and together we enjoyed an interlude of real happiness. We were delighted when Arthur Karp brought us ice-cream cones, which we devoured sitting cross-legged on his fire escape, overlooking the rooftops of New York. We loved our lunches with my actor friends, in particular my *Ryan's Hope* costar Nancy Addison, whose dazzling beauty and salacious gossip held my sister spellbound. The cool, dark silence of the television studio intrigued Jenny, but in Stratford she blossomed.

We had company picnics on the shores of the Long Island Sound, where I learned that Jenny's shyness about pulling off her cover-up and jumping into the water was actually born out of a very reasonable terror. She couldn't swim. How was it that my mother had overlooked this fundamental life skill? I discovered that while I might know a great deal about my mother's vulnerabilities, I knew next to nothing about my baby sister's. I knew only that she was thrilled to be with me, far from a home that was no longer safe. She was free to be young and silly, to love and be loved in return.

But darkness had its way, as we knew it would.

The phone rang on Arthur Karp's kitchen wall and I answered, "Hello? This is Kate Mulgrew speaking."

"Kitten, this is your father." His voice, strained, distant, determined. "Tessie died last night and we're going to bury her tomorrow, so don't even think about coming home. It's best if you just stay there and look after your sister."

"But, Dad," I interrupted, "we can get on a plane this afternoon and be there late tonight, it's not complicated."

I heard a long, controlled intake of breath, and then my father closed the argument. "It's done, Kitten, it's all over. The burial is a formality. We just want this thing over. Please stay in New York with your sister. We'll be in touch soon." There was the briefest of pauses, not even air enough to breathe, and then he hung up. I turned to my little sister, already in tears, and put my arms around her.

"I'm staying with you!" Jenny cried, slipping precipitously into an anguish she could not understand, knowing only that she did not want to return to a place where everything would be permanently changed, where the missing pieces would make the puzzle impossible to put together.

Suddenly, the doorbell rang. My friend Nancy Addison had come by to say hello and had stumbled unwittingly onto our grief. Nan and I were partners in crime on *Ryan's Hope,* despite the fact that we came from entirely different worlds and had, on the face of it, almost nothing in common. This complicated girl, this ravishing Jewish beauty from New Jersey, whose father was a furrier and whose mother lay in bed wasting away from a disease no one could name, knew a thing or two about the inequities of life. She knew she was the apple of her grandfather's eye and wanted only to please him when he had placed her, at the age of seven, ever so gently atop a sable rug and, with his fingers and his mouth, showed her again and again just how special she was and how good it feels to be adored.

Nancy understood the vicissitudes of love and the immutable nature of loss. She touched my sister's cheek and said, "I think Jenny and I should go for a walk in Central Park, get a hot dog, and go to the five o'clock show at the planetarium. Sound good?"

I had only a few hours to spare and needed to move quickly. I flipped through my address book, found the number I was looking for, and dialed. A man's voice answered.

"Come over," I said. "I'm alone."

Within minutes, he was there. Nothing was said. I took him by the hand and pulled him to the floor. My memory is blunted. Was it Arthur Karp, so good, so kind, so eager to please, who helped me meet the first wave of grief? A look of surprise, no words, I didn't want words. But who was it there, on the floor beside me, on top of me? It wasn't the one I wanted, that much I knew.

It wasn't David. Nor did it matter. I needed something fundamental, harsh, and palpable to cut the pain, and I found it. But I can't remember his face.

Our grief abraded both of us, my sister and me, and for the next few weeks we clung to each other for what little comfort we could find. The summer was drawing to an end, the turn was imminent in the soft autumn air, and the play had run its course. One by one the actors in the Putney farmhouse packed their bags and set off for home. The mystery of David Bernstein's disappearance remained unsolved, but I wouldn't allow anyone to take his room, and everything in it remained just as he'd left it. I broke down when Grayce, hoisting the pink Samsonite suitcase she'd arrived with into the backseat of her station wagon, took my face in her hands and said, "I'm leaving a half bottle of Pinot Grigio as a memento. Don't forget me, kiddo, and remember who loves ya."

I knew what the next day was about to bring, but my sister didn't, and when she saw a familiar green truck coming down the lane and turning into the gate, she took off as fast as her little legs could carry her. I let her go, knowing it was just a matter of time before she reappeared.

Mother had sent her friend B. J. Weber to pick up her youngest child and drive her back to Iowa. Blond, thickset, and rough around the edges, B.J. was on a quest for spiritual enlightenment and had met my mother at Our Lady of the Mississippi Abbey, a Trappistine convent just outside of Dubuque. They instantly became friends, and in exchange for his devotion, my mother taught him manners. "Come to my house for dinner every night for six months, and I'll teach you everything you need to know," she'd said, and kept her promise. Now here he was, ready to fetch my little sister and take her home. I cautioned him to be gentle and patient with Jenny, that a child's grief was irrational.

"You may think you know her pain, B.J.," I warned him, "but this is deeply personal, and what Jenny felt about Tessie is something that maybe even Jenny can't quite grasp at the moment. It will take time, and Mother will need to help her."

At the mention of Mother's name, B.J. looked away.

"Have you seen Mother?" I demanded. "How is she?"

"She's been out at the abbey with Mother Columba, but she'll be back by the time Jenny is home."

"Back by the time Jenny is home" connoted a good deal of time that Mother had been at Our Lady of the Mississippi Abbey under the care of her great friend and mentor, Mother Columba, and whereas a period of reflection and mourning could only benefit my mother, it did not necessarily bode well for Jenny.

Eventually, weary and resigned, her face streaked with tears, Jenny came down to the kitchen from her hiding place upstairs in my closet. Very slowly, I packed her things, and then we all had a late lunch, sitting on the porch.

B.J. glanced at his watch. "We should really get moving," he said. "As it is, we'll have to stop at a motel in Cleveland." Jenny looked at me in horror, barely stifling a groan. B.J. quickly amended this. "On second thought, I think we'll just drive straight through. I've got a pillow and blanket in the truck; Jen can get some shut-eye on the road."

It was a torturous good-bye, and when at last she was in the truck and they were rolling out through the gate, Jenny suddenly threw the passenger door open and, the truck still moving, jumped out and ran back to me, crying, "I love you, Kate! I don't want to go! Please don't make me go!"

After considerable shushing and kissing and cajoling, my sister, looking for all the world like a little old woman, stooped and shuffled her way back to the truck and, climbing slowly into the cab, turned her face to look at me as they pulled away, her nose pressed against the window, her hand lifted in farewell. I watched until they were out of sight, and until they were out of sight, that little face had her eyes on mine.

I didn't know what to do with myself after she'd gone. The house was empty; loneliness touched everything. While Jenny was hiding, I had pressed B.J. for details of Tessie's funeral, and he had told me four things: that during the reading of the Song of Solomon, as the priest spoke the words "My beloved spake, and said unto me, Rise up, my love, my fair one, and come away," a doe had come up from the timberland and stood at a little distance, watching. That my father's knees had buckled under the weight of the coffin as he carried it to the hearse, and he had fallen on the casket, sobbing, "I never thought you'd go out like this, sugar." That Father Kevin O'Rourke did not attend the funeral service but instead sent his regrets, explaining that he was needed at a fund-raiser in Colorado. That it was not my father at all, but a woman with black hair and sad eyes who helped my mother into her car and watched as she drove off to the Trappistine convent.

I poured myself a glass of Grayce's Pinot Grigio, watched as the last of the day's sun burned diamonds in the dappled orchard, and made my way upstairs for my last night in Putney Woods, at the end of a summer that had defined me as an actress.

I had fallen into a deep sleep and woke to the first notes of birdsong. Opening my eyes, I saw long fingers of light weaving a gentle pattern on the wooden floor. I saw him before I heard him; he'd been so careful and light-footed as he climbed the stairs. And then David was there, standing in the doorway, unsmiling, looking at me with those grave black eyes. It had all been weighed and gone over a thousand times, I could tell. And I could also tell that whatever battle he had waged with himself, he had lost, and that this disturbed him still.

He moved then, crossing the room swiftly, never taking his eyes from mine, and not a word had been exchanged—not one—when he leaned down and, against his better judgment, kissed me.

On the Spears

David resisted me, even when he found me irresistible, which I realize now must have been exhausting. Such is the diabolical nature of sexual chemistry, and ours was powerful. Besides which, he was exotic.

"You're Jewish, okay, I get it, but there are a *lot* of Jews in this world. Where, exactly, do your people come from? Are you a peasant or a prince?" I demanded, propped up on an elbow, lying next to him in his narrow bed. Midafternoon delight in an early spring Manhattan, the sounds of traffic, children being let out of school, James Taylor playing on the stereo in the living room. David fixed his features into an inscrutable mask, something he often did when I brought up the subject of Judaism. I was undeterred. "What are you thinking, David? I want to know. What is it you're afraid of? My Christianity, or your mother's wrath?" This prickled him, as I knew it would, and, predictably, elicited no response.

We were playing a high-stakes game of chicken, and we both knew it.

Six months earlier, I'd met his parents under less-than-favorable circumstances, when David and I were forced to impose on their hospitality as the result of a riding accident. Freud might suggest that we had intended to visit his parents all along but that it was first necessary to drive into the countryside outside of Philadelphia, break into a strange barn, saddle two massive Tennessee Walkers, and take them out for a trot in a snow-covered orchard on an arctic day in December. The sudden sound of a motorcycle gunning down a parallel path spooked my horse, and before I knew it, I was tearing through the orchard on the back of a wild thing, barely able to hold on, the horse kicking and bucking so violently that within seconds I was thrown from my seat and landed with a thwack on the frozen ground. When David ran over to help me up, I discovered, first to my chagrin, and then to my horror, that I couldn't move.

An ambulance was called, I was taken to the nearest hospital, and after I was examined by a syndicate of orthopedic surgeons and had suffered a harrowing few days of no feeling whatsoever below my waist, it was determined that I had severely bruised my lumbar vertebrae and would be unable to walk for a number of weeks. This put me in a bit of a pickle with my job, but seeing as there was no way around it, I called Claire and told her the whole story, only slightly downplaying the criminal aspect of our little adventure.

Claire, with her customary sangfroid, told me that it would be impossible to write me out for an extended period of time but that she would be willing to accommodate this mishap by redirecting the story line.

"Meaning what?" I asked, suspicious despite the delicious effects of morphine strumming my veins.

"Well," she mused, "we could do any number of things. Mary is investigating a crime as it is. Let's say you go undercover, and I mean *way* under, and catch something."

"Catch something? Like the flu?" Not terribly dramatic, I thought.

"No, no, no, of *course* not the flu!" I could feel Claire's excitement through the phone line. "I'm thinking something terrifying. I'm thinking rats. You know, urban legend has it that the rat population in Manhattan equals that of its human population. Let's get down and dirty and give Mary a dose of rat poisoning. Put her on her back with a case of leptospirosis. You'll be acting up a storm from a hospital bed—you can still *act,* can't you?"

"Yes, I suppose so," I responded weakly, a cloud of morphine-induced euphoria stealing over me. "Whatever you say—you're the genius."

My paralysis, however temporary, rendered me unable to travel back to New York, and after due consideration it was decided that I would spend the weekend with David's parents in nearby Wilmington, Delaware.

"This should be interesting," I said to him as the paramedics slid me into the ambulance. David attempted a smile, which, given his natural pallor, came off as a ghostly grimace.

David's parents were glacially polite. His father, tall and balding, was dark featured and not unkind, but his mother was clearly the dominant personality, and it was obvious from the moment our eyes met that she could barely tolerate me. She, too, had stature, but carried herself with great pride, a quality that imposed on her a certain stiffness. When I had been made comfortable in the guest room and given a cup of tea, the Bernsteins left me alone to rest. Fighting anxiety, I took a painkiller and drifted off to sleep.

It couldn't have been much later, maybe an hour or two,

when the sound of muffled voices raised in argument woke me up. The door had been left open a crack, so I could clearly hear the exchange that was taking place in the living room. I could even see the top of Mrs. Bernstein's perfectly coiffed salt-and-pepper bob as she sat rigidly in a tall armchair. I held my breath so as not to miss a word.

"You bring us this girl, this *Irish* girl, and expect us to take care of her," Mrs. Bernstein was saying, her voice spiking like a slap.

"I didn't think you'd mind, given the circumstances," David countered, high on the defensive. "For God's sake, Mother, she's had a serious accident."

Mrs. Bernstein cut him off. "There wouldn't have been an accident at all if you'd walked away from her in the first place. But no, you couldn't resist the temptation. It's bad enough she's an actress, but, David, what on earth do you think you're doing with this *shiksa?* It can't last, you know, and it won't."

I strained to hear David's response, but there was only silence. In that moment, something inside me shifted. This, I suddenly understood, was where his people came from.

Mary Ryan was soon out of her hospital bed and wanting more.

"*More?*" Claire looked at me, incredulous. "We've got you working in almost every show — don't you want a day off now and then?"

"Absolutely not," I replied, standing in her office. "I don't need time on my hands, I need to work. I need to grow. And since this job won't allow me to do theater, I need to find other ways. So, yes. Please. More."

Claire studied me for a moment, thoughtful, and then with a sly grin she said, "You asked for it."

I was invited to Claire's house in Brooklyn the following Saturday night, and as soon as I entered, she placed a glass of white wine in my left hand, a script in my right, and instructed me to go downstairs and read.

"Dinner should be ready by the time you're finished," she said, and then, as she disappeared into the back of the house, "with any luck."

She'd written a screenplay based on the legend of Tristan and Isolt, the classic Celtic tale of tragic love. In the twelfth century, King Mark of Cornwall decides to marry the Irish princess Isolt. He sends his most loyal and beloved knight, Tristan, to fetch Isolt and bring her to Cornwall. Along the way, the two of them ingest a love potion that causes them to fall madly in love, and though Isolt marries King Mark, she is bound to Tristan "through life, past death, and into the hands of God."

I flew upstairs and found Claire in her cramped but surprisingly productive kitchen, putting the finishing touches to a Virginia ham.

"I'm offering you ten thousand dollars, the role of a Celtic princess, and a summer in Ireland." She beamed at me, pot-holder aloft. "You *did* say you wanted more, didn't you?"

For a certain kind of actress, nothing serves romance better than a new part. When separation is imminent, suitcases are just about to be packed, and the script, marked and highlighted, lies on the bed, love is at its most tender. I ran my hand through David's silky black hair and pulled him into a long kiss, after which he rolled onto his back and put his arms behind his head, staring at the ceiling with characteristic intensity.

"Don't pout," I said, "it's unattractive. Besides, if anyone knew what he was getting into, *you* did. I'm an actress; this is what actresses *do:* they *act*. And look on the bright side: two whole months to do whatever you want. You're free! You should be delighted."

He looked at me darkly. "Freedom isn't everyone's idea of happiness."

On the plane, waiting for takeoff, Claire slid into the seat next to mine and whispered, "Order champagne—we've got Richard Burton!"

"You're unbelievable," I said, already beckoning the flight attendant. "How on earth did you manage that?"

She rested her head against the seat back, closed her eyes, and, smiling to herself, told me the story. She'd flown down to Puerta Vallarta, where Burton was living at the time with his wife Susan Hunt, and simply threw herself at his head.

"You didn't." I laughed out loud. "What cheek!"

"He probably needs the money, or maybe he's just bored, or maybe he really likes the screenplay."

At which I guffawed and said, "You think?"

"But at any rate," she continued, "he agreed, and he'll be in Ireland in a week."

I could see that Claire was on the verge of sinking into a well-earned sleep, but I needed one final piece of information. "Tell me, Clairabel, does he look very old?"

She grinned. "Are you kidding? He's divine." And with that, she fell into a beautiful slumber.

Divine was everything Irish, as God had intended. I'd never seen such light, incandescent and mystical. Lambent sunsets, and suddenly the heavens would open and a soft rain would fall, seagulls soaring upward, the ocean spray meeting the clouds in a dazzling display of beauty. I sat for hours, mesmerized by the play of colors.

Mesmerized, too, by the people and the singular way they have of pulling you in. *Craic,* it is called in Gaelic. Irish chit-chat. But the Irish never simply chat; they're incapable of it. Instead, they lean against the bar in the pub, nursing a pint of

Guinness, and with eyes downcast, start a slow-burning fire with a single provocative, and often mumbled, observation, igniting a conversation that loops and lashes and dances from man to man, as each in turn orders a round, cigarette smoke filling the room, turf fire glowing in the corner. Not many women can be found at the bar, but the men are capable of leniency, if they are flush with beer, and the face beside theirs is young and pretty, and the voice distinctly American.

A Welshman in Ireland is a dangerous thing, being temperamentally stuck, as he is, between two fractious cultures. Richard Burton was kind, complex, and deeply shy. His talent was remarkable, and in our scenes together I often found myself captivated by his tenderness, his perfect control, and his ability to hit grace notes I didn't know existed in the text. He took a liking to me, which was a very good thing, because he did not tolerate fools and often, when he was in his cups, did not tolerate anyone at all. One night, at a very lovely dinner Claire hosted in a farmhouse that had been beautifully converted into an intimate restaurant, I watched as Burton drank himself into a fury.

Wine did not mellow Burton; it enhanced his volatility, so that everyone felt the slow, inexorable descent into the vortex but was helpless to do anything about it. Suddenly, Burton slammed his fist on the table and shouted, amid glasses shattering and candles sputtering, "Everybody get the fuck out! Except Katerina"—here he put his hand over mine—"Katerina stays. The rest of you can fuck off!" Mercifully, his lovely wife had elected to stay at the hotel and work on her music. It occurred to me that Susan Hunt's keyboard may have been her salvation.

When the room had cleared, Burton turned to me and, taking my hand in his, said, "Listen to me, Katerina, and listen closely. Get. Out."

I stared at him, immobilized with fear and confusion—get out of where? Get out of what? Then, drawing the candelabra closer, he whispered, "This business will kill you. Strip you of your soul, steal your humanity, leave you a shell of what you once were. It's no place for a real man"—he pointed to himself, head bowed—"and it's death to a good woman. Get the fuck out before it's too late." With that, he lifted my hand to his lips, kissed it, and said, "Now be a good girl, and bugger off."

There were threads of the familiar already lacing themselves through my professional life. Geraldine Fitzgerald, who had so beautifully played my mother in *Our Town*, had been hired to play my nurse in Tristan and Isolt. Bronwyn was more than a nurse; she was also a witch, and it was she who, albeit reluctantly, composed the magic potion that would be Isolt's undoing. Although I was comfortable with Geraldine and admired her intense concentration, I found her to be slightly detached from the real world, as if she were observing life rather than sharing it. It was unlike me, then, to approach her on a level of friendship, let alone intimacy. And yet one morning, as we were driving to location in a shared limousine, and the dawn was breaking in its inimitable and breathtaking way across the stony Burren, I turned to her, smiling, and asked, "Geraldine, what kind of life do you think I'll have? Be honest."

Whereupon she turned away from me and, for what seemed an inordinately long time, stared out the window in silence. Finally, she adjusted herself so that she was facing me directly and said, without inflection, "You'll be all right, if you don't throw yourself on the spears." And then, without another word, she folded her hands in her lap and turned her face to the window.

My mother came over to celebrate my twenty-first birthday and to subject herself to Burton's somewhat dubious affections. Immediately upon meeting her, he dubbed my mother "Monkeyface," which she absolutely loathed but was powerless to change. I thought it was rather dear, but it infuriated Mother, who said to me again and again, "Mine is *hardly* the face of a monkey—the man's insane."

But he didn't strike me as insane on the night of my birthday when he gave me a small box containing two tiny gold butterfly earrings studded with diamond chips, draped a mink coat over my shoulders, sat me on his knee, and sang, a cappella, "How to Handle a Woman." He struck me in that moment as the most extraordinary man in the world.

My mother found his gifts in questionable taste, however, and the following week, when the film wrapped, she insisted that I return the mink coat. I promised her I would, but of course I did no such thing.

Stripped of any hint of Irish lyricism, New York hit me hard when I returned, the city an apiary of impossible energy. In my absence, my lawyer had found and purchased an apartment for me. "It's time," Leonard explained, "to provide you with an asset that will never depreciate. A little New York real estate." Leonard had chosen for me a studio apartment in a modern high rise on Central Park West at Sixty-Eighth Street and, though it wasn't my taste at all, it was my first apartment, and I was proud of it. David came over and, as I prepared beef stroganoff in the thimble-sized kitchen, he opened a bottle of red wine and toasted my return. After dinner, lying in each other's arms on the one piece of furniture I'd managed to not only buy but to have delivered, an emerald-green pullout sofa, David suggested a weekend away.

"I just got back!" I laughed. "Do you really loathe New York that much?"

"We haven't had any real time alone together for months," David argued. "Let's just jump in the car and drive to Jersey, Maryland, wherever—find a little B and B, take a weekend. What do you say?"

I said yes, and four days later we found ourselves renting a small, worn, whitewashed cottage overlooking Lake Garrison in Monroeville, New Jersey. We went grocery shopping; we held hands; we laughed; we walked to the water's edge and looked at the glorious moon; we slept late, tangled in each other's arms. In the morning, I made coffee and toast, and we sat across the kitchen table, and I watched as he licked the cream off his upper lip with a pink tongue, then raked his mustache clean with even white teeth. His mouth tasted of peppermint, and when he was aroused his cheeks turned a rosy pink, which embarrassed him and delighted me. He was blushing now and, jumping up, said, "Come on, lazy—race you to the water!"

Before we knew it, we were up to our chins in a lake full of Boy Scouts. "How romantic." I laughed, urging David deeper into the water. The Scouts seemed oblivious to us, despite the fact that I was cradled in David's arms like a baby, we were kissing unabashedly, and under the water our hands were everywhere at once, stroking and teasing, becoming hopelessly aroused. Suddenly, David shifted me in his arms so that I was forced to steady myself by hooking my legs around his waist. We faced each other under the melting September sun and, as my arms dropped helplessly to my sides, he kissed me with that mouth of intoxicating peppermint and, pulling me closer and lifting me high, we disappeared into each other.

This Cup

The young investment banker lured me to his lair on Fire Island. His name was Marty Segal, and he was nothing like David.

Smooth talking, aggressive, entitled, with perfectly starched monogrammed shirts and a Mercedes convertible, he was shark-smart and brutally honest. I knew that I neither thrilled nor delighted him. To the contrary, I seemed to push his buttons at every conceivable turn. Driving back to the city from a messy theater party in Bucks County, Pennsylvania, at which I'd intentionally ignored him for hours, he suddenly said, "You getting back at someone for something? Because if you are, and that someone isn't me, you're acting like a real bitch."

Yes, I wanted to shout, *I'm getting back at someone! Someone who is nothing like you! Someone who is deep and dark and difficult, whose love torments me. Someone who is brooding, misanthropic, someone who needs to be taught a lesson. No, he is not at all like you, Marty,* I hissed to myself, *with your thinning pate and your snake eyes and your perfect tan. I'm getting back at David, and I'm using you to do it.*

"Then come to Fire Island," Marty continued, remarkably inept at reading minds, "and stop with the excuses."

The gauntlet thrown, I stared straight ahead as we raced down the freeway, and said, "Fine. Let's go."

He shared a house with several other young Wall Street turks, all of whom I found repulsive. They talked about nothing but money and stared at me with open lasciviousness and a kind of animal hostility, as if to suggest that conversation was an unnecessary and unwanted skill at their table. After dinner, when Marty and I were alone, I said, "You know, Marty, I like you, but I have no intention of sleeping with you—I hardly know you. It would be coarse and pointless. But we can have a perfectly nice weekend, if you'll just show me to my room." He blinked at me, momentarily disarmed.

Leading me down a short hallway and into a spartan room containing a single bed, a naked window, and unadorned walls, Marty said, "You're a real nut job, you know that?"

I switched on my brightest smile. "And what does that say about you? I'll see you in the morning, Marty. Good night."

The sun woke me, shining hard and bright through the open window. My limbs felt strangely heavy and, longing to slip back into sleep, I pulled the sheet over my head and turned over. Then, as if from a great distance, I heard someone clearing his throat and, forcing my eyes open, realized that Marty was standing there, leaning against the doorjamb, hands stuffed in Polo Ralph Lauren pockets. He looked at me for a long moment, during which many scenarios presented themselves to my imagination, none of them desirable.

Finally, he spoke. "You went to bed on Friday night and it is now Sunday morning, which means you've been asleep for thirty-two hours. What are you, pregnant?" It was as if he'd pulled the pin from a grenade and casually tossed it to me.

I waited, didn't want to act precipitately. Patience, I counseled myself, as one week moved inexorably into the next. And the next. On my way home from the studio one afternoon, I found myself standing in front of the Church of Saint Paul the Apostle on Amsterdam Avenue, near Sixtieth Street. My personal faith had long since limped into oblivion, and yet I felt compelled to go inside. Finding a deserted pew close to the altar, I knelt. Why do we pray when we are terrified? Why do we reserve this ancient and primitive ritual for moments of great distress? It is always the same supplication: O my Father, if it be possible, let this cup pass from me.

And then how quickly it all happens. My good friend Nancy provides me with the name of a reputable gynecologist, I schedule an appointment, I take a taxi to New York University Hospital, I meet Dr. Robert Morris, and he examines me, takes blood and a urine sample. Afterward, I wait for him in his office.

Such a long wait. I'm aware of the dust motes dancing in the afternoon sunshine, which is slatted into the room through venetian blinds. Peering between them, I observe a group of nurses sitting on the stone benches in the courtyard below, white-stockinged legs crossed, sandwiches being unwrapped, and then a sudden burst of laughter as two doctors stride past them, putting their hands up in mock surrender. I am filled with envy. Bob Morris enters his office, carrying a clipboard.

His eyes are kindly, his manner efficient, and he just misses attractive. What a killer this guy would have been had he been handsome, I muse, because it is clear that he likes women.

He faces me and says, "Well, you are most certainly pregnant. About ten weeks, by my calculations."

I'm sure he has said these words many times, perhaps that is why he delivers them so smoothly. But the words do not come at me smoothly; this is not linear information. These are words that strike the solar plexus first, then find the heart, and, passing through that organ with knifelike urgency, finally lodge themselves in the throat. I am speechless.

Dr. Morris assumes he understands my silence and, reaching for the phone, says to me in a voice full of authority and resolution, "We can take care of this next week, no reason to wait any longer than necessary. Mornings are best. I'll schedule the procedure for next Wednesday." He reaches to push a certain button, the button that will alert the secretary, whereupon she will come into the room and, appointment ledger in hand, ink in a time to undergo a procedure that will be convenient for both Dr. Morris and myself.

Only I stop him first. "Dr. Morris," I say, standing in the middle of the room, "I'm not going to have an abortion. I can't explain it and I don't want to argue about it, but I know I'm not going to have an abortion. I won't change my mind. I need a doctor who will see me through to the end, whatever that means. And if you can't do that, I would appreciate a referral."

He studies me carefully, and I can almost hear his mind turning: young actress, the beginning of her career, out of her mind, must be a religious fanatic. But he says, "Then I'm your man. You and I will become good friends over the next seven months. Eat well, get plenty of rest, work hard, and the baby will be here before you know it."

*   *   *

I walked home, very slowly, and for an hour tormented myself with unanswerable questions, such as: Why did this happen to me? How did this happen to me? I'd been so careful, so very careful, to prevent just such a mishap, and still the unthinkable had happened. I combed through my memory, examining and reexamining my days, meticulously recollecting my nights, extracting every moment of intimacy from the past and bringing it under the harsh light of the present. I came to an abrupt stop at the corner of Fifty-Ninth Street and Fifth Avenue. Steadied myself against a streetlamp. The lake, it was the afternoon in the lake. On fire, helpless. That subtle shift in the position of my diaphragm, the sensation of cool water between my legs. I felt it—did I feel it? But I didn't stop, I didn't stop.

That evening, I climbed the two floors to David's apartment and confronted him in the middle of the living room as he was preparing to leave for the theater.

"I'm pregnant," I said, and giving him no time to mount a defense, I continued, "It happened in Monroeville, when we were in the lake. There is absolutely no other possibility."

He looked at me, then, with eyes reminiscent of his mother's, already seeking distance, and still he approached me and tried to take me in his arms. I swatted him away and demanded, "What are you thinking, David? How do you *feel* about this?"

He took a deep breath and, trying his hardest to compose himself, said, "I can imagine how confused you must feel, and how frightened. Of all the things that could happen to you, this..." He didn't finish, because he wasn't quite able to articulate what I must be feeling, but he understood what *he* was feeling, and after a generous and thoughtful pause, he put his best offer on the table. "Kate, you know there are other ways to...take care of this. It doesn't have to be so black and white, so life changing. There are options."

I stared at him, waiting. He was silent. "You mean abortion?" I asked. "You want me to have an abortion, David?" So odd, what he did then, when everything I felt about him hung in the balance. He did exactly what he had done a year before, when his mother had condemned him for choosing me. He did nothing. I lifted my hand and slapped him, hard, across the face. Then I left.

My mother, I knew, would understand. She would be disappointed, very disappointed, but she would hear the terror in my voice, and she would respond with patience, and with love. At first, I thought there was a disconnect on the phone, the silence was so attenuated.

"Mom? Are you there? Did you hear what I said, Mom?"

"Oh, Kitten," she replied. "Yes, I heard you. You've made a mistake, and now you have to face the music. The only solution is to give the baby up for adoption, dear. There's no other way."

My heart folded in on itself. "But, Mom, I thought maybe, if you were willing to help me, I could continue working and saving money, and I'd give you the money and provide a nanny, and maybe the baby could stay at Derby Grange with you, just in the beginning, just for a while, until I can figure it out."

Very quickly, the answer came. So quickly it took my breath away. "Oh no, honey, I couldn't do that. Your father would be furious, he'd never allow it...and, frankly, I'm just not up to it. I mean, we're still adjusting to Tessie, and...no, no, that's not a good idea. You need to call on your best and strongest self and give this baby up for adoption. You can do it, Kitten. You have the courage to do it, and it would be best for both you and the baby."

Choking back tears, I pleaded, "Mother, I don't know how to do that. How do I do that?"

"Well, honey," said my mother, the mother of eight, "you go to Catholic Charities and you find a very good social worker, someone who will see you through this. You're not the first actress who's had an illegitimate baby, you know, and you won't be the last." Then she put the phone down. My mother never said good-bye at the end of a phone call, she just—hung up.

Huge waves of terror overtook me. There wasn't a glimmer of hope in this impermeable darkness, no possibility of reprieve. I couldn't fathom how I would get through the next week, let alone the next seven months, so I did the only thing I knew would give me instant relief. I reached for my touchstone.

Having found biology insurmountably difficult, Beth had relinquished her pursuit of medicine and was now living on Thompson Street in the Village and waiting tables at Kenny's Castaways. When she heard the barely restrained panic in my voice, she called in sick, jumped on the subway, and knocked on my door an hour later. I opened the door and fell into her arms.

She said the only honest thing she could say: "Oh my God, Katie, you poor thing."

Words so basic, so completely of the Midwest, so utterly without guile, that I had to laugh. "How many women are saying those very words to their best friends all over the world right now? In Iowa alone, it's got to be in the hundreds."

"No, no," Beth countered, "it's hundreds in Paris—thousands in Iowa!"

For hours, we examined every conceivable scenario. Marriage was out of the question; I was too young, and I knew our marriage would never surmount the odds. Neither David nor I was prepared to agree to a commitment we both knew had no chance of lasting. I could attempt to raise the baby by myself. I could continue working, hire a full-time nanny, and spend every spare moment caring for the child. But what would this gain the child, and what would I become? Both of us would be subjected to a life of denial and frustration, the baby without the unconditional devotion of the mother, and the mother deprived of her freedom and perhaps her career. My work defined me, and I knew it. My mother had made it very clear that there would be no support from my family.

"I'm scared, B," I said. "There doesn't seem to be any way out."

"No," Beth corrected me, "there are, in fact, several ways out, but all of them are painful. You have to know your own tolerance for pain, what you can endure, what you know you can live with, and what you can't live without."

It was early morning when we crawled into my emerald pull-out bed. We lay there, side by side, eyes wide open, holding hands, and finally Beth spoke. "You know, sweetheart, whatever you decide to do, I'll be there for you. I don't really think there's a right way to do this, but there is a best way for you to do it. Like every other tough choice you've had to make, be total. And be honest with yourself." I knew that she was turning over in her mind her own regrets, and I also knew that her idea of goodness transcended what most people considered morally unimpeachable.

"I can't have an abortion," I said, at last. "You know that. So the only absolute is the baby."

"And what is best for the baby," my best friend murmured, closing her eyes. "That's the real test, isn't it?"

The morning brought with it an icy clarity. What I could live with, what I couldn't live without. Beth had left for work at the crack of dawn, dropping a soft kiss good-bye on my cheek. I dressed slowly, had a cup of coffee, and headed to the studio on West Fifty-Third Street. Hailed a taxi and sat in the back ruminating over the number of fates that had been decided in the backseats of taxis.

When we pulled up to the curb, the cabbie looked at me. "You okay, hon?" Preternaturally grave young women were not unfamiliar to this guy, but he hadn't yet become impervious to their pain.

"I'm fine," I answered. "Thanks for asking."

I stepped off the elevator at the second floor, and instead of taking the customary turn to my dressing room, I headed in the opposite direction and found Claire bent over her desk, brow furrowed in concentration.

"We need to talk," I said, closing the door gently behind me. "Listen, Claire, there's no other way but to just say it straight. I'm pregnant. So I'm going to have to quit. I wanted to give you enough time to write me out before I begin to show. I'm sorry."

Claire stared at me, wide eyed. "Oh, sweetheart," she said at last, "what are you going to do?"

When I opened my mouth to respond, to tell her that I was confused, terrified, what came out was this: "I'm going to have the baby, and I'm going to give it up for adoption."

"Of course you are," Claire said, with such simplicity and conviction I almost burst into tears. Claire was a devout Roman Catholic, but I knew her response had less to do with the mores of the Church than it did with her authentic love for me. "Sit down, honey," she went on, "and let's talk about this."

After dispensing with the details—when did I find out, how far along was I, did David know, had I spoken to my mother— she leaned forward and, taking my hand in both of hers, spoke in a near whisper. "Katie, I have an idea. Just hear me out." Claire rose and started to pace. "We'll write the pregnancy into Mary's story. She and Jack are madly in love, she gets pregnant, he isn't ready for a baby, they break up, she decides to go it alone, lots of turbulence with Jack until, ultimately, she has the baby and names her (it has to be a girl)...*Ryan Fenelli.* Not only is it fabulous material, so much to play, but you can work straight through to term and return as soon after the birth as you like. What do you think?"

What I thought was: Once again, dear Claire, you have saved me. What I said was, "Thank you. I accept."

And so it was that millions of people witnessed life imitating art.

The ratings soared as Mary Ryan faced her trials with courage and unwavering conviction. The audience suffered with her when she was cruelly abandoned by Jack, and they despised Jack for his weakness. Their hearts were full of pride when she elected to have the baby alone, without Jack's love and support. They applauded her independence, they respected her morality, and they adored her guts.

Looking back, I wonder how many viewers—the faithful, the devoted—guessed the reality of the situation. It was, mercifully, kept out of the press, but still—the suddenness with which I popped, this was not at all merciful. One night, I was about to step into the shower when, to my horror, I saw the beginning of a small purple hand crawling under the skin of my abdomen.

Inexorably creeping upward, each magenta finger branding my skin, so that there could be no possibility—ever—of denial.

My days were full. I worked hard. My nights, increasingly empty.

David was kind, even solicitous, but our mutual sadness was such that it precluded any kind of enjoyment or comfort we might have found in each other; so more and more, he stayed away. And I wanted it that way. The course I had set myself on was not one my sweet young lover was built to stomach.

I followed my mother's advice and made an appointment with a social worker at the Catholic Home Bureau on the East Side of Manhattan. A lovely young woman, with wild red hair and cerulean eyes, rose to greet me. Her name was Susan Smith.

"Is it *really* Susan Smith?" I asked when we shook hands, and she laughed.

"Lucky, aren't I? So simple."

"Simple," I replied, lowering myself uneasily into a chair, "is not something I'm very familiar with."

Then the lovely smile disappeared and was instantly replaced by a genuine, if studied, expression of sympathy. She read me my rights, so to speak, which were archaic, primitive, in keeping with the history of the Catholic Church: after the birth of the baby, Susan would come to the hospital with legal papers, I would be given the opportunity to change my mind, but, once the papers were signed, the baby was no longer mine. It was an act of renunciation. I would not be allowed to hold the baby; I would not be allowed to see the baby. If the delivery was routine, I was expected to leave the hospital the same day. I would be given no information as to the whereabouts of the baby. I was not to appeal to the Home Bureau after the birth of the baby. The decision to give up my baby was unalterable.

"However," said Susan Smith. Full stop. The eyes again turning soft. "You will be able to actively participate in the choice of whom you would like to parent your baby. We have many couples on file, and we—you and I—will go through them carefully and choose which ones you find most suitable, most desirable. Then we will limit this choice to one or two couples. The upside here is that you have six months to comb through these files. At the end of this process, you will be very sure which woman and which man you have most confidence in, which couple you feel can best raise your child. Many couples, I am sure, will want this baby."

Such foreign, ill-fitting words coming out of that lovely girl's mouth. I had the sudden urge to hit her, but I took the high road and shook her hand instead.

We met often over the next months, Susan Smith and I. She pulled card after card from a file on her desk and told me the story of many men and women. She explained why they couldn't have children or even, in some cases, why they preferred adoption. She described to me their jobs, their backgrounds, their hobbies, their deepest wishes.

"Now, this couple," Susan said one day, tapping the card in front of her, "is amazing. And they've been through it. Eight years ago, they were promised a baby, but at the last minute, the birth mother changed her mind. No sooner did they get here than they had to turn around and go home. They were brokenhearted."

"Tell me about them," I urged.

"Well, they're both Irish-Catholic, midthirties, passionate about each other and about having a family, and did everything in their power to conceive a child, but it just wasn't to be. He is a very successful brain surgeon, she's an artist, and they live in a beautiful house in Westchester County. She probably calls me twice a month, and has for years, still hoping for a baby. She was in despair when she lost the baby girl they thought was theirs eight years ago. Inconsolable. And such a lovely woman, so full of life and hope. I wouldn't do that to her again."

I swallowed. "What does she look like?"

Susan Smith smiled, looked me straight in the eye. "Oh, she's a wild Irish rose."

I made my decision, and the day came when I was allowed to sit in Susan Smith's office while she phoned the prospective adoptive parents with the good news. Susan indicated that I was to sit close beside her and listen in on the exchange.

A woman answered.

"Molly, this is Susan Smith at the Catholic Home Bureau. How are you?"

Silence on the other end. "I don't know," said a voice, dropping to a whisper.

"Well, I think you're going to be fine, more than fine, when I tell you to prepare the nursery. Your baby will be coming to you in just a few weeks."

Another silence, then the woman gasped, I heard a cry, a muffled shout, the phone dropping to the floor and being picked up seconds later by a man, who said, "Who is this? What's going on? Molly's running upstairs crying and laughing and shouting at the same time, she's lost her mind, and I want to know what the hell is going on!"

Susan Smith was very direct with the husband. "Hello, Jack, this is Susan Smith from the Catholic Home Bureau. I'm calling to tell you that you are about to be a father."

Seconds passed. "Holy Mother of God," the man said, and Susan responded, "Exactly."

My mother came in for the birth. I flew her to New York first class.

My due date had been an educated guess, and Dr. Morris was kind enough to inform me that it might be as much as a week to ten days off. So Mother and I entertained each other. In an effort to encourage labor, we sneaked into a porno movie in Times Square called *Defiance,* and afterward we were so weak from laughter that I could barely move.

"Walk! You need to walk! Let's go!" my mother sang out.

And so we walked until I was forced to sit down on the curb at the corner of Forty-Second Street and Ninth Avenue. Not an ideal part of town for a hugely pregnant girl to take her ease. My ankles were so swollen I couldn't wear shoes at all, so I had bound my feet in three pairs of men's woolen socks. My mother, studying me, said, "Let's pretend you're my very eccentric daughter who loves porno movies." We looked at each other, me down below, she up above, and then we did what we always did when faced with the absurd, or the unbearable. We laughed.

My due date came and went, and one morning I woke to find my mother putting the last of her things into a suitcase. "Kitty Kat, this is the longest pregnancy in the history of the world. I need to get home or your father will shoot me. You'll be all right, won't you? I mean, kid, I've been here for a *week*. At this rate, you'll have to put *me* in the hospital."

Pointless to ask her to stay. My poor little mother had had enough. Enough of babies being born, enough of babies dying. And as for babies unbidden, well — she'd come to New York, she'd done what she was capable of doing, and now it was time to go.

We rode the elevator to the lobby, and I asked the doorman to flag a cab. Mother put her long, cool fingers to my cheeks and said, "My friend Mother Columba says that God is Everythingness. Who knows?" I put her in the cab, handed her a fifty, stuffed another in her purse, and kissed her on the cheek. The taxi pulled away, and I wondered what my mother must be thinking.

It's hard to know what's in a person's heart when she never says good-bye.

Deliverance

When it begins, I am alone. I am lying in my emerald-green pullout bed, and it is just before dawn, the darkest hour. I lie as still as death, waiting for life to announce itself. Distant stirrings arise, unfamiliar, neither pleasant nor harsh, then settle and subside. I lie in wait, patient and wholly unprepared. The stirrings swell into tight waves, and I know that, very soon, it will be time, and still I don't move. I watch the dawn almost hungrily as it blossoms outside my window, and I watch as my abdomen ripples and hardens, a tiny fist or maybe the ball of a foot suddenly distorting the skin with a sharp kick, a swift poke, and all the while the waves are undulating and surging, and I am playing for time, but there is none, and so I reach for the phone and dial Beth's number.

"Sorry to wake you, sweetheart, but I think you should come. They're about ten minutes apart."

"What!" she cries, from the bowels of Lower Manhattan. "I'm on my way! Don't move!"

And so I don't, even though now it is uncomfortable in the bed and there is much to be done. The sun illuminates the room; I sit on the edge of the bed, try to stand, sit again, not so much defeated as unable to go forward. I wait.

At last, a knock at the door. I push myself up and cross the room to let Beth in. She drops her bag, takes hold of my arm, and guides me toward the bathroom.

"Let me feel your tummy." A practiced hand, a good hand, resting lightly on my stomach. "Hmmm, uh-huh. Let's get moving. You're going to shower while I pack you a bag. Come on."

The faucet is turned on, my nightie is off in a flash, and Beth is leveraging me into the tub, itself a small masterpiece of choreography. I let the water run over my face, my breasts, my heaving stomach. Everything is leaking at once. I climb out of the shower, and Beth hands me a towel, does her best to dry what I cannot possibly reach.

"What do you want to wear?" she asks, as if I might be going on an audition, because the closet is, indeed, full of lovely clothes, but none of them have fit me for months, and I point at the one garment that has been my steadfast shroud: a commodious and badly soiled off-white cotton dress that slips on and off with the ease of a large cape. Beth frowns.

I say, "Just help me put it on." Once dressed, I lean against the wall and instruct Beth to pull two pairs of men's woolen socks over my feet, which is again met with resistance.

"You have to wear shoes—it's a hospital!" she objects, but I am already opening the door and shuffling toward the elevator.

On the street, despite the unremitting piercing of the doorman's whistle, there is not a taxi to be had, and even those that look like they might be empty hurtle by, dismissing us. Without warning, a contraction overwhelms me, and I am forced to sit on the curb.

Beth grows frantic and runs into the middle of Central Park West, waving her arms and screaming, "Taxi! Goddammit, I said, Taxi! Taxi! *Taxi!*" The doorman takes offense at this and, stepping back on to the sidewalk, crosses his arms over his belly.

Beth prevails, and a taxi swerves to a stop in front of the building. She shouts to the cabbie, "Just wait a minute, will ya? We need a *minute* here!" And all the while she's trying to pull me up because the men won't help, the cabbie and the doorman absolutely do not budge, frozen in a kind of primordial terror (or is it disgust?), but Beth manages to get me to my feet and with considerable effort wedges me into the back of the taxi, runs around to the other side, and jumps in, shouting to the cabdriver, "New York University Hospital, and step on it!"

He does, and we fly through Central Park at sixty miles an hour, swerving to avoid cyclists and pedestrians. The cabbie peppers the silence with a series of invectives, until Beth leans forward and says, "Could you please just shut up and drive?" He glowers at her in the rearview mirror. This is not how he sees his part in the movie.

Beth reaches over and takes my hand. She understands that I cannot talk. It is such a gloriously beautiful May morning, I put my hand to the window and hold it against the glass; I want to see what my hand looks like before it becomes another kind of hand. I press my face to the window, and I think to myself, There will never be another day like this day. This day will end. Everything passes in front of me with alarming speed, and though I recognize the splendor of the trees and the radiance of the sun, I am detached. This startles and unsettles me.

The taxi driver, disgruntled now, speeds through traffic with careless velocity, cracking gum and swerving and braking until, finally, he screeches to a halt in front of New York University Hospital. Beth throws a twenty-dollar bill at him, and we walk away from the turmoil of the morning into the cool, clinical confines of a foreign place.

Beth steers me to the admissions desk. "My friend is in labor, she needs a wheelchair. I would appreciate a wheelchair immediately, and then we'll do the paperwork." She is masterful, and a wheelchair quickly appears, I am placed in it, and the process of admissions begins. It is all in Beth's hands now; I am simply a young pregnant girl in a wheelchair.

It happens fast. I am stripped, given a hospital gown, hoisted onto an examining table. Dr. Morris come in seconds later, pats my hand, and says, "Well, Kate, so let's hope today's the day," and straps on a rubber glove. "Yes, indeed," he continues, "you're almost fully dilated. Let's get you prepped, it won't be long now." Leaning down, and most unprofessionally, he kisses my cheek and whispers, "You're a good girl. I'll get you through this as quickly and painlessly as possible."

A nurse comes in, all business. She neither smiles nor engages (does she know what will happen to the baby?), but in short order I am subjected to a process that is so fast and so brutal, I submit to it like a lamb to the slaughter. Legs are spread wide, an electric razor applied, and then an enema inserted, and I am told: "Do *not* go to the bathroom until you absolutely have to." Within seconds, it is unbearable, and, lumbering down the hall, hospital gown flapping, I find a bathroom and stagger into the stall like a crazed animal.

Beth helps me out, and we make baby steps back to the examining room, where I am greeted by a cadre of medical residents, who have come to observe and to learn. They do not meet my eyes, to them I am a specimen (do they know what will happen to the baby?), and then Dr. Morris enters the room, now brusque and distant, separates my legs, and describes in clinical detail the condition of my cervix and the state of my labor. There is a collective leaning in, a general acknowledgment of having gotten what they came for, followed by a brisk exodus.

I turn to look out the window, think there might be tears. No tears, I promise myself. But Beth has turned her face away. Suddenly, and without explanation, two orderlies come in and begin to wheel me to the delivery room.

I say, quickly, "Beth, you have to come with me—don't leave me."

She is holding my hand, saying, "I'm here, don't worry, I'm here, Katie."

Doors swing wide, a new room, disturbingly bright, and everything is fast now, feet in cold metal stirrups, nurses bustling, hidden behind masks, Dr. Morris looming over me, and I whisper, "Beth, please let Beth stay," but I don't hear his answer because a nurse is shouting, "Don't push, breathe!"

And there is the sense of a hive at its most agitated, and I am in it but not of it, when I hear Dr. Morris say, "Okay, that's enough. Let's get this girl out of this thing," and without warning a black rubber mask is put over my nose and mouth and I hear an already distant but still-urgent voice ordering me to "Breathe deeply, Kate—on my count, take three deep breaths, in and out!"

But there is no second breath, there is only oblivion.

I am quite alone, and it is over. The room is different. It has the dimensions and character of a closet; it is small, dark, and quiet. I run my hand over my loose, flaccid stomach and then lower, to find padding, thick and unwieldy, between my legs. On the floor beside the bed sits a pair of white espadrilles. Beth, the smuggler, slipped them into my overnight bag before we left the apartment.

Very slowly, I roll onto my side and prepare to sit up, anticipating agony. There is none. When I lean over to put on my shoes, there is a sudden rush of blood, but no pain. Gingerly, I rise to my feet and pull open the closet door. Hanging there, in solitary confinement, my white cotton dress. Carefully, I slip it over my head. In the bathroom, I splash water on my face and brush my teeth. Then I look. Matted, lusterless hair, pale skin, dark circles under empty eyes. I run a comb through my hair and smooth it with my hands. I touch my cheek.

In the corridor, I am lost. A doctor is passing, and I stop her: "Excuse me, but I'm looking for the nursery. Is this the maternity ward?"

She cocks her head, appraising me, steel-gray eyes beneath a helmet of black hair. "You're a long way from the nursery," the doctor replies, as if slightly put out. "This is the oncology ward. Take the elevator to the third floor and you'll find a directory there, and a bridge to the nursery, but it's a hike."

It is a long way to the nursery, and on this journey, turning over and over in my mind, is the question: Why did I wake up on the oncology ward? I follow the bridge to another building, where I am told that the maternity ward and the nursery are two distinct units and that I must go back, and down, and then straight ahead through a passageway. That is, if I'm looking for the nursery, and not the maternity ward.

At the end of the passageway, double doors open into a long, cool, dimly lit corridor. In the distance, I make out the solitary figure of a nurse sitting at her station. I slowly walk toward her, trying to quiet the flapping in my brain, as if something has been let loose in there that wants to sit still but can't. As I approach, the nurse looks up. She is pristine, from white-capped head to white-shoed toe, and she is smiling.

"Can I help you?" she asks, standing. She is young, no more than thirty, and she exudes calm. For a moment I hold my breath but then realize with relief that, no, she doesn't recognize me.

"Yes, I think so," I reply. "I had a baby this afternoon, and I was wondering if I could see my baby."

The beautiful young nurse with the warm brown eyes now stops to consider me. A shadow crosses her lovely face and she asks, "What is your name?"

"Kate Mulgrew."

She pauses and says, "Let me see." She consults the large white journal sitting open on her desk. A minute passes, during which she intently studies this journal.

Finally, she closes the book, looks at me, and with a modulated voice says, "The birth record shows that your baby is to be put up for adoption."

I nod, and place a hand on the countertop.

The nurse is glancing furtively up and down the corridor while she speaks. "Hospital policy forbids the birth mother to see her baby under these circumstances. You understand."

I do not nod. I see the brown eyes harden, and my pulse races, but the good nurse—the infinitely good nurse—whispers, "If you go quickly down the hall you'll see the nursery on your right. Stop in front of the window and I'll come and pull up the blinds. But you need to hurry."

Down the hall a little way, quickly, and there's the nursery, just as she promised, concealed behind venetian blinds. The nurse comes up behind me very softly and, again looking to her right as if expecting someone who might disapprove, she manipulates a tangle of silver cords and choosing one, pulls, and the room is instantly revealed.

"Just look for your name on the bassinette. Your daughter is there," and she points to the front row. Daughter. She said daughter. And there on the front of the bassinette is the label clearly marked: BABY GIRL MULGREW.

I press my face against the glass. Strain to see her. Tiny brown face under a pink cap, pink cap over black curls, miniature fists suddenly escaping from the blanket, opening and closing. I put my hands to the window, can't be helped, and the little fists are opening and closing, opening and closing, and my face is flattened against the pane and then *thwack!* The venetian blinds are dropped, the nursery disappears, I turn in bewilderment, but the nurse is adjusting her cap and saying just under her breath, "That's enough now, you need to go," and hurries off in the direction of a group of doctors, coming in to make their rounds.

I stand there, just outside the nursery, but as the doctors draw closer, I lower my head and, averting my eyes, make my way down the corridor, through the passageway, across the bridge, and up six floors to the cancer ward, where I know Susan Smith will be waiting for me.

Ransom

Three days after the baby was born, I returned to work. I entered the studio and was greeted by the floor manager, Briggsie, who lacked his usual exuberance. Neither Claire nor any of the other producers was present. Lela Swift, the director, embraced me and asked, "Are you okay?"

"Yes," I replied, "I'm fine."

"Well," Lela went on, "this is the scene where Mary comes home from the hospital with her—baby. While she waits for the family to arrive, she has some time alone with her child. You got the script, right? It's a bit of a monologue."

I nodded, and said, "Let's get going. Roll tape on the first take."

I took my place behind the living room set door. Suddenly, the studio nurse approached me, carrying an infant in her arms. When she attempted to give me the baby, I held up my hand and said, "Wait until the red light goes off." At my cue, I signaled the nurse to give me the stunt baby, took her in my arms, and entered the living room of the Ryan family home. Standing in the middle of the room, I delivered the monologue to the baby, as directed. A monologue about love, a monologue about courage, a monologue about, above all else, loyalty, ending with the words: "I will never leave you, Ryan. We will never be separated. That is my solemn promise."

The first take was flawless, not a word out of place. I looked up at the control room, where often, if the scene was particularly difficult, the producers would flip on the lights and stand up, clapping, in a collective show of appreciation. But today, after this scene, there was nothing.

No one spoke. The control room remained detached and silent.

I turned to Lela and asked, "Acceptable?"

She nodded.

I beckoned to the studio nurse and, handing the stunt baby to her, said, "Take it."

Claire had written me only one scene on my first day back. Not even a scene, really. A monologue. A beautifully crafted monologue that would, everyone knew, go a long way toward improving our sagging ratings.

My work done, I gathered myself and walked toward the open door.

Skating

The elevator door opened, and there he was. I'd seen him so many times, this curious blue-eyed, sandy-haired creature with whom I shared a common elevator, and not once had we exchanged words.

Today, however, was different. Though not tall, he gave the impression of size and was always impeccably dressed, from his elegant three-piece suit to his tailored pink linen shirt (replete with monogrammed cuffs) to his custom-made English shoes. He turned his head, gave me the once-over, and, smiling, said, "So, looks like you survived."

Ah, yes, the baby. Of course. He had ridden the elevator with me countless times throughout the past year, had been what one might call a silent witness to my ordeal, and here he was, acknowledging it openly, almost cavalierly. "In a matter of speaking," I said.

Strange man. He had a face that radiated intelligence, and although he was standing still opposite me, he possessed a kinetic energy so palpable I almost wanted to ask him to slow down. The door opened, ushering us into the lobby, when he turned and said, "Today's my birthday and I have no plans. Wide open. Why don't we step across the street to the Tavern on the Green and have a glass of champagne? You game for that?"

It was the middle of the afternoon in the middle of the week in New York City, the sun was shining, and he seemed kind, so I said, "Why not? You can tell me the story of your life."

So much sympathy was evident beneath those gaudy, glittering chandeliers that much that should have been withheld was not. He listened with infinite patience, and not once in the unfolding of that long, luxurious afternoon did I feel the sting of criticism.

His name was Richard Cushing, he was a defense attorney, and there was nothing about which he was not passionate.

Immediately, I sensed a wildness in him, but what I could not have foreseen was his capacity for tenderness. He was a tough New York lawyer, born and bred on Long Island, fully aware of his flaws, but oh, how he loved to win. An obsessive love of the game was at the core of his nature, and while he approached the courtroom like a predator, as a friend he turned out to be generous and fiercely loyal.

Balm in Gilead, he was. Undemanding, and without judgment. Still reeling from the baby, and having just left *Ryan's Hope* after two years of unremitting upheaval, I sought refuge in Cushing's constancy.

That he wanted and expected more from me was, I suppose, inevitable, and yet I was not prepared when, one night at dinner,

I found a diamond ring at the bottom of my glass of champagne. With the guilelessness of a child, I slipped it on my finger and said, "Oh, Richard, I don't know what to say," to which he replied, "No pressure, just wear it for a while, see if you like it." This was the beginning of a game I justified as whimsy, and would come to play adroitly.

My tenure on *Ryan's Hope*, however brief, was sufficient to confirm my suspicion that television, while lucrative and enjoyable, was not enough to satisfy me creatively. I missed the theater, and so, in the winter of 1978, I accepted the role of Desdemona opposite Ron O'Neal in a Hartman Theatre production of *Othello*, in Stamford, Connecticut. Mr. O'Neal, famous for having created the iconic role of Youngblood Priest in the movie *Super Fly*, insisted on playing the role of Othello in blackface, a perplexing choice that no one had the guts to argue but that proved a nightmare for the wardrobe department. To add insult to injury, on opening night, after Othello had rather violently "put out the light," I rolled center stage and, covered with sooty fingerprints, lost my wig to the front row. Convulsed with laughter, this Desdemona simply would not go gentle into that good night and faced her curtain call bald, besmudged, and beside herself.

One afternoon, I got a call from Stark Hesseltine, who told me that Fred Silverman, the head of programming for NBC, was in town and wanted to have lunch with me. When I demurred, Stark said, "One meets with the premier executive of a major network out of courtesy, if nothing else, so put on your prettiest bonnet and be at Thirty Rockefeller Plaza tomorrow at noon."

I wore an Italian cream-colored pleated skirt, black stockings, and a black turtleneck sweater, and slipped on a pair of Ferragamo heels. I tied a black satin ribbon in my hair. The elevator let me out on the penthouse floor, where I was greeted by a plump middle-aged woman wearing a bright smile and a string of pearls, who led me down a short hallway and, after pulling open two heavy mahogany doors, ushered me into the executive dining room.

The table of twelve men rose as one. Immediately stepping forward, Fred Silverman extended his hand and introduced himself. He was full faced and brown eyed, and I thought him polite, straightforward, and avuncular. His eleven henchmen introduced themselves by turn. Nothing about this group promised a luncheon full of laughter and bonhomie, but I was famished and figured I might as well enjoy my meal. Silverman remarked on my unconventionally hearty appetite, to which I responded, "I must introduce you to my father. Those are his sentiments exactly."

This was met with guffaws of appreciation (clearly most of these gentlemen were married to Hollywood wives who ate, on average, exactly nothing), after which the mood became noticeably more somber. Then Silverman cut to the chase. After carefully folding his napkin and placing it on the table, he leaned forward and said, "You know, we were all very impressed with your performance on *Ryan's Hope,* thought you were terrific as Mary Ryan. So terrific, in fact, that we were thinking about developing a nighttime series for you, a spin-off of the *Columbo* series, but this time our protagonist will be Mrs. Columbo."

"Peter Falk?" I interrupted. "But he's old enough to be my father! Or maybe, if he was really precocious, my grandfather."

Laughter, dampened by what I'm sure they all considered my cheek. Chuckling, Silverman persevered, "No, no, nothing like that. His wife, perhaps, but the beauty of it is that they'll never be together on screen. He does his thing; she does hers. Mrs. Columbo will be a journalist by day and a sleuth by night. They may talk occasionally on the phone, but this is strictly her story.

She solves murders using her wit, her style, and her courage. We at NBC/Universal television think you have the talent and the charisma to pull this off—how does the idea grab you?" He stopped just short of winking at me, but in his eye there was the unmistakable glint of victory.

I looked around the table, at all those terribly important faces turned toward mine, and I was suddenly filled with an urgent need to get out of there. "Mr. Silverman, gentlemen," I said, rising, "it's very kind of you to have thought of me, and I'm very flattered, but you see, I just finished two years on television and now I want to get back to the theater. In fact, I'm dying to get back to the theater. It's what I came to New York to do, I've missed it, I've longed for it, and so really as much as I'd like to, I can't, but thank you all very much. It was a pleasure dining in the clouds with you, and now, if you'll excuse me." I reached for my raincoat, and after quickly shaking Fred Silverman's hand, I was out the door before the remaining eleven could even push back their chairs.

I jumped into a taxi and flew to 80 Central Park West, threw open the door to my apartment, tossed my bag on the table, and fell into a chair. Relief. Happiness. Triumph. All real, all true. Then I felt the merest zephyr of regret, followed by the need for a good part in a good play, which, in an ideal world, would start rehearsals tomorrow, open in a month, and run for a long, long time. Such are the cascading thoughts of the actress who has just turned down a big job when she has no bird in the hand. This pattern, common enough by now, motivated me to pick up the phone and call my agent, who, himself deeply familiar with this cycle, beat me to the punch. The phone rang just as I reached for it.

"Hello?" I answered.

"Kate, Stark here. Now listen: Leonard is waiting for you in his office. At three o'clock, he'll have Fred Silverman conferenced in. We all understand what happened at lunch, and while we respect your decision, it is never smart to walk away from the table before you've considered the deal. Courtesy, that's all. Fred Silverman is a powerful man, the day may come when we'll need him, so let's play nice and listen to what he has to offer. At the end of the conversation, if you still feel the same way, we'll accept your decision. Now get going." And with that, he hung up.

A tiny surge of excitement, followed by a stab of terror. I raked a comb through my hair, brushed my teeth, and was on my way.

Leonard Franklin's office was dimly lit, richly decorated, and intimidating. In the center of the room sat a round, glass-topped coffee table bearing two crystal tumblers, a crystal pitcher of ice water, and a very large black telephone attached to a triangular device studded with a variety of colorful buttons.

Leonard greeted me warmly. "Now, Katie, sit down. I have Stark on the line, and Mr. Silverman will be conferenced in at three. He'll be on speakerphone, so this will be an open conversation. We just want you to hear him out. Can you do that? Without interrupting? Can you just listen to what the man has to say?"

I accepted the tall glass of cool water and took a seat. "Of course, Leonard. As long as you all know where I stand." Leonard nodded, but he appeared preoccupied. At exactly three o'clock the phone rang. Leonard pushed a button and greeted Fred Silverman as if they'd served together in the Normandy Invasion. They used a vernacular that was foreign to me but evidently very familiar to them, seasoned with obscure expressions and delivered in a dialect I found surprising and strange coming, as it did, out of my lawyer's customarily patrician mouth.

I watched as Leonard paced, and slowly came to understand

that Fred Silverman was not so much talking to me as he was to my lawyer and my agent, both of whom—if silence is any indication of interest—appeared mesmerized by what he was saying. Various words emanated from the disembodied voice of the NBC guru, they glowed for an instant and then were swallowed up in the grand unspooling of promises so extravagant as to seem absurd to the mind of a twenty-three-year-old actress who had one soap opera, a movie, and a couple of plays under her belt. The men who managed my professional life, however, did not find it in the least absurd. They were galvanized, riveted, in their element. Stella Adler, green eyes flashing, popped into my consciousness and shouted, *In the banker's way! Only the work will lift you up! I worry that you'll skate into Hollywood.* But by that time, the conversation had come to an end; Fred Silverman was signing off with an admonition to think long and hard, with the implicit warning that such a conversation would not be had twice.

That night onstage, I played Desdemona as I'd never played her before, but at the curtain call I was so solemn that Ron O'Neal leaned in to me and whispered, "What happened to you? Did someone die?"

I looked at him, took his hand, and, curtsying deeply, said nothing.

Fred Silverman had made me an offer I couldn't refuse.

Before I left for Hollywood, there were things to do. I wanted to look Susan Smith in the eye and ask her for mercy, a sliver of mercy, nothing too untoward. I wanted to ask her if my baby was all right. I wanted to ask her how my baby had been received by her adoptive parents—in particular, I wanted to know what the mother had said when my baby had been put in her arms and how she had looked. Last, I wanted a photograph of my baby. Surely, requests as modest as these would be granted.

Susan Smith was fundamentally kind, so it must have required a significant effort for her to greet me so coolly. Her lovely warmth had been replaced by a steely stoicism. She did not ask me to sit but instead launched into the litany of reasons preventing her from providing me with any information about my baby, let alone a photograph.

"But what possible harm could a photograph do?" I pleaded, struggling to maintain my composure.

She shook her head. "I've told you and told you, Kate, it's not the policy we subscribe to here at Catholic Charities, and you know that. You need to learn to accept it."

I felt I had accepted enough. "This is wrong, Susan, and you know it. It's cruel. I'll go to the archbishop, if I have to, because this is untenable."

There was a moment's brittle silence in the room, and then Susan Smith said, "You do that. You go to the archbishop. Maybe then you'll understand why there are rules that, once made, cannot be broken."

On my way out, I stopped at the administrative and clerical offices on the ground floor and requested an appointment with the archbishop. The clerk told me that the archbishop was, naturally, indisposed, but perhaps I might chat with the executive director of the Catholic Home Bureau maternity services, Sister Una McCormack. I was led into a room and introduced to a tall, formidable-looking woman with short-cropped gray hair, wearing a simple black dress with a white collar, the requisite silver cross hanging from her neck. Her eyes were piercing, the color of slate. When she inquired as to the point of the meeting, I told her that I had given up a baby and I wanted to discuss the adoption policy with the archbishop.

"To what end?" she asked, gray eyes unblinking.

"For comfort, and for edification," I replied. "It's my right as a mother."

The nun folded her hands in front of her and, shifting her voice to a lower octave, said, "But you gave up that right when you relinquished your baby, didn't you? All of that, I'm sure, has been carefully explained to you. Now, here's my card if you need anything of a practical nature," she said, sliding a thin white card across the table. She tapped it with her finger, twice. "But you should know that the archbishop is a very busy man and seldom here."

Over drinks in his apartment, Richard Cushing ranted and raved about the injustices so generously served up by the Catholic Church.

"Not the Church proper," I corrected him. "Just a faction of the Church."

"Bullshit!" he shouted, his enormous blue eyes bulging with fury. "It is the mandate of the Catholic Church, and it's outrageous! Barbaric! When I hear unspeakable crap like this, it makes me proud to be a Jew."

I had to smile at him, and said, "Jesus was a Jew."

Cushing stopped in midstride and turned to look at me. "That's right," he declared, "and His Father was a wrathful God!"

This righteous train of thought extended itself all the way to Sag Harbor, where Beth was living with her lover, an unorthodox bohemian artist and a confirmed bachelor who had type 2 diabetes, which he treated with chronic disdain. Richard had suggested we make a weekend of it, but he was in no way prepared for the lifestyle that greeted us when, after many complicated attempts to find the house where they were living, we turned into a gravel drive and came upon a dwelling that looked for all the world as if it was missing only the county edict: THIS PROPERTY IS CONDEMNED.

Inside, however, Beth had converted the space into something charming and whimsical. Candlelight illuminated her lover's paintings, which hung on every wall, broken bits of colorful crockery had been assembled on makeshift shelves, a bowl of red apples sat on a Shaker table in the kitchen. Beth led the way upstairs, leaving the gentlemen to get acquainted over mismatched cups of herbal tea. We entered the master bedroom and closed the door behind us. I meant to tell her so many things. I meant to laugh. But when we sat on the bed together and she took my hand, I looked at her and said, "I don't think I can bear this, Beth. I made a mistake."

I pressed one hand to my mouth to stifle the sobs. Beth put her arm around my shoulder and held me very tightly. We sat there, like that, until the worst of it was over, then I composed myself, and we rejoined our men, who had already tired of each other's company and were eager to get on with the evening.

An emptiness and a terrible longing dogged me, and I knew there was only one person on earth who could fully understand. When I called David, I immediately sensed a wariness. It had been six months since I'd last seen him, shortly after the birth of the baby. He had taken me for an ice cream on the East Side and, as we sat rigidly on stools staring at our root-beer floats, it was appallingly clear that we had nothing to say to each other. He loved me, I knew that, and I loved him, but the baby had made anything else between us impossible. Nothing was salvageable.

And yet a few nights later, I walked slowly up Central Park West until I came to the corner of Eighty-Sixth Street. The snow was falling lightly, and there, sitting on the wooden bench that had once been our meeting place, was the father of my child. He didn't acknowledge me, barely moved when I sat down next to him. The collar of his black peacoat was drawn up around his face, in sharp contrast to his pale skin. That silky hair, wet with snow. The beautiful mouth, set. The length of him, wound tight. He looked into the distance, never once at me, and waited until he was sure I had felt the silence.

Quietly but not unkindly, David Bernstein said, "I wish I'd never met you." Then he rose, buried his hands in his pockets, and walked away.

The snowflakes danced under the streetlamp. I sat until I felt the bench growing cold beneath me and then stood, brushed myself off, and headed in the opposite direction.

On Thin Ice

Many people are of the opinion that Nature bestowed her favors on Los Angeles. I've always regarded those immutable blue skies and that fixed bright sun as a vast, thin varnish spread over a city that is not a city at all but a string of rootless villages. Some of the villages matter, but most don't. The more enduring villages bear names signifying their importance, such as Culver City, Beverly Hills, and Studio City. You knew where you were going when you entered Studio City and, almost always, you knew why you were going there. You were, of course, going to the studio itself, because that is where you worked.

In my case, entering the gates of Universal Studios at four

thirty in the morning was a powerful and mysterious rite of passage. The studio guard sitting inside a glass-enclosed booth would stand up as my car approached and lean out to greet my driver, Frank, who would smile at him and say, "Morning, Bill, another early call." Frank worked because I worked, and Bill worked because Frank worked, and the studio worked because Lew Wasserman was a genius and understood that a studio was like a Swiss watch: beautifully constructed, perfectly calibrated, and very expensive.

Frank was tall and lean and for many years had served in the military. He took his job seriously and was always punctual, respectful, and kind. On my first day, he presented me with a white coffee cup embossed, in black letters, with my name. I have it to this day. I've lost countless silver boxes and gold pendants, but that coffee cup has stayed with me through thick and thin, and I always think of Frank when I drink from it. Mostly, I think of the expression on Frank's face when he arrived to pick me up at four o'clock in the morning. A slightly sheepish grin, a short shake of the head, and Frank would say, "Time to roll."

And roll we did. Past the gates and through the studio alleys, some brightly lit, some still in shadow, until we arrived at my bungalow, which was situated at the rear of the studio. The lights would be on and the front door open, figures within bustling about. My makeup and hair team, Gloria and Jose, would have arrived an hour earlier and, having already set up, were waiting for me. Jose greeted me with a cup of coffee, and Gloria, with a wry grin, would ask, "Ice mask?" I tried, always, to be considerate to these two people because I recognized them as belonging to that underrated but noble Hollywood breed of severely sleep-deprived, modestly paid, and remarkably devoted craftsmen.

After hair and makeup were completed, Frank drove me to

the soundstage, where most of the day's work would take place. Stage 24 was a capacious piece of real estate containing Mrs. Columbo's kitchen, her living room, her bedroom, her daughter's bedroom, her study, the newspaper office where she worked, and a doghouse wherein lay her trusted canine, a giant bloodhound afflicted with bad breath and clinical depression.

In the beginning, I worked seven days a week. This was an unexpected development, but under the circumstances I felt I needed to comply. As a result, I was never late, I was never unprepared, and I never complained. I was going to show these Hollywood veterans what I was made of, we were all going to have a rollicking good time, and, with any luck, we were going to hand Fred Silverman a hit on a silver platter.

But young girls, they do get weary. In the fourth month of seven-day workweeks, my nerves began to show. I lived on a diet of coffee and cigarettes and the occasional cheeseburger, which was covertly frowned upon by the producers, who felt that Mrs. Columbo should be as trim and attractive as possible. I slept on set pieces and spent my entire lunch break (which never exceeded more than thirty minutes) in my trailer, sacked out on the couch. I began to negotiate with my makeup and hair team, begging them for an additional ten minutes of rest in exchange for which I would sleep sitting up, a towel draped over my costume, my hair wrapped in curlers. I negotiated, too, with my personal assistant, whose name was Lisa, but I called her Twink, which was, I thought, the most appropriate nickname I could bestow on someone who approached her job as she would the bar at Trader Vic's.

"Twink," I'd say, closing the trailer door and locking it behind me, "do *not* let anyone come in and do *not* wake me up if the PA knocks. I do *not* need to run lines with the guest star, I do not need a touch-up, I need *ten more minutes of sleep*. You will be rewarded, trust me."

The Swiss watch, unbendable and unbreakable, was beginning to feel unbearable. Frank took me to lovely places, but I couldn't enjoy them. There was never enough time. No time to sit on the patio of my sweet house nestled in the hills of Benedict Canyon, no time to zip down Sunset Boulevard in my own little Nissan convertible 280ZX, no time to spend an afternoon at the beach, or go to the movies, or eat in a restaurant other than the Universal commissary. No time for old friends, no time for new friends, and certainly no time for boyfriends. Richard Cushing came for a weekend and we brawled. He'd read my diary while I was working and, rigid with fury, shouted, "Are you seeing someone else? Are you? Tell me, goddammit!"

And I, too tired to argue, simply said, "You should be ashamed of yourself. I'm going to bed."

I was seeing someone else, of course, because weariness is by its very nature compromising. It wasn't a normal relationship at all, just a small piece that fit well into the Swiss watch and didn't disturb its rhythm. My private life was of little concern to anyone on the *Mrs. Columbo* set, and, in fact, I often wondered if the pursuit of the illicit was not tacitly encouraged among those in charge, devoted, as they all were, to profit. I could have been carrying on with a psychopathic serial murderer, and no one would have blinked an eye as long as I knew my lines and hit my mark with efficiency and a modicum of verve.

These and other sentiments were shared with my costars, in the brief moments we had between setups, and often it was the actor playing the murderer who would reduce me to helpless laughter. Who knew that Armand Assante and Fred Forrest were ruthlessly funny raconteurs? Or that Bob Dishy, famous for his wit, had a heart of gold? My friend René Auberjonois showed up and, twirling a fake mustache, created the character of Mrs. Columbo's French teacher, never missing a beat as he chewed every conceivable piece of scenery on that set. Donald Pleasence was the master, however, and during a five-minute scene consumed no less than eight cream puffs in quick and perfect succession while delivering an alibi so exquisitely funny that it brought the crew to its knees.

One night, we wrapped early so that I could attend a ball in honor of Lew Wasserman, a Hollywood mogul of the highest order, the man responsible for merging MCA with Universal Studios. I don't know quite how I plucked up the nerve, but I crossed the vast ballroom to the Wasserman table and, after introducing myself to Edie Wasserman, asked Lew if he would do me the honor of a spin. He rose, offered his arm, and gallantly escorted me onto the dance floor. We didn't say much, the music was dauntingly loud, but it gave me an opportunity to study this man who had begun with so little and had accomplished so much. His eyes were nearly hidden behind his signature thick-lensed, black-framed glasses, but there was a lightness to his step and a gentleness to his touch that evoked in me a respect for what this son of Russian-Jewish immigrants had overcome and the heights to which he had soared. When the music stopped, he very lightly kissed my hand and said, "Thank you, Miss Mulgrew, for your considerable talents, one of which, I now know, is dancing."

As we approached the end of the first thirteen episodes, I laughed when it dawned on me that the set decorator had managed to place either a sofa, a chaise, or a bed in nearly every interior scene, thereby serving as an accomplice to my stolen moments of repose. It's a curious truth (and one I've noted with regularity in the four decades that I've been acting) that when an actor is present on the set, she is somehow acquitting herself in a professional manner, whether rigidly awake or fast asleep. My crew on *Mrs. Columbo* subscribed to this peculiar philosophy, and while I was not encouraged to fall into a dead sleep in the middle of a working set, I was nonetheless conveniently ignored when I slipped into a coma on the very sofa Mrs. Columbo had just used as a confessional.

One night, while the company was on location in the hills just outside of Universal and had taken no fewer than three meal penalties, I curled up in an armchair between scenes and fell into a profound sleep. Evidently, this was the endgame for my subconscious, because despite every attempt, no one could wake me up. I was bundled into my car, and Frank drove me back to the lot, in the middle of which sat the studio clinic. Supported by Frank, I was led into a small examining room, whereupon a middle-aged nurse (herself a study in functional narcolepsy) came in, pulled up my skirt, and gave me a shot of B_{12} so potent that within seconds I was calling for Frank to grab my script and start the car. On the way out, I happened to glance into an adjoining room, and there, pants down around his ankles, chin in hand as he leaned against the examining table, was John Belushi, also receiving a "midnight constitutional." He caught my eye, and we exchanged weary smiles.

Well intentioned but misguided, *Mrs. Columbo* could not survive its many incarnations. Its evolution was evident in its ever-changing titles: from *Mrs. Columbo* to *Kate Columbo* to *Kate the Detective* to, finally and most baffling, *Kate Loves a Mystery*. I suppose the producers were hoping that if they planted the wilting flower in an altogether new garden, the audience might suddenly regard it as exotic.

My producers possessed many skills, but, alas, horticulture was not among them. The plug was pulled in the middle of a scene on a cold winter's night in the Hollywood Hills. I shook the hand of every member of the crew, embraced Gloria and Jose, and, jumping in the car, instructed Frank to take me to the airport. "I'm going home," I said to him, unable to resist a smile.

As a postscript, I gave the contents of my Benedict Canyon

house to my older brother, Tom, who had dropped in to visit me for a few days on his way to greener pastures in San Francisco.

"What about the booze?" Tom asked.

"Drink it."

"And the Jacuzzi?"

"Jump in."

When he asked me what he should do with the key, I told him to leave it under the mat for the next actress who, I felt sure, would be along shortly.

"So maybe I should leave a light on," Tom suggested.

"Wouldn't want her to stumble," I replied.

My older brother, not one to put off a cool drink in a hot tub, chuckled and said, "Roger that."

La Donna è Mobile

Stark Hesseltine, whose passing I shall mourn until I die, behaved rather irresponsibly on a hot afternoon in Beverly Hills when he accompanied me on a shopping spree and encouraged me to buy a ten-thousand-dollar white mink coat with a dazzling fox collar from an absurdly expensive furrier on Rodeo Drive.

"Why not?" said my agent, who was himself attired in his customary mustard turtleneck and dark Valentino sport coat. "You deserve it. You've worked hard, haven't had a break in over three years—wear it in style, nap in it, see the world, for God's sake! I hear the upcoming opera season in Venice is supposed to be extraordinary—now, that's a coat made for a night at the opera!"

My mother did not agree, and as we picked our way around the puddles of autumnal Venice on our way to see *Rigoletto* at La Fenice, she deliberately let go of my arm, saying, "I didn't know I was going to the opera with *Cher* tonight. When did you change your name to *Cher?*" Ah, she's back to herself, I said to myself, and half smiled as I led the way across the Ponte di Rialto.

Just five weeks earlier, Mother had visited me in New York and, as was our habit, we had dined one night at Asti, a small family-run Italian restaurant, of the kind endemic to Manhattan's Lower East Side. It was a large and convivial gathering that evening, with Richard Cushing serving as host, as he so often and so unsparingly did, a vivacious Beth beside him laughing into my brother Joe's ear, siblings Jenny and Sam in conspiratorial bliss on the other side of the table, and me next to Mother, who sat at the head opposite Cushing.

My father, as usual, was absent. He and my mother never traveled together. This was understood and accepted by all of us.

My mother loved this particular establishment for the singular sweet it offered at the end of the meal, by which I mean, of course, a singing waiter. On this night, it was Oscar who stepped up to the table and, white linen napkin meticulously folded over his left arm, opened his mouth and produced a magnificent a cappella rendition of "Danny Boy." My eyes traveled from face to face, registering the delight of each person, because "Danny Boy" was clearly intended as a special gift to us, this Irish family so crazy about this Italian restaurant.

When I turned to Mother and saw her face, all pleasure instantly drained from me.

"Danny Boy" had stirred up both the vivid memory of Tessie, and her keenly felt absence, and all of it showed in my mother's face as she sat and listened to Oscar sing: agony, grief, despair. No tears, there were never tears, my mother didn't cry, but in that moment her face was fractured with longing and hopelessness, and I made up my mind, then and there, to take her far away and for as long as was needed to stitch that face back to happiness.

So it was that we found ourselves in a city of singular decadence and beauty, skipping over footbridges to make our way to the opening night of *Rigoletto* at La Fenice.

Afterward, sitting at a table in the Piazza San Marco, Mother said, "There's no point in having an espresso after dinner—as your friend Richard Cushing would say, let's cut out the middle man and go straight to the *digestivo,* and let's cut out the glassblowers on Murano and go straight to Florence." She was longing for the tombs of Santa Croce.

We entered the lobby of the Excelsior Hotel in Florence at night, tired and hungry. To Mother's chagrin, I was again impersonating Cher and, taking her by the hand, swept through the dining room in my ostentatious fur, past the bar, and into a small anteroom where she could rest and have her *digestivo* in peace.

"Now, Mother," I said, helping her off with her raincoat (a real find at Goodwill, as I was daily reminded), "just relax and drink your Averna quietly. If anyone approaches you, please resist the impulse to engage, okay? Just until we get our bearings and I get us checked in. I need a minute. Promise?"

Mother sank into the rose damask-covered armchair and said, "Oh, Kitten, don't be silly. But I wouldn't mind a tiny panino with my *digestivo,* I'm having a sinking spell." I stopped by the bar on my way to the lobby and ordered a drink and a sandwich for mother, as requested. Seated at the bar were a number of well-groomed, well-heeled Italian gentlemen, all in postures of repose, exuding entitlement, smoking and drinking and engaged in what sounded, to my uneducated ear, like a sustained and heated argument. I put my head down and walked quickly toward the lobby.

When I returned, twenty minutes later, Mother was no longer reclining in her chair but leaning forward, happily engaged in conversation with a man who was literally kneeling at her feet, cigarette in one hand, drink in the other.

"Kitten!" Mother cried as I approached. "This is Roberto, he's utterly divine, and if you don't want him, I'll take him."

The stranger was unabashedly grinning at me, to which I

responded with practiced indifference. I sat on the ottoman beside Mother's chair and beckoned a waiter. The "divine" Roberto leaped to his feet and addressed the waiter with a passionate outpouring of words, hands gesticulating wildly in every direction, at the end of which tirade the waiter looked curiously unmoved and, shrugging his shoulders, mumbled *"Va bene, signor"* and slid out of the room.

It was then that he turned to me and introduced himself as Roberto Meucci, from the house of Sesto Meucci, a Florentine born and bred, and an artist. Although it was clear that he considered his English impeccable, it was, to my ear, liberally seasoned with Italian idioms and eccentricities.

As he spoke, I took him in. A man of medium height, with thick salt-and-pepper hair that continually fell into his hazel eyes, dressed with the casual elegance of his class in a gray mock-necked ribbed sweater pulled over beautifully tailored trousers, which broke perfectly across the tops of exquisitely made Italian shoes.

"Oh my, what heavenly shoes," I said, to which he immediately responded, "Your mama thinks I am divine, you think my shoes are heavenly, and so I think we need Prosecco to celebrate my sainthood, no? *Ecco, Luigi, bottiglia Prosecco pronto!*" he shouted in the general direction of the bar. He then explained to me that he was very particular about shoes because that is what he did; he designed shoes, beautiful shoes for women.

"My father, Sesto Meucci, started this line of shoes, and now that he is gone, it is my brother Massimo, my sister Gabriella, my mother, and myself. But I am the designer of this line," he qualified, "and very, very elitist about shoes. Now those, for instance," he said, pointing to my Ferragamo heels, "tell me that you are *tipa classica*, comfortable and safe. Not a risk taker with shoes, not a connoisseur, so I will have to teach you what to buy and what not to buy."

I laughed, disarmed. "Shopping isn't really my thing. Not when there are bookstores to be plundered and tombs to be explored. Mother's crazy about tombs."

Roberto handed first Mother and then me a glass of Prosecco. "Ah, tombs! I, too, love the tombs, and I will take you first to Santa Croce, then we will walk over the Ponte Vecchio, and we will eat something in Giardino di Boboli. Joan," he said, addressing my mother, with whom he was immediately on a first-name basis, "we will go to Palazzo Pitti—the Medici sent everybody, even their children, *especially* their children, to tombs—you'll like that, no?"

Mother looked at me and said, "He's dangerous, but he's got the right idea. I say yes."

Before I collapsed into my bed that night, Roberto had teased from me our passports, our itinerary, and our plane tickets. He ripped the itinerary to shreds before my eyes, pocketed our tickets and passports, and stated, with unequivocal confidence, that from now on he would be showing us Italy *come i cognoscenti*.

La Signora Meucci, Roberto's mother, was American born, but her years in Italy had done nothing to soften her disposition. On first meeting, she struck me as being singularly unhappy, as if she had fought to overcome a long and debilitating malaise and, having lost the battle, had set her face in rigid disapproval of anything that suggested pleasure. She was an imposing woman, well dressed and magnificently shod, of course, but running through her jet-black hair was a streak of white so startling in juxtaposition to the rest of her head that I found myself mesmerized by it. She looked like an eagle.

It was clear to me, almost from the beginning, that Roberto was the black sheep of the family, whose behavior was tolerated only because of his remarkable expertise, without which the shoe business would cease to exist. His skill as a shoe designer was outmatched only by his talent as a painter, but this gift was discouraged by his family. La Signora Meucci carefully measured her kindness to her oldest son and doled it out sparingly. Over lunch one afternoon at Harry's Bar, she pointed a rigid finger at Roberto and said, "When that one was a boy and got out of line, I stuck pins in his tongue." Theirs was a cold war, unwinnable and bleak, and it occurred to me more than once that Roberto stirred up memories in his mother of another black sheep, his father, Sesto, who was also brilliant at the drafting table but was, I suspected, cruelly disappointing as a husband.

The prodigal son courted me with an intensity and skill I'd never experienced before. Roberto's extravagant nature appealed to my sense of abandon; it suited the actress to be wooed in this manner, and allowed me to imagine myself free of the girl I had been only months before. While a master at the game of romance, Roberto was almost childlike in his indefatigable urge to conquer, and I, the presumed target, equally tireless in my practiced evasions and silly manipulations. I withheld my favors, which had the desired effect of intensifying Roberto's attentions, all of which kept the romance at fever pitch.

For weeks, my mother and I were captivated and captured, both, by Roberto's munificence, his extraordinary capacity to lavish upon us gifts of all kinds, his seemingly inexhaustible resourcefulness. We were driven to Siena to see the tomb of Saint Catherine of Siena; we were taken to Pisa to see the Leaning Tower; we were ensconced in the Hotel Principessa in Santa Margherita Ligure, where Mother, after investigating the suite, quipped, "I see he has consigned me to the servant's quarters."

It was tightening, this romantic noose. One night, sitting in the Piazza della Signoria, it started to rain. Neither of us moved. Looking straight ahead, Roberto said, "*Ti voglio molto bene, amore.*"

Very softly, I asked him exactly what that meant.

"It means I will meet you at the Hassler Roma in one week, at exactly six o'clock, in the Palm Court Bar, and then you will give me your answer. I will make all of the arrangements."

My mother was waiting up for me at the Excelsior, sitting on her bed in her pajamas. I told her what had happened and was stunned when she looked out the window and said, "It's your turn now, isn't it? It was mine for a long time, but now it's yours. I'm surprised how hard it is to let go of that. You will be, too, one day."

This was the first time in my life that Mother had exposed this kind of vulnerability, in revealing the last vestiges of her vanity, and I wasn't at all sure what to say or how to behave. Mother took my hand and started to lightly play with my fingers, which, for her, signified affection at its most demonstrative.

"Well, Kitty, let's see this through to the end. I'll spend the week in Rome with you, but then I'm going home. It's time. What does she say in *The White Cliffs*? 'I've had enough of lovely, foreign lands,... I'm going home to those who think the way I think, and speak as I do.' But first, let's nip downstairs for a nightcap."

One hour before six o'clock on the following Friday night, in a grand suite at the Hotel Hassler in Rome, I asked my mother to come into my room and talk to me while I dressed. She sat on the bed, hands folded, looking at me as if the curtain were about to go up on a play she had committed to sitting through, but wasn't at all sure what the critics would say. I was nauseated and clammy as I pulled a white linen skirt over silk hose, buttoned myself into a fitted black velvet jacket, and fastened a string of pearls around my neck. At precisely five minutes before six, I kissed Mother on the cheek, tried to smile, failed, and walked out of the suite.

I saw Roberto before he saw me. Just as he'd promised, he was leaning against the bar, smoking a cigarette, and next to him was a bottle of champagne chilling in a silver bucket. The atmosphere in the Palm Court was lively, and Roberto himself appeared to be in the middle of an animated conversation with several tables adjoining the bar.

When I entered the room, it was as if the lights had been dimmed. There was a sudden lowering of voices. I walked slowly toward this man I hardly knew, who was waiting for me with such composure, and with every step I took the room became quieter and quieter. He held my gaze with almost defiant green eyes and, unsmiling, stood there in silence until I leaned in to him and said, simply, "Yes." Roberto pulled a small box from his pocket and, opening it, revealed a band of diamonds, which he slid onto my finger.

Then he turned to face the room and shouted, *"Champagne per tutti!"*

The room erupted into laughter and cheers. Roberto grabbed the house phone and called my mother as I stood there, understanding that something momentous had just occurred but having absolutely no idea what was going to happen next.

Two days later, as Mother prepared to board her plane at Fiumicino–da Vinci, I appealed to her as a friend and implored her to tell me if she thought I was doing the right thing.

"I don't know, Kitten," she said, zipping up her money belt, "but I'll tell you one thing—if it were a book, I wouldn't be able to put it down."

Sidesaddle

On a cold winter's night, and after many whiskeys at Harry's Bar, Roberto jumped on his motorcycle and headed home, toward his villa in Scandicci. He hurt more when he was drunk and drove fast to prove that he could withstand the pain, that he was impervious to life's blows and indifferent to fate. Those winding country roads on a dark night were treacherous even when conditions were favorable, but this was not a temperate, clear night, and Roberto's mood was very black. He hit a large rock, swerved hard, and flew high into the air, landing in a gutter at the side of the road. They say he lay there for almost two days before he was found and rushed to the nearest hospital. They say he nearly died, having lain in a ditch for almost forty-eight hours with a broken neck. Incredibly, he survived. They stapled him into a reasonable facsimile of himself, propped him up in a wheelchair, and gave him a full-time nurse. They say he never complained and that one day, when the nurse had momentarily left him alone in the garden, he simply decided he'd had enough and stopped breathing.

But I'm getting ahead of myself. Many, many years before this incident occurred, and on another motorcycle, Roberto and I flew through the hillsides of Scandicci, stone-cold sober in the face of imminent danger, not willing to concede an inch. For brief moments, we were airborne, and then it seemed that time stood still, until we would find the road again, and, satisfied with our invincibility, slither home at top speed. It was late to bed, then, or — and this depended on the season — we would veer off-road and find ourselves behind someone's farmhouse, where a midnight fire was seen burning bright inside the barn. We'd call out a greeting and receive one in return, *"Viene, Roberto, venite qui, amici!"* The barn doors would be opened wide, revealing a rustic wooden table that ran the length of the room and that bore the fruit of the gentleman farmer's labor. The hearth warmed the room, and when at last we sat, red wine was poured, glasses were raised, and rough voices sang out in unison: *"Salute! Cent'anni, cin cin!"*

Roberto owned several vehicles, but my favorite was a green vintage army jeep. This we took into the higher hills when the *fragoline di bosco* were in season, and everywhere the eye could see, the ground shimmered with rosy crowns. A checked blanket would be thrown on top of this masterpiece, and we would lie on it, sipping champagne from the bottle and eating tiny, perfect strawberries, mouths ruby red under a warm afternoon sun.

In the villa, I was given a room of my own. Roberto converted one of the bedrooms on the second floor into a study for me, bought me an electric typewriter, ordered a desk, and placed both of these under a window that looked out over the rolling fields of Scandicci. A woman came and measured the room for a chaise, which arrived one day and was settled against the far wall. Slowly, over weeks, it dawned on me that I was essentially a glorified prisoner and that the room of my own was merely another enhancement to my gilded cage. Roberto knew what he was doing. Whole days were spent in that room, reading, keeping a journal, and pouring out my heart in long letters to friends on the electric typewriter.

The days assumed a sameness. Roberto left the house around nine in the morning, at which time Sara, the dour Lebanese maid, would bring me an espresso and a hard roll on a tray. She would place this on the bedside table without acknowledging me. I would read and write for a few hours, and at two o'clock exactly, Roberto's car came through the gates, and we would have lunch downstairs in the dining room, just the two of us. The table was knotted, of dark wood, large enough to seat twelve. On the table sat two high brass candlesticks, mismatched hand-painted ceramic pitchers of olive oil and vinegar, a large saltcellar with a silver spoon, and a pepper mill. Lunch was a three-course meal, without exception. Soup or antipasto to start, followed with a pasta dish, and then an entrée. Dessert was almost always a bit of fruit and hard cheese. Wine was poured with each course. Espresso signified the end of the meal. Conversation was not mandatory, but the afternoon siesta was. I would follow Roberto up the stairs to the master bedroom, where the door would remain closed for an hour and a half. Roberto would then shower, change, drop something on the bureau for me, and leave. His gifts were varied. Sometimes a strand of pearls, sometimes a few thousand lire, sometimes a pair of shoes. Three times a week, a car came for me at dusk, and I would be driven into Florence to meet with my Italian tutor, a young man with brilliant black hair, a pleasant, affable manner, and infinite patience. Often, and with little provocation, we would dissolve into helpless laughter. I suspect that he was lonely, too.

It was a world of privilege, but it was neither warm nor welcoming. I was a twenty-four-year-old American television actress, lacking both nobility and fortune, without even passable Italian to recommend me. The Italian women, in particular, were wary, and I often caught them appraising me with cool, critical eyes, as if to say, How on earth did you stumble into this, you little fool? Roberto was completely at ease wherever we went and expected me to comport myself with grace and confidence. Speak Italian! was his constant admonition, and so I did, often to the amusement of everyone present, most of whom spoke little to no English. I learned, very quickly, that the Italian upper class does not need to exert itself; it simply is. The caste system in Italy is rooted in antiquity, and it was breathtakingly clear that I would never be embraced by this rare and elite society. I experienced the first genuine pangs of sympathy for Roberto's mother, who must have endured years of isolation and yet, somehow, had persevered.

That white streak in her hair, I now understood, represented survival.

In the depths of the night, my agent called from faraway Los Angeles over a telephone connection so broken as to render his words incomprehensible, and I found myself on my knees shouting, "*A part!*" And heard, as if through a mangled tube, the barely audible response, "Yes, a part!"—words that filled me with joy. In less than four hours, I was packed and on my way to the Galileo Galilei International Airport.

Roberto, baffled by this sudden turn of events, was understandably unhappy and cross-examined me all the way to Pisa.

"Let me put it to you this way, Roberto," I explained, slipping my ticket into the jacket of my passport. "In my business, I am not the designer, I am the shoe, and the production company is the buyer. Hence the expression 'If the shoe fits, wear it.'" I left him standing at the gate, but I had little doubt that his sorrows would soon be drowned in wine and the sympathy of others.

Three days later, in County Cork, Ireland, corseted, bedecked, and beribboned, I put my high-buttoned boot in the silver stirrup of a sidesaddle and allowed the wrangler to hoist me aloft. From my precarious perch atop the thoroughbred, both legs angled and tucked to the left, I could see miles into the Irish countryside, and what I saw didn't please me. Holding the reins in a death grip, I whispered to the wrangler, "But where will you *be* when I *need* you? It's wide open, there's nowhere for you to hide, the camera will pick you up."

"Now, miss," the lying, conniving miscreant assured me, "sure, there's nothin' to do but sit there and enjoy the ride, nice 'n' easy like," whereupon the assistant director shouted "Action," the wrangler slapped my horse's rump with a hard, flat hand, and the animal took off like a creature possessed. It was a ride to hell, not a wrangler in sight, one of my feet dangling like a broken doll and the other digging into the horse's flesh, my riding crop useless in my hand, which was soldered to the pommel, and images of my tragic demise looming before me, when out of nowhere, a strong hand reached over and yanked the reins out of my hand. The horse came to an abrupt stop, and I slid off the sidesaddle and into the arms of a laughing and lovely Pierce Brosnan, who was shouting, "Cut, the man said, cut! Jaysus, woman, but you're a terror on that feckin' thing!"

Later, nursing my bruises in a hot tub, I mused that there were worse ways to spend an afternoon than playing Pierce Brosnan's love interest in an epic miniseries that would keep me in Ireland for almost six months. *The Manions of America* was conceived and written by Agnes Nixon, whose penchant for the melodramatic showed itself in every frame, but it catapulted Pierce Brosnan to almost overnight stardom and forged friendships that would last forever.

Pierce, a true Irishman, was not averse to practical jokes at five a.m., especially if the target was Simon Rouse, or T. P. McKenna, and we often found ourselves convulsed with laughter before the first shot was pulled at seven o'clock. We minded our manners around Anthony Quayle and Hurd Hatfield, well-respected veterans, but we all wore wellies under our costumes, and those wellies walked us to many a pub of a damp Irish evening. It was as if some mysterious power had unzipped me and out poured weeks of unbridled laughter.

Roberto visited me on weekends. Like most of the civilians I've introduced to show business over the years, he was initially fascinated by the process of filming, then baffled, and, finally, bored. A set can be disappointing for visitors, who come expecting to witness high drama or, at the very least, some degree of questionable behavior but are unprepared for the discipline and repetition that are required to get a film made properly. Roberto found it particularly difficult to maintain silence through multiple takes and could often be spotted stirring up trouble close to camera or chatting too loudly over coffee at craft service. He was accustomed to being the center of attention, and this make-believe world of mine, filled with people concentrated on tasks that did not require his involvement, held no appeal for him.

All too soon, the filming came to an end, and I left the world I loved to return to one with which I was increasingly at odds. Roberto lived at a speed and height that could dazzle from a distance but, up close, threatened to scorch. It was nothing to fly to Paris or London for a weekend, to dine at Maxim's one night and have lunch at the Connaught the next. It was madness, or so it felt to me, but then I was just the sidekick, and my opinion was seldom sought. I was dragged from restaurant to restaurant, from club to club, from overcrowded bar to overcrowded bar. The evening almost always ended in some terribly chic discotheque, an amphetamine-induced riot of sound and touch. I would sit on a banquette in a shadowy corner of a plush underground club in Kensington sipping champagne and longing for a hot bath and a good book. These comforts were withheld until (not unlike Chinese torture) my every sense had been thoroughly assaulted, and often even then Roberto would insist on going to an after-hours club somewhere in the bowels of Piccadilly, where a peculiar breed of pasty-faced Englishman would stare at me as if observing a large and rather hardy vegetable.

Unpleasant incidents began to occur, and I began to note them.

Roberto was particularly fond of his business colleagues in London, and it was not uncommon to spend long evenings in their company, over lavish dinners that lasted for hours. It was excruciating for me, watching Roberto in animated conversation with one of his more attractive female buyers and enjoying himself immensely. One night, I felt ill and begged to be excused. When Roberto failed to respond sympathetically, let alone respectfully, I stood up and excused myself. Roberto caught up to me outside, just as I was getting into the limousine, and took me roughly by the arm.

"*Cosi fai,* eh? What do you think you are doing? This is important to me, to my business, you cannot just do whatever you want whenever you want to do it! *Ecco,* you!" he called to the driver. "You take her back to the hotel, and make sure she doesn't go anywhere."

I looked at him, stupefied, but held my tongue and climbed into the backseat of the car.

Once in the hotel room, I wasted no time in calling my mother, who advised me to get on the next plane to America.

"Don't go to New York," she instructed me. "Go directly to Chicago, throw him off the scent. I'll meet you there."

Very quickly, then, I packed my modest bag, took the elevator to the kitchen level, located a door that opened onto an alley, and walked until I found a high street, where I flagged a taxi and ordered the driver to take me to Heathrow. Within hours, I was on a plane to O'Hare.

One of the most interesting and, one might even say, endearing qualities of certain Italians is their singular ability to work effectively while feeling rage and desire at the same time, and one of the most peculiar and pathetic traits of an actress is her compulsive need to check her answering service for messages at every conceivable opportunity. This I did upon arrival in Chicago and learned, with no little satisfaction, that Roberto had left ten frantic messages, all of them alternately hot and cold, plaintive and bitter. I was to call him back immediately, I was to forgive him unconditionally, I was an impossible brat and a prima donna, he loved me madly, was intoxicated, helpless without me, I was to inform him of my whereabouts pronto or there would be serious repercussions. But I was loved. No, I was adored. In fact, I was *honored* above all women. I was the future mother of his children, the secret Madonna of his heart, the fire of his loins. My answering service operator, to her infinite credit, actually read these messages aloud without bursting into laughter.

When I walked into the bar of the Drake Hotel, I was astounded to find both my mother and my father sitting at a table, sipping Manhattans and smiling conspiratorially. It was one of the rare times in my life that I actually saw them out together, alone, and openly enjoying themselves. Clearly, my father had risen to the occasion and, having learned of my dilemma, had gallantly offered my mother a lift to Chicago. It was, after all, the city responsible for bringing them together (after Mass, on a cold Sunday morning, my father had approached my mother and asked her to dinner, to which she famously responded, "I don't date short men"). I was delighted to see them in such a companionable state, and I promptly launched into the saga of my Italian love affair.

An hour later, after many drinks had been consumed, my father excused himself and walked over to the piano, which he considered happier territory, saying as he rose, "Do whatever you want, Kitten. You and your mother are responsible for this one. I'm staying the hell out of it."

Mother looked at me when he'd gone and said, "A veritable pit of compassion, your father." We smiled, shrugged, and then Mother went on, "I think you should ask Roberto to come here, to meet you in Chicago, and tell him you'll be under the protection of your parents. Then we'll find out what he's made of. But he needs to hop to it because your father, as only he knows, has a very full schedule."

I had to admire the decisiveness with which Roberto responded to my call. He was on the next available flight to Chicago, and the following evening he walked into the bar at the Drake Hotel, kissed my mother's hand, introduced himself to my father, and then knelt at my feet and said, "Katerina, I am begging you to come back to me. *Amore,* please, don't be foolish. I love you too much, we are meant to be together. Please. Look at me, *amore.*" I did. He took my hand, kissed it, and placed it over his heart.

At this point, never before in his life having witnessed such an extravagant display of romantic passion, my father shook his head, held up his hands, and said, "I'm out."

As my father made his way to the bar, stopping on his way to chat with the piano player, my mother looked at Roberto and said, "You have to remember, kid, Kitten Kat is an *American* citizen. American women are emancipated. And this one," she continued, patting me on the head, "is not only emancipated, but she is a member of the American workforce. Very important not to fool around with that. I think the two of you should consider spending more time in this, a free and democratic, country. Now, Roberto, be a good guy and get some drinks. I think we should have *lots* of drinks tonight, don't you?"

This was the full extent of my parents' intervention, and from their point of view, it was not only sufficient but generous. It was never wise to overdo anything, according to their philosophy, and always best to leave on a high note. Roberto could not have agreed more, and so it was that the four of us had a liquid and loquacious dinner at the Drake Hotel. The next day, Mother and Dad drove back to Dubuque, and Roberto and I returned to Florence.

The seed had been planted, however, and before our plane touched down in Pisa, Roberto had conceded that it might be best, after all, to take an apartment in New York.

Seeking Absolution

We were in a hurry to forget, Roberto and I, and we were good at forgetting. He never named the demons that plagued him, but he knew of my affliction and did everything in his power to dismiss it. There was to be no residual sadness about a baby I had willingly renounced. It was pointless, and in poor taste. Instead, we flew the Concorde from Paris to New York, which was very chic. Before boarding, we were invited to consume spoonfuls of beluga caviar from a deep silver urn on a linen-covered round table, accompanied, of course, by many flutes of champagne. Once seated, we were each served an ice-cold glass of ouzo, which was constantly refilled by a very attractive flight attendant who, at supersonic speed, appeared to be slightly drunk herself. In three hours, we landed at Kennedy Airport and staggered off the sleek jet looking, and behaving, very much like the Italians I had come to despise, which is to say we were loud, inebriated, and demanding. Barely acknowledging the driver, we would fall into the backseat of a waiting sedan and pass out, not to be awakened until we reached our new home, at 122 West Seventy-Sixth Street.

While living with Roberto in Italy, I had instructed my lawyer to sell 80 Central Park West. The blond-brick high-rise condo had never suited me, and, in the end, the memories it stirred up proved to be overwhelming. But this was charming, this classic brownstone apartment, and it was mine to do with as I wished. I chose the furniture, the paintings, and all of the linens with great care and made sure that Roberto's stamp was felt only in the back room, which I converted into a studio for him. That studio opened into an L-shaped garden and provided an illusion of pastoral charm for the many diversions we enjoyed there. Roberto was a master at throwing parties, although he never seemed to actively participate in the conviviality and would loop from room to room, glass in hand, searching for something he could never find, some missing piece of himself he thought might pop up at the bar or over the canapés or in the eyes of the gypsy fortune-teller he'd hired for the evening. When he ran into me at these parties, he would smile winsomely, as if to suggest that the mysterious missing component, the part that would make him whole, had eluded him once again.

I usually waited until the parties were over, and the cleaning up had begun, to begin my downward spiral. It was then, when the wine had dissolved my natural defenses, that feelings about the baby would ambush me. Carrying glasses into the kitchen, emptying ashtrays, folding cheeses in plastic wrap, were all very effective ways of concealing anguish. No one, least of all an Italian male accustomed to a privileged way of life, will interfere with a woman as she goes about the business of tidying up after a party. The detritus, the silence, the anticlimax, all served to place him squarely in the garden, where he could be seen through the window, smoking a cigarette and nursing a tall drink. It was then, with the water running and the stereo still blasting, that I would indulge my dark side and pull my finger from the dam, opening the floodgates, as each glass was meticulously washed and dried, every corner of the counter scoured and sparkling. In the time it took to put the place to rights, immaculate and shining, I had reassembled my heart sufficiently so that, to a stranger's eye, to Roberto's eye, it appeared almost normal.

Mercifully, Roberto was often in Florence, and I was left to my solitude, a state I welcomed with almost pathological gratitude. As soon as Roberto was out the door, I collapsed with relief and would putter around the apartment for hours, lost in blissful reclamation of myself. He was gone, and I was free. It would seem that work would threaten this state of release, but, in fact, it did the opposite, just as Stella had prophesied. The work lifted me up. A good thing, too, because the movie I was involved in was a study in psychopathy on every level.

A Stranger Is Watching, based on the book by Mary Higgins Clark, was a thriller involving the kidnapping of a woman and her fiancé's eleven-year-old daughter. The two are held captive in a bunker below Grand Central Station and desperately plot their escape while the police try to track the kidnapper/killer, who leaves his hostages alone during the day but returns at night to terrorize them.

If there was one actor in the world expert at terrorizing, it was Rip Torn. He had only to stand still and look at you, hands thrust in pockets, dirty Irish flat cap pulled low over his eyes, to fill you with an unspeakable anxiety, the kind that blooms into horror when he opens his mouth and mutters the first of many threats, always delivered with a smirk. This was the Artie Taggart that Rip Torn created and whose skin he slipped into from the moment we walked onto the set in the morning until the moment the assistant director called out, *That's a wrap*, at the end of the day.

Most of the movie was filmed in the catacombs of Grand Central Station, a haunting netherworld I had no idea existed. Whole communities lived beneath the vast train station, and I was stunned when one night I watched as an entire family— father, mother, and two children—scurried through the tunnel and, not once looking back, disappeared down a dark passageway. The station's massive steam generators created an atmosphere of surrealism, a nightmare quality of being buried alive. Rip adjusted to this bizarre lost world with surprising equanimity, whereas I, playing the damsel in distress, did my best to conceal a very genuine discomfort while underground. I was always relieved as soon as the day's work was over and I was led through the labyrinthine pathways to my trailer, parked on Forty-Third Street.

One afternoon, when the lunch break was called, Rip asked me if I'd like to join him at the Oyster Bar. He was meeting Gerry Page there, he told me, and thought I might enjoy making her acquaintance. It was a known fact that, although they were still married, Rip and Geraldine no longer lived together. What I could not have anticipated was the understated but very real affection they displayed for each other. Rip stood when Geraldine came through the door of the Oyster Bar and, spotting us, slowly made her way to our table. The famous actress of stage and screen did not create so much as a ripple as she crossed the room draped in a long raccoon coat, her waist-length graying hair hanging in loose coils. Clad in faded denim jeans and Birkenstock sandals, completely unadorned, she looked like an aging flower child. When she reached across the table to take my hand, her coat opened for a moment and I glimpsed her breasts, also unadorned. The eccentricity of genius, I thought, observing the two of them.

Rip's intensity flashed hot and cold, as did Roberto's, so it was a real roll of the dice when Roberto visited me on the set one night and I introduced the two men. In the role of Sharon Martin, the brave and long-suffering heroine, I had been shackled to a food cage in a defunct deep freezer by an enraged Artie Taggart. When I spotted Roberto, I was forced to call out the formalities while restrained. Rip, sitting near me on an apple box, was casually polishing an ice pick when I said, "Rip, that's my fiancé, Roberto Meucci. Roberto, this is Rip Torn!"

Roberto shouted back, "How do you do, Mr. Tear?"

"Torn!" I corrected him.

"Tear, torn, who gives a shit?" Roberto responded.

Rip leaned forward on his apple box and, turning the ice pick in his hand, whispered to me, "I don't give a shit, as a matter of fact, but maybe *you* should."

Rip planted this red flag squarely in my field of vision, and still I could not see it. The blindness peculiar to my affliction prevented me from distinguishing the good from the chaotic and created a kind of helplessness in which I found myself swimming with the current rather than risk being dragged under. Sooner or later, I speculated, circumstances would spit me out on dry land.

Those circumstances unfolded one night at the Essex House Hotel, where Roberto and I were to be married in a civil ceremony. He had been pressing me to marry him from the beginning, but it was clear that the more I worked, the more he felt compelled to legalize our union. My career was a source of agitation to him, and he wanted to bring it, and me, under his full control. Any misgivings I had about his character I put down to my own insecurity. I was clinging to an old notion of self and needed to move on, I told myself, to a new way of life. Two weeks earlier, after another heated argument about our living situation, I sat up in bed and said, "All right, then, let's do it. Let's get married. And the sooner the better."

Champagne glass in one hand and cigarette in the other, I stood in a corner of the hotel suite, which, although pleasant enough, nonetheless felt suddenly clinical and forbidding, as if I'd stepped into someone else's bad dream. I had been in the middle of a conversation with the woman who had been taking care of my finances since I was twenty years old, someone I had always pretended to like very much but who now struck me, with instant and startling clarity, as nothing more than a paid acquaintance, someone I wouldn't go out of my way to greet if she stopped paying my utility bill. The entire room, in fact, was full of people I not only didn't love but (and this I realized with the abruptness of a slap in the face) didn't like very much, either. They were appendages, business acquaintances, sycophants, and servants. The only face in the crowd I recognized with love belonged to my old friend Claire, and when I caught her eye she looked both perplexed and slightly frightened, as if the party had gotten out of hand and she couldn't find the exit. With the swiftness and sureness of fingers lifting a latch, I suddenly knew what had to be done.

I sidled up to Roberto and, taking his arm, drew him into the corridor, where I looked him directly in the eye and said, "This doesn't feel right to me, Roberto, so please tell me how it can feel right to you. My parents aren't here, Beth isn't here, none of my siblings are here. It's absurd. What are we doing? What's the mad rush? Let's wait until we can do this the way it needs to be done. Please, *amore*, I'm begging you."

Roberto did not seem alarmed, or even saddened. Instead, he looked irritated: he'd gone to the effort and expense of throwing a lavish party that wasn't going to end with a bang, after all, but something more like a whimper, and whimpers were an insult to his Italian joie de vivre.

He studied me for a moment and then, using his hands in a classic Italian gesture of surrender, proceeded to reenter the suite and announce to all present that the wedding was temporarily postponed in deference to the bride's wish to have her family present but that the party had just begun, the champagne would continue to flow, and, in the tradition of big-hearted Italians everywhere, it would be a night to remember!

The party, as promised, lasted long into the morning, and when Roberto and I finally stumbled out of our clothes and into bed, I felt as if I had been caught in an undertow that had somehow, mercifully, released me and that I had been given a second chance. I knew I had narrowly escaped another punishment, a punishment masquerading as happiness. Roberto, resigned to the fact that we would have to put off the wedding until it could be properly organized, returned to Florence.

While he was away, I had lunch with my agent. Stark loved to dine in a small, dark Italian restaurant on West Fifty-Seventh Street, close to his office. Impeccably dressed, as always, he greeted me with a kiss and looked me over. "Well, how are you liking the life of a jet-setter?" He studied the menu and, gesturing for the waiter, said, "I think we'll have wine today. Don't you think a glass of wine would be appropriate, Kate?"

"I think a glass of wine is always appropriate, Stark, but you're obviously on the verge of celebrating something. What is it?"

Stark pushed his menu aside, waited until we had glasses in hand, and then lifted his, saying, "If it's not terribly beneath you, how would you like to get out of Italy for a while and go west? The Seattle Rep is doing a production of *Another Part of the Forest* with Kim Hunter and Keith Carradine, and they want you for the role of Regina Hubbard. You know the play, of course. Lillian Hellman at the top of her game. Commitment is two months, ten, tops, with an extension, and then you're back in the arms of your inamorato. What do you think?"

I clinked his glass. "When I'm with you, Stark, I don't think, I just sign. Sounds like manna from heaven. When do rehearsals start?"

Stark laughed. "In three weeks. They'll be thrilled, didn't think you'd bite."

"I'm absolutely delighted," I said, "not to mention suddenly ravenous. I'll start dieting tomorrow—we can't have Regina waddling onto that stage."

"Certainly not, my dear." Stark chuckled. "Svelte and smooth as silk. Never had a bowl of *pastasciutta* in her life."

That night, I told Roberto how I had always longed to play the part of Regina Hubbard, and what a cast! A golden opportunity! After the initial, and by now predictable, show of resistance, Roberto acquiesced, but on one condition: when the play was over, we would get married and begin to think of our future in Italy.

"You need to become a proper mother now," Roberto announced. "It's time. Enough of this nonsense. But go and get it out of your system, *amore*." There was a pause, and then he added, "One last time."

One Last Time

A good theater is like a petri dish, cultivating all sorts of surprises within the confines of a very limited space, and it is of paramount importance that this process be disturbed as little as possible by the vicissitudes of the world at large. That is why you will seldom hear an actor expounding on the vagaries of his personal life unless, of course, that personal life has been cultivated in the aforementioned petri dish. When rehearsals begin, there seems to be an unspoken agreement among all involved that anything not directly related to the play is unimportant. However, it is crucial to remember that in the theater everything that might enhance the play is permissible.

This was my thinking as I approached the rehearsal studio where the first read-through of *Another Part of the Forest* was to take place. I had just spent a half hour in the theater itself, familiarizing myself with its contours, feeling its bones. The Seattle Repertory Theatre gave the impression of intimacy but boasted a capacity of eight hundred seats.

The stage was wide and deep, the space was dark and muted, and I was home.

I have always been early for rehearsal, but I'm particularly vigilant when it comes to the first read-through and like to get in the room and comfortably situated well before the reading is actually scheduled to begin. The rehearsal room I entered that October morning was typical of its kind: a large, well-lit room, devoid of furniture, with one mirrored wall facing another wall covered by a floor-to-ceiling crimson velvet drape. In the center of the room, a long table had been devised by pushing three or four smaller tables together, and around this table about twenty chairs had been placed, with large binders and glasses of water marking the seats reserved for the directorial staff.

The assistant director approached me and asked if I would like a cup of coffee. When I nodded, she pointed to the snack table across the room and told me we'd get started in about five minutes. Assistants in the theater, unlike production assistants in the movies, will never fetch an actor a cup of coffee, because, first, it is beneath them and, second, they simply don't have the time.

When I arrived at the snack table and attempted to pour myself a cup of coffee, a very tall person standing next to me bent down and whispered, "Don't drink that, it's shit. Unless, of course, you prefer your coffee to taste like shit, which, believe me, I can appreciate under certain circumstances."

I was about to respond when another tall, angular figure approached and, shaking his head, said, "I don't know if putting you two in the same production is a good idea. Maybe we should rethink this."

The first tall man drew himself up to his full, imposing height and wagged his finger in the other's face. "What you should rethink is your shitty coffee. How do you expect to get good actors to come here if you serve them this crap?"

Dan Sullivan, the artistic director of the Seattle Repertory Theatre, laughed and said, "Kate Mulgrew, allow me to introduce your brother, Oscar, otherwise known as John Procaccino. Oscar, be nice to Regina, or she might—"

"What?" Procaccino interrupted. "Threaten me with drinkable coffee?"

Clearly, this was a relationship of long standing, and it was immediately apparent to me that the people who worked at this theater loved it. I sensed none of the hierarchical tensions that were so pervasive on a film set.

Dan Sullivan excused himself, whereupon John Procaccino pulled his chair up next to mine and began a running commentary on everyone seated around the table. "That's Keith Carradine across from you, he just finished an Altman film, they say he's great in it, he's playing Ben, of course, and then there's the lovely Kim Hunter who might look like a deer caught in the headlights this morning but just wait until she gets in front of an audience, an absolutely brilliant actress, and that's John Kellogg down there, he's playing our father and I hear he's a real nut job, watch out for him he could be trouble, standing up at the other end is Mark Jenkins, he plays your lover boy, nice guy, local, but a good actor, and then seated right next to you is the delicious Miss Birdie played by the very lovely Donna Snow. Donna, meet Kate Mulgrew, your nemesis. Now, I need a five-minute break."

Dan Sullivan was clearing his throat at the far end of the table and calling the reading to order. His was a long, craggy Irish face with dancing eyes and the perpetual suggestion of a smile so that, regardless of what was being said, you were convinced that Dan found it amusing. He welcomed everyone to the theater, introduced the director, Ed Hastings, and then added, drily, "We should probably get started. My esteemed associate Bob Egan is apparently otherwise engaged and will join us when he can. So, without further ado, let's begin at the top. *Another Part of the Forest*. Act one. Scene one."

Heads bowed over binders, the Hubbard clan began to bond. Even at the table, my rapport with John Procaccino was natural, playful, as if we'd known each other for years, whereas the restraint I instinctively felt playing opposite John Kellogg planted the seed that would soon take root, both onstage and off. Kim Hunter, too, lowered her voice to a near whisper when she had a scene with Kellogg, and although it was a perfect choice for the dynamic between husband and wife, it was strangely premature that first day, when all that was expected of the actors was a clear and honest reading of the text.

Suddenly, my attention was diverted by the studio door opening, and I watched out of the corner of my eye as a man approached the table and quietly slipped into the chair beside Dan Sullivan. An inner alarm sounded. Don't be absurd, I counseled myself, steady on. With actors surrounding me on all sides, my privacy was protected, and I could steal looks without danger of suspicion. So I stole, and stole again. He was, I assumed, the associate to whom Dan had referred earlier, someone too busy to be on time for the first reading of a main-stage play. Too busy doing what, I wondered, and with whom, and why. All of these questions leapfrogged through my mind as I surreptitiously studied him. What struck me first was his beauty, so evident as to be almost redundant Black Irish looks of the most dangerous, and therefore the most appealing, kind. My kind of looks, the kind I had been raised to appreciate, the kind that would last. The face was clear, the eyes a deep blue, the mouth full, the nose prominent, the hair, thick and black, brushing his shoulders. A thirty-something Prince Valiant, wearing a black cotton smock with deep pockets in the front. As he concentrated, he toyed with his pencil, drumming it lightly against his lips.

At the first break, I turned to the actress beside me, the lovely Donna Snow, and whispered, "Do you know anything about that guy?" I nodded in the direction of Prince Valiant.

"Not a thing, but he sure is cute, Miss Regina," she replied, affecting a Southern accent.

Slipping into character, I leaned in and said, "Now, Miss Birdie, you need to find out about that man, a few of the more important details, if you understand me."

Miss Birdie understood completely and rose to get herself a cup of tea at the snack table, where Prince Valiant was conveniently helping himself to a bowl of mixed fruit.

At the start of act 2, Miss Birdie, hiding behind her binder, said out of the corner of her mouth, "He's the associate artistic director, he's not married, but he's got a girlfriend. It's serious."

I reflexively lifted my binder to cover my face and, without thinking, responded, "And I have a fiancé. That's serious, too." It wasn't even lunchtime and already I had broken the unspoken rule of the theater and brought what belonged outside inside.

After the read-through, as I was gathering my things and wondering how I was going to create the opportunity to talk to Prince Valiant, the company manager appeared at my side and asked if I would like to pick up some groceries on my way to the apartment the theater had provided for me.

"Where's the closest market?" I asked.

She abruptly turned away from me and called across the room, "Hey, Bob, you live around here—where is there a good market? Kate needs to stock her kitchen."

Bob Egan acknowledged us but took his sweet time crossing

the room, stopping to greet John Procaccino and having a word with Dan Sullivan, so that when he finally extended his hand to introduce himself, I had made up my mind that he was arrogant and self-absorbed.

Our shopping expedition was brief and unremarkable. Robert Egan comported himself like a gentleman, despite a certain aloofness. There was a wariness in his manner that I didn't like, a guardedness that suggested to me a distaste for actresses. Maybe he'd had one or two unfortunate experiences with my kind, but if that was the case, I concluded, he shouldn't be in the theater, where actresses tend to proliferate.

The next day, rehearsals began in earnest, and it was soon evident that *Another Part of the Forest* was going to evolve into a beautifully realized production. The company camaraderie was so organic, so easy and uncontrived, and John Procaccino was so completely accessible as a partner and a friend, that one day I suggested to him that he should have a dinner party and invite a few members of the company, as well as Robert Egan. He looked at me, a slow smile starting, but I beat him to the punch. "And *no* significant others," I emphasized. "It wouldn't be fair to those of us who have come so far, and with only ourselves to show for it."

Invitations were extended for the following Sunday night, which was the company night off, leaving all of Monday free for recovery. I arrived with the wardrobe mistress, a tough but tenderhearted creature who adored the theater.

Procaccino answered the door and pulled us inside. In the kitchen, a young woman with lively brown eyes stood over a busy stove. Seeing us, she shouted, "Well, Jesus, John, take their coats already and give 'em a drink! Hi, I'm Joanne, and yup, I'm John's wife," and threw up her hands as if to say she had fought the good fight and lost. I laughed, handed my coat to John, and peered into the next room, which was already crowded with people from the theater. Keith Carradine, beer in hand, had his guitar strapped across his chest, and next to him stood a beautiful blond, whom I took to be his significant other. Oh, dear, I thought. Donna Snow, blushing scarlet, was enjoying a joke with the assistant director, and it was then that the door opened behind me and I heard Procaccino call out, "Egan! You honor us with your presence. Now help yourself to a fucking drink and join the party!" In the ensuing charade, while pretending that we didn't see each other, I realized, with relief, that he had come alone.

That night was the first of many nights at the Procaccino home, full of laughter and stolen bits of flirtatious chat with Robert Egan, but this one I would remember in particular for the tears it brought to my eyes when Keith Carradine, after dinner, sat cross-legged in the middle of the living room floor and sang "I'm Easy," a song he had composed and performed in Robert Altman's film *Nashville*. The hour was late and we'd had a lot to drink, but that song by candlelight cast a spell over all of us. When he finished, we burst into applause and demanded encore after encore until finally, at three o'clock in the morning, Procaccino staggered to his feet and bellowed, "Okay, everybody out! And Egan, make sure Mulgrew gets home all right, will ya?"

Egan took me home on the back of his motorcycle, slowly bumping our way down Queen Anne Hill. Inebriated, he was careful and deliberate, the very opposite of Roberto Meucci. He was, as usual, quiet and restrained, so that when we pulled into the parking lot I was surprised to find myself suggesting lunch the next day, and doubly so when he accepted, albeit grudgingly.

"Well, we don't have to, if it's a hardship for you." I laughed, slipping off the bike and adjusting my skirt. He didn't seem to find this amusing, didn't even crack a smile, but told me he would pick me up at noon tomorrow.

"*Noon?*" I cried. "What about my beauty sleep? It's crucial, you know, for ticket sales."

Again he was not amused and, revving the accelerator on his handlebar, said, "See you tomorrow."

Inside, the phone rang. The only person who could possibly be calling me at three thirty in the morning had to be living in another time zone. My relationship to the telephone has always been prickly, at best. When it doesn't involve work or is not an emergency, the phone fills me with a peculiar anxiety, and my tone can often be interpreted as almost hostile. Roberto, thousands of miles away, was equally abrupt, and words that were meant to be sweet and conciliatory ended up sounding harsh.

"Where have you been, *amore?*" Roberto demanded. "It's very late where you are and I have tried calling two or three times."

I explained that I'd been to a party, but he wouldn't let it go. He pressed until finally I said, "It was a great party, and then the associate artistic director drove me home on his motorcycle in the pouring rain."

Predictably, this ended the inquisition but was the start of something else. So far away, I felt a courage I didn't feel in Roberto's presence. Not to mention a freedom. He hung up, stung, and I went to bed, thinking of what I would wear for tomorrow's lunch with the enigmatic Mr. Egan.

He was late picking me up. This time, it felt intentional, although I said nothing when he leaned across the gearshift and opened the passenger door to his Volkswagen Bug. Not one to get out of his car and open the door for a lady. Not one for old-fashioned courtesies. He made it crystal clear that he didn't go in for any of that antiquated nonsense, that we were two equals who shared a common love of the theater, and who, because they also needed to eat, were free to share a table.

The restaurant boasted a strong Indian motif but served food that somehow defied description. The beer was legitimate, however, and we both kept our glasses filled, sitting by the window at a small table, in shadow.

We talked of nothing important until, quite suddenly, Robert Egan said, "I have a girlfriend, her name's Ky. We've been going out for about a year. I don't like to fraternize with the actresses working at the theater. Not on that level. I just wanted you to know that, so that there's no misunderstanding."

I looked at him, and I knew. He was protecting himself, from me. When I had fully absorbed this, I relaxed and, smiling, said, "Let's just have a nice lunch, then. Tell me about yourself. Where are you from? And why the theater?"

It was a learning experience, that afternoon, at that table, and one I was fairly sure I enjoyed. Egan talked at length about himself, and I could see that he was very proud of his accomplishments, particularly regarding his education. It was an impressive résumé. Boston College, followed by a stint at Oxford University, and finally Stanford University, where he had worked on his dissertation, a thesis on Marxist aesthetics.

"Ah, so you're not only a socialist but a doctor, too," I said, lifting my glass in obeisance.

"Not quite," Egan responded, with a wry smile. "I didn't actually finish my dissertation."

"Why on earth wouldn't you finish the job and take home the prize?" I asked, genuinely puzzled.

Robert shook his head, as if slightly embarrassed, and shrugged. "Life gets in the way."

I didn't buy this explanation but decided not to pursue it; we were getting along so well, and I didn't want the conversation to end on a sour note. Then I spoke, and said something I hadn't planned to say. I think I must have said it to alleviate any discomfort Robert felt about his unfinished dissertation. I think I must have said it to bring us closer. "I know a little about life getting in the way. I got pregnant a few years ago, and I had the baby. I gave her up for adoption."

Robert didn't know what to say.

He sat there, silent and still, but something shifted in his expression, a subtle softening, which made me feel he understood. And something else was shared, more difficult to explain, something hundreds of years old, a crossing over, a sadness, almost a reluctance. The strange shorthand between members of the same tribe, who certainly never expected to run into each other so far from home.

In the middle of rehearsals, Roberto came for a visit. He complained loudly about the weather, the rehearsal schedule, the apartment, and my attitude. I realized that it was pointless to explain to him, as I had done countless times before, the sacred nature of the rehearsal process and the need to protect my space while I was developing a character. He scoffed at this, in his dismissive Italian way, and suggested we throw a party instead.

Roberto rented a car and drove maniacally around Seattle, abruptly pulling over and double-parking while he ran into some obscure market to acquire items for his inimitable *pastasciutta*, which was to be the pièce de résistance of our dinner party. He bought huge arrangements of yellow roses, a beautiful cashmere throw for the living room sofa, and a sophisticated boom box for our listening pleasure. I was sure that my bleak concrete apartment, in all its pathetic history, had never known such glory.

The party was a great success. Everyone came, with the exception of John Kellogg, whose near psychotic mood swings and caustic behavior had alienated the entire company. The actors drank, the designers danced, and everyone ate Roberto's magnificent pasta. Robert Egan arrived late, as was his custom, and stayed close to the front door, where the bar was situated. At one point, I introduced him to Roberto, who looked him over as one would an attractive puppy. Roberto may even have said, "Nice boy," before walking into the living room, where the actresses were gathered in a knot, gossiping. Egan and I exchanged a look, and then he left.

Roberto came one more time, for opening night. By then, the tension between us had grown into something constant and ugly. By then, too, Robert Egan and I had met several times outside of the theater, and one night, when he was again late picking me up, I raised my voice in frustration and he stopped my mouth by kissing it. So it wasn't a disappointment, or even much of a surprise, when, at the opening-night party, Roberto accused me of flirting with Egan, and I confessed that, yes, I was guilty of wanting another man. Roberto glared at me and then, enraged, declared, "This is a joke! You will never last with this boy, never!"

He was wrong, but we recovered ourselves sufficiently to salvage the evening, and when it grew late, we crawled into bed and, like exhausted children, held each other tenderly.

One last time.

Cut

It's not late, but the sky is already darkening on a January afternoon in 1982. I am walking home after having drinks with
some friends in the neighborhood. It is cold, and even though
I'm dressed in my workout clothes, I hurry. My arms are laden
with grocery bags; my purse is slung over my shoulder. When
I turn off Columbus Avenue and start walking west on Seventy-
Sixth Street, I realize, too late, that my keys are in my purse
and I will need to put the bags down in order to retrieve them.
I approach my building and adjust the bags to set them on the
stoop while I find my keys. My apartment is on the ground
floor, and the bedroom window faces the street. I usually leave
the light in the bedroom on, but today, for some reason, I
didn't. It's dark. When I have my keys in hand, I take the two
steps down that lead to the front door, but have the second key

ready. Between the front door and the door leading into the apartments, there is a closed foyer where the mailboxes are, and above these are the buzzers that are necessary to push in order to be let in. I need the second key for the second door. I insert the key into the front door and, just as I push it open, struggling to hold on to the grocery bags, I feel something cold pressed against my neck. Then I hear a voice, and it says, "Get inside, now." I enter the foyer and stand there while the man who has followed me decides what to do next. He is young, maybe twenty, and black, and he has a serious bruise under his left eye. There is a knife in his right hand, and he holds it close to his side, as if trying to hide it but at the same time letting me know he has it. He's wearing a quilted green jacket, not very warm, and a checked hunting cap with flaps. His head is on a swivel, back and forth, back and forth. I lower my voice so that it is flat and level and I say, "You can have my necklace, it's a diamond, and my diamond ring. I just went to the bank and there's three hundred dollars in my wallet. I'll give it all to you, if I can put these bags down." He nods sharply, and flashes the knife, wants me to get on with it. I put the grocery bags on the floor and slowly reach behind my neck to unclasp my Elsa Peretti diamond pendant, then I slide the band of diamonds that Roberto had given me off my finger, and hand them to him. He takes them roughly and quickly and avoids touching my hand. When he has stuffed them in his pants pocket, he gestures toward my purse, wants the money. I take out my wallet and give him all its contents, credit cards and everything, and I say, in the same low voice, "The jewelry is good and you can pawn it for a lot of money. Take it all. I'm just going to sit down here, on the floor, and do nothing. I won't do anything for a long time, and then I'll go inside, but I won't do anything. I mean it." He looks at me, and I can see that the knife is shaking in his hand. He's nervous, maybe even scared. I slowly and deliberately sit on the floor, never taking my eyes off him. He has a wild look in his eyes, almost like he's about to cry, but he doesn't. He moves toward the front door and puts his hand on the doorknob, then he looks at me and says, "You move, cunt, and I'll kill ya. I know where you live and I'll fucking come back here and kill ya, if you even move, bitch." His voice is as low as mine, but not as level. He talks to me the way he talks to women, I think. I get as small as I can in the corner and say, "I won't move for an hour, I promise you that. And I will not call the police, or anyone. That's a promise." He looks at me for what feels like a long time, and then he turns the doorknob with his hand and opens the door a crack. He looks outside for maybe thirty seconds, and I know he is trying to figure out what to do. He opens the door a little wider, and just as he puts one foot out to hold the door in place, he turns and stares at me, as if he is just now seeing me sitting there in the corner. Then he moves his foot, not even an inch, and the heavy door closes. He says to me, "We goin' to your place, so get up and open the door inside." My apartment is on the ground floor, just a few feet away, and it is empty. I never take my eyes from his face, and I say, "We can go inside, but my husband's in there — he works at home — and he carries a gun. He's Italian. Volatile. The minute he sees you, he'll shoot." He gets mad then; I can see his face changing. He doesn't want to believe me, but he can't take the chance. The knife is flashing in his hand, and he looks me up and down, for what seems like a long time, and then he says, "Take off your shoes and pull out the strings." I don't want to do this, but he moves toward me a little, and I bend down and undo my sneakers, then I pull out the laces. He yanks them from my hand and tells me to stand up, "Fast, and turn to the wall." "What do you mean, my back to the wall?" "To the wall, bitch, you fuckin' know what I mean." I stand up and turn around.

He does something I can't see, and one of the bags of groceries spills. I feel him close behind me, and then he pushes me and orders me to put my hands against the wall and to shut up. He has the shoelaces and he is trying to tie my hands together, but he needs to put the knife in his pocket to do this, and then he binds the laces, tight, around my joined wrists, and knots them. Time is going fast and slow, fast and slow. I can't see him. It feels too long and I think someone else will come home and I know he's scared, but then he grabs my sweatshirt and cuts it straight up the back, so that both sides of the shirt are just hanging there. He pulls the waistband of my sweatpants out and cuts through the elastic, rips it until the pants fall around my ankles. I feel the blade of the knife against my back, and he severs my bra strap. He has one hand around my waist, and the other, the one holding the knife, he is running up and down my breasts; he draws the tip of the knife across my nipple and I whisper, "Please don't cut me." He doesn't stop, but then he suddenly jerks me up, off my feet, and enters me from behind. It hurts, but I don't want to struggle with him because the knife is everywhere now, and I can sense that he's losing control and getting more and more furious and so I say, "If you're going to kill me, do it fast. Please be fast." The knife goes slack, then, and he's out of me, and I fall to my knees, facing him. He's adjusting his pants and slipping the knife into his jacket pocket. The door is opening, and he is about to step outside, when he suddenly turns, looks down at me, and says, "Fuckin' cunt."

It's dark now. The eye above the bruise glistens; he looks like a young kid. He opens the door just wide enough to snake through, lowers his head against the cold, and is gone.

The Handshake

I heard voices, muffled. Muted. Voices I recognized, just down the hall, tantalizingly close. One voice belonged to my mother, and the other to my boyfriend, Robert Egan.

These two voices, above all others, had the power to move me out of my state of torpor. Drugs, I was sure, had laid me low. They must have given me tranquilizers when I got back from the hospital, or maybe after the police lieutenant had questioned me for the third time. Someone must have taken pity, at last, and said, Oh, for Christ's sake let her sleep. It must have been Beth, or maybe my landlady, who lived upstairs, they were both there, though Beth had come much later. It fell to

Beth to make the necessary phone calls, and now look, here they both were, my mother and Robert, talking in the living room.

Then I remembered that it was I, in fact, who had called Mother, but Dad had answered the phone, and when I told him I'd been raped, he said not a word, I sensed the briefest internal scuffle, and then only, "Here's your mother." I can't recall what I said to her, but she got on a plane, pronto, like a good mother. So Beth must have called Robert Egan, and there was certainly some back and forth about it, and tranquilized as I was, I must have said, Let's not bother him, he won't come, and Beth must have cried, He will too come, he has to! He didn't have to, of course, no one has to do anything unless he's married and not necessarily even then, but we weren't married, far from it, we'd only just begun. In fact, Roberto Meucci's things were still hanging in the closet, his easel in the back room displayed an unfinished seascape, paints were scattered everywhere.

But Robert had come, and now he was facing off with my mother in the living room, and I could hear them going at it. My legs were like leaden weights, but I managed to manipulate them over the side of the bed, and then I lifted myself up, using the bedpost for support. I crept along the hallway, leaning against the wall, moving along like a ghost in my long white nightgown. I needed to be as quiet as death; the part of me that had always been drawn to trouble needed to hear what they were saying.

I stopped at the end of the hallway, and although I couldn't see them, I could hear them very clearly. Mother's voice was rising and falling, as if she were having trouble modulating her tone, so I pressed my head against the cool plaster wall and held my breath. Mother was explaining to Robert that there was not room enough for the two of them in my apartment, that there was only the one narrow bed in the studio and the small sofa in the living room and that both of them squeezed into the same space for two days would make for uncomfortably close quarters. "My friend Jean Smith lives across town, and I'll be staying with her, but I'll be back first thing in the morning," Mother said, as if reading from an itinerary. "Kitty's been sedated, so she'll sleep through the night—good God, I hope she sleeps for a week! She needs rest more than anything. The poor thing's been pretty heavily sedated."

There was a low murmur of acquiescence from Robert that, for some reason, seemed to irritate my mother. "You do understand, Robert, how serious this is? "

Robert took offense: "Yes, Mrs. Mulgrew, I do understand the seriousness of what's happened, that's why I came."

"You came," my mother interrupted him, "because you're a gentleman, and because it's the right thing to do. But you must leave her alone. Do you understand what I mean? She needs to be left alone for a long time, Robert."

I couldn't see Robert's face, but I knew he was smiling. The kind of smile that would grate on my mother's nerves. Then he responded, "Don't worry, I know what to do."

My mother was silent for a moment, then there was a rustling, perhaps she was reaching for her coat and her bag. Mother lowered her voice to its most stripped-down level, where there was a touch of menace, and real ice.

"I want your hand on it, then," Mother said, and I could feel her moving closer to Robert. "That you will sleep in the studio. Give me your promise that you will leave my daughter alone."

I thought I heard the lightest of chuckles, as if the sound had escaped Robert's lips before he'd had time to recapture it. "Of course, Mrs. Mulgrew," Robert Egan said, with exaggerated deference, "you have my hand on it."

I scurried back to my bedroom, just in time. The front door

was triple-locked, I could hear mother's footsteps receding in the outer hallway and then, moments later, the door to my bedroom was opened. I pretended to be asleep, but I knew that his jacket was coming off, his shoes, his pants. The blankets were gently pulled aside and Robert Egan got into my bed. He lay there for a moment, thinking. Then he put his arm around me and pulled me to him, saying, "I'm here now, everything's going to be all right."

I didn't move. Frozen. Robert moved closer, this time with more confidence, and whispered, "Come here, sweetie, let me take care of you." And I did.

The Games We Played

We stood at the back of Resurrection Church, my father and I, in the very space where sixteen years earlier I had so earnestly recited *The White Cliffs*, only this time the room was completely empty, and I was about to get married. Dad was smoking a Pall Mall, and I repeatedly took it from him, inhaling deeply and discharging the nicotine through my nose and out the slatted window into the parking lot. Not very becoming, you might say, had you been watching. Nor was the manner in which we smoked, like two old Irishmen standing outside of the pub on a wet Saturday evening, legs splayed, arms crossed, the butt held Cagney-style between thumb and forefinger, ready to be flicked fast and sharp out the window should the priest come by. He didn't come by; he was a fussy, fastidious man with a lot on his mind and was probably going over his lines in the sacristy. Looking out the window at the rolling cornfields that hadn't changed in twenty-five years, I asked my father how I looked.

"You look fine. Just fine." Typical: a measured response without music and without exaggeration.

"I look like hell, actually," I corrected him. "We were up till dawn."

"Not too smart," Dad countered, "considering the occasion. What the hell were you up to all night?"

I took another long, bitter drag on the cigarette and let the smoke escape from my mouth like a wayward cloud. "Well, Dad, we were playing a last game of Whoever Touches the Ground Is Dead."

My father lifted an eyebrow, as if the game were not altogether foreign to him, and asked, "And who, if I may ask, were the participants?"

The usual suspects, I told him, although that crew could have consisted of just about anyone staying at Derby Grange for the long weekend. It so happened that assembled in the living room the night before my wedding were my brother Tom; my best friend, Beth; and my little sister Jenny. We had all consumed copious amounts of champagne and, in a frenzy of prenuptial madness, I had permed my hair and lopped a good bit of it off, so that I looked not unlike a sepia photo of a woman who had survived the worst of the Dust Bowl. This happy band had taken pity on me and, stealing a case of champagne from the dining room, had cracked open bottle after bottle while listening to show tunes on the stereo. It was Tom's inspired idea to jump from one piece of furniture to the next, champagne glass in hand, not spilling a drop, at increasing speed, while singing along with whatever musical happened to be playing. If you touched the floor, you were dead. Tom was brilliant, or so it seemed to us, as Professor Harold Hill in *The Music Man*, holding his champagne glass aloft in lieu of a baton, never missing a beat as he leaped, from chair to chair, shouting "You got trouble, you got trouble, right here in River City!" stopping only to change the LP, and then it was Jenny's turn, and "everything was beautiful 'At the Ballet,'" which was remarkably effective because at the time she was training as a dancer, and we screamed with delight as she sprang from the couch to the ottoman to the chair, as light as a feather. Beth was too drunk to remember the lyrics to anything, so she began to make it up as she went along, which somehow made perfect sense to us until Tom demanded that we all stop while I performed "I'm the Greatest Star" from *Funny Girl*. The game came to an abrupt end when they demanded that I dramatize the number standing alone in the middle of the living room floor, at top volume, with Barbra Streisand guiding me, effervescent and incandescent with champagne, and nothing to lose as dawn intruded and the clock ran out. When I finished, the three of them sprang from the couch, applauding, crying "Bravo!" and Tom, in a moment of liquid delirium, fell to his knees, arms outstretched, and shouted, "You *are* the greatest star!"

In the back room of the church, my father shook his head, wryly amused. We were shoulder to shoulder, facing the golden cornfields and the wide-open beauty of a hot July day in Iowa. The garland I had chosen instead of a veil was irritating my forehead, and I continually plucked at it until at last my father said, "Take the goddamn thing off for a minute, you have time."

"Not much time," I replied, and then my father startled me when he said, "All the time in the world, as far as I'm concerned." This was a provocation I chose to ignore, so instead I asked, "How do you like my dress?"

He turned to study me and, after a brief appraisal, said drily, "Looks like an afterthought while fleeing Tijuana."

Not even a week before, having settled on an exquisite vintage gown of ivory lace, I changed my mind and, on my way to catch the plane that would take me to my wedding, I asked the taxi to stop while I ran into a nondescript shop on Columbus Avenue and bought a two-hundred-dollar party dress from the Latina owner, who shouted after me that I could wash it in cold water, in the machine!

"It's none of my business, Kitten," my father said, lighting up another Pall Mall, "but what the hell's the rush? You just met this guy a few months ago."

"Last October, Dad, is when we met, and a lot can happen in a few months."

"Well, I can't keep it straight. It seems like you just got rid of the Italian and, bingo, you're marrying this kid! Doesn't make any sense. What's the urgency? Unless you're pregnant. Is that it?"

No, that's not it, Dad, I thought, but you have a good nose. Just a few weeks earlier I'd been sitting in my friend Tina Ying's Chinese restaurant on the Upper West Side of Manhattan, going over wedding plans with my husband-to-be.

I had said, "We'll need to pull the wedding up. I don't want to be waddling to the altar in some size-fourteen polyester muumuu. I'm ten weeks along as it is." Egan shifted in his chair, deliberating.

"Fine, let's make it July instead of October. What difference does it make? It's not like we don't want children. What number did we agree on?"

"We didn't."

"Yes, yes, we did. We'd like five."

"Four."

"Done."

The kung pao chicken on my plate suddenly lost its appeal. When I excused myself to go to the bathroom, Tina Ying appeared out of nowhere and rested her hands firmly on my shoulders. "Just wait a minute, Kate,'" she said. "There seems to be a little problem." By now, I was feeling downright nauseous and really needed to get to the ladies' room.

Robert looked baffled. "What's up?" he asked, chopsticks poised.

"Look down," Tina replied, indicating my chair.

When I attempted to rise, I saw that the entire seat cushion beneath me was saturated with blood and that it was beginning to leak through the rush weaving onto the floor.

In short order, I was wrapped in a tablecloth and bundled into a taxi, which took us home, where I lay for some hours on the living room couch drinking large quantities of gin, as per the doctor's orders, in an attempt to relax my uterus. This method of saving the fetus proved unsatisfactory, so I was ultimately taken to the Roosevelt Hospital emergency room, where the young male ob-gyn on duty took one look between my legs and said, "Jesus Christ, this is a real mess! We're going to need to perform a radical D and C immediately." When I woke up the following morning, an IV was attached to my arm and there was no more baby. The fetus had literally come apart in my womb, requiring me to have a blood transfusion and a night's observation in the ICU.

I turned and saw someone sitting in the armchair next to the bed. It was Beth. Always there in a crisis, a stand-in for someone far less brave. She put her book down, sighed deeply, and said, "Robert had to go to a theater conference in New Jersey. He said you'd understand. He loves you." We smiled weakly at each other.

"It must have killed him to have to call you," I said.

Beth laughed as she leaned down to kiss my forehead. "No, word on the street is he's still alive. Caught the eight a.m. train to Princeton."

My father had divested himself of his jacket and had loosened his tie. He watched as the congregation filed into the hot church, dusty and wilted. The air-conditioning at Resurrection on my wedding day felt like it was funneled through an old-fashioned fan attached to an ice block. Dad wiped his brow with his signature red handkerchief and said, "The hottest bleeping day of the year. And Egan's already up there at the podium going over his homily, or his pledge, or whatever the hell he calls it. Never heard of that before, the groom giving the sermon."

"He's not giving the sermon, Dad," I interjected, "he's simply saying his piece. It's his right. He wants the congregation to bear witness to our commitment."

My father paced, as was his wont, then suddenly stopped and said, "Guy's got an impressive résumé, I'll say that for him. Boston College, Oxford, Stanford. Told me he was doing his dissertation on Marxist aesthetics, is that right? Jesus. What the hell has that got to do with your line of work?"

There was no point in playing this game with my father, who, I was fairly sure, had a pretty keen understanding of dialectical materialism but little appreciation for the way it sounded, smacking, as it did, of grandiose idealism. My father had been well educated, read voraciously, and used language like a poet, sparingly and with elegance. He had written my mother love letters, witty, ardent, brimming with confidence. No talk of socialist ideals, why should there be? It would have been redundant. My parents were dyed-in-the-wool Irish-Catholic, yellow-dog Democrats, and not without their own sense of elitism, but neither of them could tolerate posturing. I studied my father for a moment, looked at him with eyes that saw what they'd seen from the first: a face that would never lose its fascination for me.

Robert Egan, too, was one of the most handsome men I'd

ever laid eyes on. I suppose he knew this. He was a black Irish beauty, no question about it. Pedigree notwithstanding, he was smart, practical, ambitious, and gifted. But he had a terrible time making up his mind.

This had been made exquisitely clear one afternoon in May, on a green hillock in a small park where Robert and I were enjoying a picnic before the evening performance of *Major Barbara*. I'd returned to Seattle to play the lead in this Shaw play, directed by Dan Sullivan, with a serious goal in mind, and it didn't have much to do with Barbara Undershaft and the Salvation Army. I wanted to get married. Egan knew it, and so, I suspected, did everyone else.

As we finished our picnic lunch of hard cheese and green grapes, I stretched out luxuriously on the woolen blanket we'd stolen from the property department and lit a cigarette. It was a sunny day, glorious for Seattle, and the park was full of people enjoying the afternoon. As I lay there, I made up my mind that I would say nothing. Absolutely nothing. If Egan didn't have the balls or the desire to pop the question after months of romantic intimacy, then I wanted nothing more to do with him. I had my pride, I had my faction of devoted suitors, and, perhaps most compellingly, I had a six-thirty half-hour call.

Robert stood, having long ago lost interest in the picnic, and began pacing. This, I understood from years of watching my father and my brothers, was not necessarily a good thing. Either Notre Dame was losing, we were running out of scotch, or an exceptionally pretty woman had entered the room. Pacing is a form of agitation and uncertainty. It is not calming, nor does it inspire confidence.

Egan circled the tiny hillock, again and again, until the sun shifted and people began to leave the park. He had his hand in his pocket, toying with something. An engagement ring, I thought. I raised myself up on an elbow in a very leisurely fashion and said, "It's getting late." He stood for a long time looking out, past the park, beyond the theater, into the safety of his imagination, and there he must have found the same unrest he found here. So he hunkered down beside me and showed me the little ring in his hand. A slim band of gold, somehow cleaved, adorned with the tiniest diamond I'd ever seen. He looked at me questioningly. I looked back and smiled, making it clear that this was his moment. I believe he proposed formally. I think I heard "Will you marry me?" but I was so concerned about being late for the half-hour call that I only remember feeling relieved, and slightly irritated. Once the band was on my finger, and lips perfunctorily pecked, I made a mad dash for the stage door.

"Who knows, Dad, we may start our own theater, get the kids their equity cards before they're ten." Music was playing inside the church, and my stomach was churning. Beads of sweat stood out on my forehead; my frizzy hair framed my face like coils of hay; I felt ridiculous in my garland with its long blue and white ribbons—signifying what? I wondered.

After the rape, Beth had quit her job, and the two of us had fled to Barbados, where we'd found some measure of peace because no one knew us there, and we felt unshackled. Beth had left an abusive husband, and I had assisted her in the getaway, outside a Spanish restaurant in Midtown, shouting in her husband's face, "I'll call the police if you come any closer, you sonofabitch! Get in the taxi, Beth, get in!" As the taxi sped up Eleventh Avenue, Beth started tearing off her clothes and throwing them out the open window, until I grabbed her wrist and, pointing at her wedding band, shouted, "That's what you need to throw away!" So, laughing hysterically as tears streamed down her cheeks, she hurled that ring into the darkness.

Egan found me in Barbados and insisted that the hotel management inform me of his phone calls. The woman at the front desk would make her way to our bungalow, gently rap on the door, and call out, "There's a phone call for Miss Mulgrew," and I would look frantically at Beth, because it was too soon, because I couldn't bear it, because I wanted to forget, and so Beth would trudge up to the front desk where Somerset Maugham once collected his mail and return after a short while, shaking her head and saying, "You know, you're going to have to talk to him sooner or later."

I cannot remember in all of my life a time when I deliberately sought my father's strength, but as the music swelled in the church and the last of the guests had been seated, and our cigarettes were nearly burned to the nub, I rested my head on his shoulder for a moment and whispered, "Oh, Dad, I feel so tired."

My father stood straight, as he always did, but maybe this time just that bit straighter as he adjusted his tie and pulled on his jacket. Then he turned to me, looked me directly in the eye, and said, "You know, Kitten, you don't have to do this. Just say the word and I'll go in there and call the whole thing off."

Beth was already at the altar. From where I stood, I could see the blue-and-white floral dress she'd borrowed from me the night before. Robert Egan waited on the other side. The "Wedding March" had begun, and the first notes were discordant, which made me laugh. I took a last drag from the kernel of my father's cigarette, flicked it out the open window Cagney-style, and, taking my father's arm, said, "Fuck it, Daddy, let's do it."

On Our Way Home

We lived in a succession of houses. The first belonged to Robert, and it sat at the top of Queen Anne Hill in Seattle. It was small and blue, and upside down, so that our bedroom and living room were on the ground floor, and the dining room and kitchen were on the basement floor, down a flight of stairs.

Our first son, Ian, conceived on our wedding night, was brought to this house after a remarkably easy labor and delivery. It took that baby no more than forty-five minutes to come squalling into the world, whereupon a chorus of nurses burst into song, "Look at him, he's a nine-point-nine, almost a ten! A perfect baby!" I vaguely remember being served a dinner of steak and champagne in my room afterward. Robert poured champagne into my glass with the fastidiousness of a heroin dealer. I hadn't had a glass of wine or a cigarette in nearly nine months. Robert had implemented these inarguably sound rules to protect the health and well-being of the baby.

How right my husband had been. For here, in my arms, lay a perfect babe, and because I had been so good for so long and had grown so plump and indolent, nothing much mattered to me but continuing my regimen of deliberate sloth. But now I had an accomplice, whereas before—during the long, dry, uneventful pregnancy—it was just me, alone, lying in my wide canopy bed that was far too big for the tiny bedroom in the little blue house.

Ian and I were natural partners in crime. As long as we were left to our own devices, it was bliss. I'd plump up the pillows, soft drink and snack nearby, while Ian lay in the crevice of my arm, suckling away. We watched old movies, and sometimes we'd drift off, only to be awakened by some delicious urge—to eat, to suckle, to coo, to play. Ian Thomas was a very beautiful baby, and eminently watchable, and he had, from the very beginning, an unusual gravitas. Newborns do not generally inspire respect, but that is what I felt for Ian. While appreciating his utter helplessness, I could not help but admire the steadiness and intelligence of his gaze. He was not an infant to express discomfort in conventional ways. Instead, he would turn those deep blue eyes to mine and simply stare at me until I got the message. This method of communication suited both of us.

I hired a professional photographer to come and take a series of photographs of mother and son. I wanted them in black and white. The photographer lobbied for color shots, but I said no, black and white, and nothing posed. The day before the photo shoot, I called a hair salon and told the lady who answered that I'd pay any hairdresser she had available two hundred dollars to make a house call. A young man arrived, and I led him down the stairs to the kitchen, where I had draped a sheet over a chair. Holding Ian in my arms, I instructed the guy to cut my hair.

Shorter, you mean, he asked, and I said, No, cut it all off. The photos have survived, and they show mother and son staring directly into the camera, somber and alert, acknowledging the intruder but not necessarily welcoming him.

The natural tension that existed between Robert and me would periodically erupt into a spat, though seldom damaging or long lasting. The tension was a taut line tying me to him and him to me, almost a way of expressing our solidarity. Instead of touching, we teased. He didn't bark his displeasure, but bit with criticism. I, in retaliation, withdrew into myself, where I could dwell for days in a cold, distant chamber. It was a way of life we understood, despite our better instincts. We didn't sulk, we didn't complain, and we did nothing to examine the nature of our love.

Reconciliations were swift, and celebratory. There were many dinner parties, shared with excellent friends, and long nights of exhilarating conversation about the theater. We were passionate about the theater and loved talking about it. Dan Sullivan and his petite, quiet wife, Cecilia, were a staple, as were John and Joanne Procaccino. Mark Jenkins, a statutory member of the acting company, introduced us to his wife, Vicky, whose WASP-y reserve and pioneering spirit fascinated me. Tall and lanky, with long, thin ash-blond hair tucked back with a single bobby pin, she was capable of writing a chapter in a novel, preparing dinner for eight, and changing the tire on her vintage Buick, all in an afternoon. She was altogether my kind of person. In that cold, wet place, these were the relationships that sustained me.

My idyll with Ian came to an abrupt end when Robert told me that he wanted me to play the part of Kitty Strong in the world premiere of Michael Weller's play *The Ballad of Soapy*

Smith. I was contrary, insisting that it would be better for me to stay home with the baby than to be a part of such a large ensemble. Anyone could play Kitty Strong, I argued. Well, I'm directing it and I want you, Robert countered. Okay, I said, I'll do it, but then you have to let me go to Anchorage to do *The Philadelphia Story* at the Alaska Rep. Tracy Lord is a part every actress wants to play, and you know it, I declared.

"When?" Robert wanted to know.

"Rehearsals begin immediately after *Soapy Smith* closes, so I'd be on my way pretty much the next day. And, of course, I'm taking Ian with me," I responded, gaining confidence.

"We'll see about that," Robert said.

"Yes, that's right." I laughed. "We'll see if you want to be stuck with an infant for two months!"

"You're crazy," Robert demurred, "and who the hell wants to go to Alaska in the middle of winter to do a Philip Barry play?"

"I do," I said. "Obviously."

A few weeks later, I was in my dressing room at the Seattle Rep being laced into Kitty Strong's corset. For weeks I had been nursing Ian, whose appetite was voracious, and hadn't quite shed the pounds necessary to return me to my fighting weight, so the unfortunate wardrobe mistress, sensitive to all of this, had to pretend that there was a malfunction with the hooks and laces rather than admit that my waist would never be twenty-four inches again. With every agonizing tightening of the laces, Ian, resting happily in his Moses basket at my dressing station, would emit a little coo of delight, which sent a signal to my brain that my baby was hungry, whereupon my milk would let down, the laces were promptly undone, and the entire process was aborted while I saw to my infant's afternoon tea.

The stage manager stuck her head in and said, "Kate, there's a call for you in the greenroom—it's been transferred from

Administration. I'll look after the baby while you take it, but hurry up, we're at fifteen minutes."

I walked quickly to the greenroom, wondering who on earth could be calling me on a late Friday afternoon at the theater. It must be a job offer, I thought, something glamorous and lucrative—and on location! I picked up the phone, already flush with anticipation, and I heard a familiar voice on the other end of the line, a voice I did not associate with the theater, a voice I both respected and feared.

"Kate, it's Dr. Shy calling. I hate to interrupt you at work, but I thought you should know that the results of last week's tests have come back, and it looks like you're pregnant again."

"But, Dr. Shy," I sputtered, "that was just a routine postpartum visit, I didn't want a pregnancy test! I can't be pregnant, I'm still nursing! I'm still bleeding! I'm about to go onstage! What are you talking about?"

"It's unusual, I know, but not unheard of. You're about eight weeks along." Dr. Shy sighed. "Congratulations."

When I accused Robert of lasciviousness, he said, "Oh, stop complaining. You should be delighted to be having another baby! It's meant to be!" A self-congratulatory dig.

Alaska moved me. The audiences were so hungry for entertainment that I could have walked out and sung "Happy Birthday" standing on my head and they'd have been delighted. Every night, the curtain call was explosive. Boots were stomping before the curtain fell, men hollered in loud, harsh voices, wild hooting erupted from the back of the house, from the orchestra, from the mezzanine, all the way into the lobby. It was raw, and exciting.

Hidden beneath an abundance of bearskins, Ian and I flew across the Alaskan wilderness in a dogsled. We stopped at an outpost for a hot drink, and when we came through the door, a silence fell, unlike anything I've ever felt before. Not a woman in sight, and here I was, in a white fur-lined parka, holding a beautiful baby in my arms, both of us pink cheeked from the bracing air, asking for a hot toddy. The bartender shook his head, didn't smile, didn't say a thing. A beer, then, would be fine, I said. He put a thick brown bottle in front of me and stood there, waiting. I took a sip, and nodded. Eight or ten men stood at the bar, each with a beer in hand. Rough hands, dirty and callused, with blackened, ragged fingernails. As I drank, I kept my head down, but I could observe those hands on top of the bar, and as my eyes slid from hand to hand, it slowly dawned on me that every hand on the counter of that bar was disfigured. Most were missing one or two fingers, but one man looked as if his entire right hand had been mangled in something and had been mutilated. They smoked with any two fingers; they drank using their left hand. They never once looked at me, but they took in every part of me with a still and intense concentration.

Robert flew up to spend Christmas with us and gave me a present, unexpected and unique.

"Garland Wright is directing *The Misanthrope* at the Rep, and he's interested in you for Celimene. The problem is, you'll be almost eight months pregnant by the time it closes, and Celimene is a grand coquette, so it would complicate the plot, if you know what I mean."

"But look at me, Robert! I carry low and my hips are so narrow, you'd have to study me through opera glasses to catch on! Did you tell Garland how I look?" I demanded.

"He wants to see you for himself, then he'll make his decision." Silence. The beginning of a smile played at the corners of his mouth, and Robert added, "But Garland wants to set it in the French Revolution, and you know what the clothes were like for the French aristocracy."

"Commodious," I offered. "Extravagant."

"Big," Robert declared, and now we were both smiling.

Two weeks later, I stood facing Garland Wright in a fitting room at the theater. He asked me to turn around, slowly. Standing next to him was the costume designer Kurt Wilhelm. Each held a forefinger to his mouth, as if trying to solve a puzzle. Wilhelm stepped forward, asked, May I, and with a measuring tape calculated the distance from my neck to just below my breasts.

"A high whalebone corset, just above the abdomen, and a very low bodice. A robe à la française, expensive fabric with a beautiful drape, and, of course, all of the appropriate undergarments. Chemise, hoops, petticoats, drawers if necessary—will she disrobe?"

Garland looked at me, grinned wickedly, and said, "Oh, yes, indeed she will."

"And, you know, with the Fragonard wig..." Kurt Wilhelm held up his hands, the idea of the wig so marvelous that it defied description.

"Well, madam, shall we begin?" Garland came forward and lifted my hand to his lips. "It's time to meet your Alceste."

In the rehearsal studio, a man leaned over a table, intently studying a script. When he heard me enter he turned and, never taking his eyes from mine, moved toward me with the grace and confidence of a natural actor, a man born to play Alceste, built to dazzle and devastate this Celimene. Daniel Davis and I embraced each other from the first moment as if it was simply meant to be, this union, which for some reason or another, fate had annoyingly delayed.

Rehearsals for *The Misanthrope* were joyful and utterly unpredictable. Kevin Spacey brought an unexpected edge and dangerous charm to Philinte, while the scenes between Arsinoe and Celimene evolved into a kind of lethal dance, daggers concealed beneath layers of velvet, glinting only now and again, thrusting with intent at the end, when all is lost for Arsinoe. But it was my scenes with Daniel Davis that were exquisite miniatures, at once seductive, passionate, and—something else, a surprise—tender, honest, poignant.

When, each night, Alceste kneeled between my legs and slowly, sensually cut my corset up the front with the tip of his knife, and my swollen stomach was suddenly revealed in all its protuberant glory, the audience as a collective audibly gasped, and Danny and I would look at each other with the kind of lustful exultance that only two actors can feel when a moment, in front of eight hundred people, reaches perfection.

Beautiful babies and beautiful parts, however gratifying, did nothing to change the constitution of Seattle. It was a cold, rainy, provincial city where I felt isolated and lonely. We had agreed, at the beginning of our marriage, that Seattle would be only temporary. Heavily pregnant with Alec, I entreated Robert to remember our promise to each other. To live in a place where we could both thrive. I knew that New York was out of the question for Robert and was not unhappy when we undertook the long drive to Los Angeles, en famille, shortly after *The Misanthrope* closed. Robert had been offered a job as producing director of the Center Theatre Group, under the artistic directorship of Gordon Davidson. Gordon had been running that ship for many years, and he understood the value of a young man whose gifts included not only dramaturgical and directing skills but a wife who loved to throw herself on a stage and could do so at the drop of a hat.

My third pregnancy developed naturally and without incident. I worked, I played, I indulged in the occasional glass of wine, I stayed up late, I was happy. This probably explains why Alexander James was so reluctant to step onto the real stage of life. I imagined him, after his nine-month bath of endorphins and serotonin as I pranced about in various phases of creative delectation, far too comfortable to decamp for cooler climes. I labored for nearly fifteen hours before a frustrated obstetrician (presumably late for a golf game) threatened a C-section, citing fetal distress and prolonged womb worship as justification for the knife, whereupon a very Viking-like Robert Egan took me by the shoulders and practically shouted, "You do *not* want a C-section and you are *not* going to have one! You're young and you're strong and you need to fight! Now get down on your haunches, goddammit, and push that baby out!"

I did as he instructed and, lo, the angels were pleased, and a very large, very pink, very serene baby slipped out of his blissful cocoon and into his father's arms.

This little boy, my second son, had none of his brother's intensity and twice his appetite. How strange and sweet the moment when a newborn infant, with eyes that cannot yet quite see and hands that cannot grasp, still finds his way immediately and unerringly to the breast, as if it were an extension of himself. For me, this moment was unmatched in its tenderness.

"Look," I said to Robert, who was reading the birth coach's postpartum manual, "his eyebrows are absolutely white. Little running elephants of eyebrows," I cooed, stroking the baby's brows.

Robert glanced up and shook his head.

"Elephants, to the best of my knowledge, are not white. We should call him Alec, he'll prefer that growing up."

"You mean you'll prefer that," I countered, too enthralled with my offspring to argue.

"Christened Alexander James, but known as Alec. Celtic," Robert stated, with finality.

"English," I murmured, "Alec is English."

Silence from the fatherland, but as the baby suckled and I nuzzled his downy cheek, I put my lips to his tiny ear and whispered, "You may be Alec to him, but to me you will be known as Little Running Elephants of Joy."

The rented house on Montana Avenue held a certain conventional charm, in that the bedrooms were actually upstairs and everything else a floor below, opening onto a garden that, instead of sloping dramatically into our neighbor's backyard, as it did in Seattle, expanded upward, in tiers. The second floor had three bedrooms, one of which housed a peculiar young woman I had brought with me from Alaska to help me look after Ian during the run of *The Misanthrope.* When we moved to Los Angeles, she begged to accompany us on the drive down and then pleaded with me to let me stay just a bit longer, until we'd found our sea legs. While her devotion to me was clear, I couldn't be a hundred percent sure of her commitment to the babies, and so I was always pricking up my ears or lying rigidly awake in my bed, waiting with an invisible cudgel for some sign of aberrant behavior.

It was not unusual for me to gather my offspring into my arms and take them to bed with me. One night, as Alexander lay contentedly suckling my left breast, and Ian had burrowed his way into my right armpit, I saw a shadow fall across the top landing of the hallway, then another, immediately behind the first. Instantly frozen, I searched frantically in my mind for the most efficient mode of escape and, barring that, the most effective and accessible murder weapon. Just as I was about to dislodge Ian from his nesting place and reach for the telephone on the side table, the two shadowy figures fell to their knees and began creeping slowly into the master bedroom, where we lay. Risking all, I pushed the babies under the blanket, and just as my hand grasped the telephone, a mass of yellow roses bloomed in front of my eyes, and slowly, one by one, the flowers were placed on my body until I resembled a lovely corpse.

Suddenly, the shadowy figures pressed their faces forward, and one of them, a well-known playwright, whispered, "Dear Kate, I am begging you to do my play, and if you agree, I will be forever in your debt."

Another voice, far more familiar, chimed in and said, "We'll work it out about the babies, but I had to fire the leading lady—she was a fucking nightmare—and we open in two days. You've got to save us."

At this very moment, Alexander attacked my nipple with unusual ferocity, and Ian, shifting beneath my right arm, gave me a swift kick in the ribs with unnecessary vigor and precision, but I, the actress-mother, looked into the faces of Jon Robin Baitz and Robert Egan and said, "Oh, for Christ's sake, all right. I'll do it."

This established the pattern that would define my marriage, and although I was delighted to be reunited with my great friend Daniel Davis in Jon Baitz's *The Film Society*, I staggered home each evening, guilty, happy, and conflicted, as well as increasingly concerned about the girl with the wide-set eyes living in the third bedroom.

Every other week, a Mexican woman by the name of Josephina came and cleaned for me. She was tall, trim, and stern, with jet-black hair swept up into a bun, and dark, careful eyes hidden behind thick glasses. One morning, as she vacuumed and scrubbed, never pausing in her labor, I asked her if she knew anyone who might be looking for employment. I explained that I needed a woman, preferably on the youthful side, who would live with us and look after the babies while I was working. Josephina straightened, put her hand on her hip, and said, "My niece, she just come from Mexico."

"Can she speak any English?"

"No, señora, but she smart, hard worker, she learn fast."

"When can I meet her?" I asked, now offering Josephina a

cup of coffee and a cookie, which she declined, saying, "I bring next week. Okay with you?"

"*Fantastico,*" I replied, popping the cookie into my mouth.

The following Tuesday, Josephina arrived for work at the customary hour, bringing with her the young woman who was her niece. The girl could not have been more than twenty-five years old, short and stocky, with long, pitch-black hair that fell in thick sheets to her waist. The face, though not immediately beautiful, was striking. There was a certain nobility to her features. The mouth was set in a frown; the brow was furrowed. She held herself with pride, and her eyes, a rich chocolate brown, were intelligent and curious. She stood at the door, hesitant and shy, and refused the offer of refreshment with an abrupt shake of her head.

As she stood there with her arms folded tightly across her chest and her posture so erect as to seem almost defensive, I found myself at a complete loss for words. She spoke no English, and my Spanish was rudimentary, at best. Suddenly, from his cradle in the adjoining room, Alexander began to cry, and his distress had a reflexive effect on Ian, who started to howl with alarming gusto. Not missing a beat, the young girl unfolded her arms, put her purse down on the counter, and walked out of the kitchen. Moments later, she reappeared, with Alexander neatly tucked in one arm and Ian held firmly in the other. The babies were silent. She was silent. Josephina was silent.

I said, "You're hired."

She put her hand into Alec's diaper to test for dampness and then, looking at me, asked, "Pamper?"

I pointed to the adjoining room, and just as she started to walk away with my babies secure in her arms, I called after her. "What's your name?"

Back came the answer, unexpected. Perfect. "I Lucy."

"My name is Kate, please call me Kate!" I shouted, and then

came the response, as she bent over the first of thousands of dirty diapers, in words that, from that day forward, would never change.

Decisively, she said, "Sí, señora."

Lucy changed my life. Her presence filled me with confidence. I trusted her implicitly with my babies and did not hesitate to send the strange girl from Alaska on her way. I felt a new sense of freedom and went in search of opportunity. Immediately after *The Film Society,* I was offered a part in a movie starring Fred Ward and Joel Grey. It was called *Remo Williams: The Adventure Begins* and would be shot almost entirely on location in Mexico. This required a negotiation between Robert and me, and unlike so many of our interactions, this was neither protracted nor messy. Our commitment to each other as artists was an understanding more cohesive, and more respected, than any other in our relationship. The tougher negotiation demanded a confrontation with myself, but I was unwilling to subject myself to that scrutiny—not as long as I could have my cake and eat it, too.

In Mexico City I sat over drinks with the cinematographer, Andrew Lazlo, with whom I had become friendly, and on this particular afternoon we found ourselves immersed in conversation about work and parenting. I was defending my right to leave a four-month-old infant in the hands of a good nanny and a responsible father and to go on location for a few weeks. My voice rising, I told him that I was flying home whenever possible, and that the money I made working in movies was our financial bedrock.

"You don't have a leg to stand on in this argument," I bristled, "since your wife—*without discussion*—stayed home to raise your five children, leaving you free to go off to work, wherever it might take you, doing whatever strikes your fancy.

So please don't tell me that your relationship with your wife is one of equals. You're the alpha male, and she's the beta who stays at home, putting a brave face on it."

Andy leaned forward and, cupping my chin in his hand, whispered, "You're a very attractive woman and a lovely actress, and I am exceedingly fond of you, but you'll never be a natural mother."

Shocked by the unexpected venom of this opinion, I jumped up with such force that my chair tipped over and, tears streaming down my cheeks, ran from the room. Andrew tried hard to make amends, protesting that he'd meant nothing by the remark, but the alpha had bared his teeth and I, with my tail between my legs, had gone into hiding.

When I returned home, after having been in Mexico for nearly three weeks, I ran up the driveway and into the kitchen, shouting to Lucy as I approached that I needed money for the taxi and did she have any, and when I entered the kitchen and dropped my bag on the floor, I was greeted by a stranger sitting in a red rolling chair, eating a banana. The child appraised me with cool hazel eyes, and what had begun as a smile on his face now suddenly faded and fastened itself into a frown, a serious frown, a frown of righteous disappointment, and those bright eyes, at first glance so merry under those running elephants, turned into dark pools of fury, and with nary a backward glance, my shockingly ambulatory baby turned his chair around and skittered away from me, as fast as his little legs could propel him. I stood there, devastated, with Andrew Lazlo's words echoing in my mind. *You'll never be a natural mother.* And then I felt before I actually saw the whirling dervish that was Ian, as he hurtled into my arms, miniature Superman cape attached to his shoulders with safety pins, flying through the air, shouting, "Mama! Mama! Mama!"

That night, I knew to leave the babies in their cribs, and

when at last I heard Robert's weary step on the stair, I sat bolt upright in bed, snapped on the light, and said, "Hi there. You know, I made a few bucks in Mexico, Lucy's room is nothing more than a glorified closet, and Alexander isn't speaking to me. We need to buy a house."

Egan ran his fingers through his hair and, sitting heavily on the bed, said, "We should also discuss a play I'm directing. Shakespeare's *Measure for Measure*. There's a part in it for you."

"But I just got home—" I began to interrupt.

"Shhh," my husband said, turning off the light, "sometimes you talk too much."

Foxboro Drive

It is strange to me, even now, that a house that brought me so much happiness also stirred up a yearning I could neither understand nor articulate. I wanted to imbue it with the charm and grace of Derby Grange, but I wanted my house to have, unlike the chaos I had known as a girl, a sense of order. It was meant to be a place where all were welcomed, and none were judged. It was a house bustling with activity, from the early hours of the morning until well past midnight, when Robert would come through the front door with a few of his cronies, ready for music, for drinks, for talk. If we were working on a play together, then we would arrive home at approximately the same time, famished and buzzing with adrenaline. Lucy had transformed herself into a superb housekeeper, as a result of which the kitchen was always spotless, stocked, and inviting. Robert and I and whoever else we'd invited over at the last minute would make our way into the kitchen, clattering pots and pans into submission, pouring wine, piling plates high with bread and cheese.

If it was an opening night, I knew to expect a full house and that many would not leave until dawn, not until the last paper had been found and delivered, the last review dissected with surgical precision, the last hope dashed or confirmed. Egan was a gifted director and an exceptionally talented dramaturge, so his productions quickly acquired a reputation for their visual elegance, their unexpected boldness, their capacity to tell the story on a high and intelligent level without having to lead the audience by the hand.

Measure for Measure was a success at the Mark Taper Forum, particularly among the cognoscenti, many of whom joined us after the opening in our living room, until the first light of dawn crept through the windows and our little boys ran helter-skelter into the room, clamoring for attention, for breakfast, for nickels hidden in the crevices of couches. Robert and I walked the boys to their preschool, just a few blocks away, urging an exhausted but exhilarated Kelsey Grammer to stay put, assuring him that we'd be back in no time and would prepare him a breakfast fit for a king. His electrifying performance as Lucio, opposite me as a passionate and strong-willed Isabella, had created a stir in the theatrical community, as a result of which Kelsey and I had developed a mutual admiration, and it wasn't long before Kelsey had arranged an appointment for me to meet with James Burrows, the creator of a television sitcom Kelsey was on called *Cheers*.

I was hired to play Ted Danson's love interest in a multi-episode arc. The half-hour show was taped weekly in front of a live audience. The money was fast and easy, although hardly what the stars of the show were making, I learned as I stood backstage waiting for my cue to enter, listening to the actors' rather glib chatter regarding their exorbitant salaries. Later, I passed Kelsey's dressing room, where he sat tinkering on a baby grand, and blew him a kiss. I was going home. How much simpler it was in the theater, I thought, where there was never any talk of money because there was never any money to be had. Simpler, I mused, but not necessarily fair.

When I came through the front door, I saw Robert's long silhouette reclining in a chair in the backyard, close to the pool. He had his feet up on an ottoman and was smoking a cigarette. I stood for a moment weighing the odds and then, as was so often my habit, dropped my bag on the floor and made a beeline for the backyard, itching to pry the lid off Pandora's box. A bottle of wine rested on the glass coffee table, next to an ashtray overflowing with cigarette butts.

"How did it go?" he asked, perfunctorily. He was always much more interested in my career when it was directly involved with his own.

"Fine," I answered, "fun. Boy, are those actors raking it in. Hundreds of thousands per episode, or so a little birdie told me tonight before we went on."

"No kidding," Robert said, drily, as if the subject of expansive salaries was somehow beneath him.

"Yeah, good for them. And good for me, too, don't you think?" I asked, lighting a cigarette. Robert chuckled, uncertain as to where this was going but feeling the first tightening of a long noose. I poured myself a glass of wine and took a deep breath.

"Robert, I know that you think it is best to pool our resources and to work out of a single account, and I know that you feel in better control of the household money when you're in charge of paying the bills, but the thing is—I don't. I don't feel better giving you my paychecks. I've always made my own money, I've worked hard to make it, and I've always had my own manager and my own accounts, and that's what I want again. So that's what I'm going to do. I'm going to hire a money manager, and she can cut you a check for my share of the household expenses. Okay?"

There was a long and uncomfortable pause.

Finally, Robert stood up and, not looking at me, demurred, "I think it's bullshit. We're married or we're not. It's common money, for a common purpose. Who makes what makes no difference. It's called a shared life." He lifted his wineglass to his lips, drained it, and walked into the living room.

A shared life. Does this include all that came before, as well as all that comes after? Are memories shared, are sorrows shared? Or, when someone refers to a "shared" marriage, do they mean strictly the obvious—children, money, acquisitions? And why is the mention of money between spouses so unsettling, so divisive? Money, by its very nature, does not seek to be shared, any more than old memories do, or deeply hidden sorrows. If an independent nature is cut in two, is it then shareable? I didn't think so. The next day I hired a business manager.

Blind to its implications, but aware of its incomparable beauty, Robert presented me with the Hope diamond, for surely Hedda Gabler is that jewel among all the roles written for women in modern literature.

It was virtually impossible to say no, although careening through my memory were snatches of reviews of this play, historically famous for its difficulty, notoriously challenging for the actress playing the central role.

"We'll take the journey together, and I'll guide you. You have her in you, you know you do. We'll coax her into perfection," Robert said, triumphant. "What's more, I've got Michael Gross for Tesman, Linda Purl will be perfect as Thea, and we've decided on George Deloy for Lovborg. Dark, handsome, dangerous." Robert paused, then added, "You should enjoy that."

From the beginning, from the moment I sat at the table in the rehearsal room for the first read-through, I knew that I was looking at Kilimanjaro. And it was not the play alone that filled me with trepidation, but something else, something I couldn't quite put my finger on, something that I sensed might have the power to change the nature of my marriage. Robert approached *Hedda* with rigor and passion. He hired the head of the Scandinavian department at UCLA to edify us about Henrik Ibsen, the master of modern theater, and the world of the Norwegian middle class in the late nineteenth century. She was lithe and reserved, with a head of hair gone wild in salt-and-pepper curls, and I instantly sensed in her the long-lost friend I had been impatiently waiting for since we arrived in Los Angeles. As we listened to Robert explain his ideas for the play, the relationships within the play, the set that would frame the play, and the marvel that would be the play, Mary Kay Norseng and I looked at each other across the table and grinned. As of that moment, our allegiance would be to each other.

Rehearsals were demanding, Robert unrelenting in his need to realize exactly what it was he'd sculpted so meticulously in his imagination. He was tough and exacting with all of the actors, but he was merciless with me. Maybe he assumed that our relationship was sufficient to protect me from the exigencies of his directing, but in this he was misguided. I felt as if I was dancing on the head of a pin.

In the little time we had off, which usually fell on a Monday, Robert would ask to go over a certain scene with me in the backyard. It was always the same scene, always the same lines, always the same direction. At one point in the play, Hedda looks out the window and says, "The leaves, they're so yellow, so withered."

Invariably, Robert would pounce on me. "What are you *doing?* Just. Say. The. Lines. It's not sad, it's not reflective, it just *is.* Now, walk around the pool and say it over and over until it's falling out of your mouth like it should, simply and organically."

And I did; I did walk around that pool, saying those lines over and over until I felt that if I had to say them one more time, I would scream. Was this Robert's idea of guidance? Did he intend to fill me with frustration and loathing and then watch as I, the skilled professional, took the antipathy I felt toward him and channeled it into a magnificent performance on the stage?

I grew wary of him.

At night, it was our habit to have a glass of wine when we got home from the theater. Often, we discussed the day's work, but increasingly I wanted to share with him my feelings about my daughter. Feelings that would not change and that would not go away. Perhaps some of the terror and pressure I felt playing Hedda heightened my sense of loss, but I was caught in a private cycle of sadness, and the only conceivable relief I could find was in the telling.

Robert shifted in his chair, always uncomfortable with my tears. He didn't want to hear about the daughter I'd given up, and how this continued to haunt me, the futility with which I fought the sense of regret, the sadness that had become malignant. I didn't blame him, but I yearned for the comfort and shelter of his empathy. "You need some sleep," he said, standing and crossing in front of where I lay sobbing on the living room floor. "Go to bed."

Mother flew out for the opening of *Hedda Gabler* and, at the dinner party that followed, said to me, "Oh, Kitten, I thought it was exquisite. In fact, I thought it was Robert Egan's valentine to Kate Mulgrew."

Stella Adler was in the audience as well, and I greeted her after the show in the lobby of the theater. "Well, darling, you've done it," she said, looking at me with those piercing gray eyes, "you've done what few have managed to do. You found Hedda Gabler."

The morning after *Hedda* closed, I woke with a splitting headache. Robert lay next to me, dead asleep. I slipped out of bed and tiptoed from the room. Downstairs, I found my purse, opened my wallet, and pulled a small, tattered piece of paper from its folds. Written on it was the number of a private investigator that Richard Cushing had given me years earlier, after he had witnessed my distress firsthand. He had stuffed it into my wallet himself, saying, "Just in case." I stared at the paper for a moment and then, carefully closing the kitchen door behind me, picked up the phone and started to dial.

Occasionally, on the spur of the moment, we would pack a bag, collect the children, and drive up to Santa Barbara for the weekend. We would stay at a cozy little dive off of Main Street that offered a hot tub and cinnamon rolls, or sometimes at the El Encanto Hotel, which truly was enchanted, nestled in the hills overlooking the bejeweled city and valley below. Sometimes, Robert would challenge me to walk into one of the swankier beachfront hotels, inform them of our nonexistent reservation, and when they would express their surprise and confusion at finding no such reservation and their regret that the hotel was fully booked, I was to assume an air of disappointment and frustration, as if my assistant had screwed up yet again or, even more effectively, look directly into the manager's eyes and say, "You know, I've had problems with your hotel in the past." Sometimes it worked; sometimes it didn't.

When it did, Robert grinned slyly as if we'd pulled off another clever heist.

On the way home, tired and sun-kissed, Robert would engage the boys in made-up games. One of his favorites was called Katy at the Beach, and it ramped up pretty quickly to a level of hysteria, all at poor little Katy's expense, because Katy was always doing something naughty or stupid or even vulgar at the beach. At some point, it always became overextended and calculating. It was then I would cry, "Enough, enough, not fair!" and would spend the rest of the drive staring out of the window, deaf to the ongoing taunts of the two little boys in the backseat and the big bully of a boy in the driver's seat.

Dinner parties were a staple of the early years of our marriage. We had ceaseless energy for entertaining, and did it on a generous, if not lavish, scale. I learned to cook wonderful dishes in that narrow galley kitchen, which I sometimes preferred to the actual event itself. Planning the menu, doing the marketing, filling the house with fresh flowers, music, and silver coolers of wine, gave me a sense of order and satisfaction. The boys would have been fed and bathed by the time the guests started to arrive, and the cocktail hour was an opportunity for everyone not only to become acquainted with one another but to admire my offspring, who looked so fetching in their striped pajamas, smelling of soap and baby powder. Of course, thirty minutes of this was sufficient to satisfy my guests, and invariably the boys went off to bed tired and annoyed, baffled by the injustice of their house being overrun, yet again, by strangers.

It was generally at this moment, when the drinks were winding down and the children had been put to bed, that Robert chose to make his entrance, bedecked in his running clothes, bandanna around his forehead, dripping with perspiration, fresh from a five-mile run. If the invitation was for seven, Robert invariably loped off around six fifteen, which by necessity protracted the cocktail hour until, by the time Robert had showered, changed, and rejoined us, dinner was served late, tepid, and to a group of inebriated and slightly irritable guests.

Spearing a limp shrimp with his fork, Robert would say, "And what, I wonder, is this mystery fish?"

Later, in the kitchen, while dumping the "mystery fish" into the trash, Mary Kay would come in and, putting her arm around me, whisper in my ear, "Well, I thought it was delicious."

The Westside of Los Angeles was dominated by industry professionals, and many of these men chose the soccer field as a means of expressing their paternal integrity. Robert took to coaching with a singularity of focus I have seldom seen matched. He whipped those little boys into fighting shape within weeks. Every Saturday was spent at the soccer field, from early morning until dusk. It was relentless, joyless, and, in keeping with the spirit of the privileged Westside, the unspoken mantra was *Win, or else.*

The boys were now in grade school, and it was made clear to me by the association of devoted mothers at Saint Martin of Tours that it would behoove me to spend a little less time on my career and a little more time helping to shape the futures of our beloved children. To this end, I taught a poetry class to Alec's second grade and Ian's third grade for six months. I chose Emily Dickinson as the poet who I thought would best enlighten these youngsters, and they responded to my teaching methods with joyful abandon. The goal was to understand the poem by acting it out, and so, inevitably, the classroom erupted in a chaos of overturned desks, paper airplanes sailing through the air, children leaping onto the teacher's desk, shouting, "'I'm *nobody, who are you!*'" Wild laughter, crocodile tears, startlingly passionate embraces upon "'Then there's a *pair* of us, don't

tell!" Then, ardently whispered, "'They'd *banish* us, you know.'"
At the end of the semester the principal thanked me for my
efforts and, leaning in to take my hand, said, "I just can't wait
to see what you'll do next—on television."

The compulsion to work was unremitting, an unscratchable
and often unbearable itch. Everyday life, in all its sameness,
was not nearly as rich or exciting as success, and in an industry
town, this meant that personal stardom was every bit as significant as personal decency and certainly more relevant. L.A.
was a laboratory designed to breed and advance success in the
motion-picture industry, which is why thousands of people
spent whole days in their cars, searching for impossibly hidden
offices, labyrinthine studios, obscure trailers in back lots, stalled
for hours in freeway traffic, always late, always lost, always
anxious. The burden of rejection weighed on the shoulders of
everyone I met, surpassed only by the burden of hope.

Occasionally, there would be a flash of lightning, and all
of that drudgery would be converted into a contract, the terms
of which were so delightful it was all I could do to sit still and
wait until someone in a three-piece suit passed me a pen.

HeartBeat was an exceptional idea, inspired by true events,
following the hardships and professional challenges of female
doctors who decide to open a medical center in response to a
health-care system that has failed to address many of the problems presented by female patients. I played the lead, Dr. Joanne
Halloran, based on Dr. Karen Blanchard, who quickly became
my personal ob-gyn. She allowed me to shadow her for a week
in her Santa Monica clinic, observing as she performed Cesar-
ean sections and deliveries, listening quietly during patient
consultations. I was captivated by her skill and sense of self,
and I learned that an excellent doctor, though exhausted and
perhaps frustrated, will always maintain her composure in the
face of bad news, particularly when she is about to deliver that

news to an anxious patient. I tucked these lessons into my bag of tricks, used them to shape the character of Joanne Halloran, and had the time of my life. It was a series ahead of its time, written with audacity and intelligence by Sara Davidson, produced by Aaron Spelling and Esther Shapiro, and costarring Lynn Whitfield, Gail Strickland, and Laura Johnson. But like many precocious series, it was canceled after just two seasons.

To assuage my disappointment, I bought a house nestled in the San Jacinto Mountains in a village called Idyllwild. Robert was livid when I insisted that my name, and my name alone, be on the title. As we meandered through the back roads of that mountain community on our first trip to the house, there was a palpable chill in the car, but I was firm in my resolve and simply said to him, "You understand practicality and fairness as well as anyone I know, Robert. I am paying for the house, so it is only fair that I should own it, and I will maintain the house, so it is practical, as well." He said nothing, but as we pulled into the driveway of our beautiful new weekend house, with its long and deep front porch sheltered by tall pine trees, a coolness had settled between us, and it prevailed through the long evening and into the days ahead.

One night, as I prepared to leave for the theater at the end of a long week, the phone rang. The private investigator I had called two weeks before announced himself. I asked him if he'd learned anything, and he replied, "Well, I'll tell you this. Your daughter didn't go to any couple in New York. She was moved out of state and adopted by a couple living in Massachusetts." I was too stunned to speak. Finally, the man said, "It shouldn't be too hard to find out who they are and exactly where they live."

"Yes," I responded, "I need to know."

The man was quiet for a moment, then I heard him cough. "I can do that, but it will cost you."

I had given him one payment already, and I realized, suddenly, that I was in dangerous, uncharted waters. I gripped the phone with a clammy hand. The blue vein on the inside of my wrist jumped. Lowering my voice, I said, "The cost has been high enough."

Suddenly, the front door banged open downstairs, and my sons called out, "Mama!" I went to them and, looking at them sternly, said, "The time has come." Ten minutes later, after the chase, the tackle, and the tumble, I put them in the tub and went to it with gusto, scrubbing first Ian, the more resistant, and then his brother. Predictably, they wailed as if they were being burned at the stake. When the worst of the torture was over, I sat on the rug in front of the bath tub and just looked at them. My two little beauties, suds in their ears, washcloths on their heads. So smart they were, so vital. I decided to tell them a story.

"Only, it's a true story," I whispered, "so you must remember that as I tell it. And I must have quiet, because it's a very important story. Do you understand?" Both heads nodded, and Ian, very intense, leaned on the rim of the bathtub, head in hands. I told them the story of how I had, long before I'd met their father, had a baby, but that I wasn't expecting to have a baby and that I didn't think I could take care of her very well, and so I had finally, and very sadly, given her to another family to raise. "But I am looking for her, and I will not stop looking for her until I find her, and then you will meet her and she will be your sister. She is your sister, and you are her brothers."

The boys stared at me, mesmerized, until finally Ian asked, "But is she *really* our sister?"

"Yes, darling, she is. I'm *her* mother, too."

The boys seemed to be considering this when Robert suddenly appeared at the bathroom door and said, "I don't really think that was necessary, do you?"

I called Sister Una McCormack the next morning and demanded an explanation.

"Why was my baby taken out of state and adopted by a couple I knew nothing about? Why did I have to learn this through a private detective? Why was I not told?"

Sister Una sensed the panic in my voice and tried to calm me.

"We should have informed you that your files were destroyed in a devastating fire last year but we didn't want to add to your distress."

This, to me, was simply amazing. I waited.

"And Cardinal Cooke made a special request regarding your baby, one that we could not have foreseen, and one that we needed to fulfill."

"Above and beyond your promise to me — your *only* promise to me — that my baby would go to the couple I had chosen?"

To her credit, she did not equivocate.

"Terence Cardinal Cooke has the power to make or change policy within the Home Bureau. There is nothing more I can tell you."

And, true to her word, that was the last thing she said to me before hanging up.

We lived well, but ours was a marriage without sympathy. We enjoyed our tribal affinity and encouraged this is in our sons, who, like their parents, took pride in physical courage and intellectual curiosity. Tenderness was something we were forced to leave behind. The construct of our marriage could not accommodate it. But, like most Irish-Americans, we were sentimental to the core.

At the beginning of our marriage, when I was very pregnant with Ian, Robert and I attended a fund-raiser at the home of a rich board member in Seattle. At the end of the meal, the host rose and told us that, in honor of our coming, he had prepared a poem by the great W. B. Yeats. It was my favorite. Halfway through, the man stumbled, and when it was clear he had forgotten the verse, Robert nudged me. I stood up and, looking out over the candlelit room, finished the poem.

"And bending down beside the glowing bars
Murmur, a little sadly, how Love fled
And paced upon the mountains overhead
And hid his face amid a crowd of stars."

Less Traveled By

We were driving across the Mojave Desert, toward Mammoth Mountain. Ian was in the front seat, next to me, and Alec was in the back. It was late afternoon, I could feel the sun withdrawing, so I accelerated, hoping to make it to the mountain before dark. The energy in the car was high, lit by a strange, blue flame.

"Why isn't Dad with us?" Ian demanded. "When is he coming up?"

"Yeah," Alec chimed in, "where's Dad?"

"Yeah, Mom, where's Dad?" Ian asked again, but this time it was provocative. Threatening.

"Where's Dad, where's Dad?" Alec intoned from the backseat, and immediately his brother joined in. As the two of them chanted, and the sound grew in volume, the car filled with a wild, unbearable tension, and although I struggled to hold on, to maintain composure, to hold tight to the awful secret, the voices of my children cracked me open, and I suddenly swerved and pulled the car off the road.

Even then, I said to myself, there was time. Hold on. Hold on. But the sun had now turned a deep orange and sat heavily above the horizon. The children were silent, looking at me with dark, curious eyes. I turned off the ignition and turned to face them.

"Boys," I said, softly, "I wanted to wait until we got home next week, when your father and I could do this together."

Ian interrupted, loud and sharp. "Do *what* together?" Alec instinctively clapped his hands over his ears.

"Your father and I love you very much—"

"Ohhhh!" Ian shouted.

"We love you very much, but we have decided that we can't live together anymore."

"*Ahhhhhhh!*" Ian screamed, and I forced my voice over his, stifling the sounds he was making.

"We haven't been happy for some time, and we've decided to get a divorce."

Ian was the first to go. He unsnapped his seatbelt and threw open the door. Then he started to run, as if running for his life, disappearing into the desert.

Alec, in the backseat, looked at me. He didn't understand, he couldn't at first grasp it. His eyes were pleading with mine. But that was no more than a moment. Then his little face fractured as quickly and shockingly as if I'd taken an ice pick to it.

He wept quietly, strapped into place. He did not howl, or shriek. He wept very quietly.

I looked out the window and could barely make out Ian's figure as it melted into the sun. I knew that I must go after him, but for the moment, I could do nothing. It was enough to stay in that car, with my youngest child, and do nothing. It was enough.

It takes a very long time to sever a marriage in which children are involved. There is a table, two chairs, and a small pile of bargaining chips. This is how it begins, but it ends with one chair in an empty room. The days darken. The children are sliced open and split down the middle. Someone takes an arm; someone takes a foot. The car pulling into the driveway on a Friday afternoon becomes a hearse, and everything is couched in lies. The house of old assumes a silence.

Friends come less often to visit. Lucy goes about her chores with a carefully composed face. She loves the boys with a devotion that barely conceals her ferocity. I am often in bed, reading or begging my agent to get me work. Work, now, is rare. I go to auditions and am so overcome with anxiety that I fall asleep in the chair before I am even called into the room. I need money, and there is none coming in. The divorce is expensive. California law is strict, because divorce is so common. The breadwinner pays the heaviest price, but in the end, it all equals out.

Mary Kay sits opposite me on the patio in the backyard, sipping white wine. Her face is fixed, gentle, and serene. She is an exceptionally good listener. I complain about the absence of work, of money, of trust. I tell her I'm fed up, at my wit's end, just want out of this marriage, once and for all. She regards me with measured sympathy. All of my closest friends know I am having an affair with a Mexican bullfighter who, I am beginning to feel, spends considerably less time in the ring than I do. No one approves of this liaison, least of all myself, but I can't seem to end it. He is adoring, weak, and always available.

I look at Mary Kay and suddenly am struck by an idea. "I'll sell the house, we'll move to an apartment in Westwood, I'll get a day job, we'll start over, the boys and I, and I'll be free!" I am on my feet, almost shouting. It has been a year of whitecaps, breaking gray and relentless, and now I think I spot land. Mary Kay's instinct is to urge caution, but I am already up and out of my chair and calling my real estate broker. I tell her to put the house on the market. In the same hour, I call my business manager and demand to know how much cash I can get my hands on. She is startled, laughs uncertainly, says she'll call me back.

When she does, I learn that all the ready money I have in the world is ten thousand dollars. Twenty years of steady work and I am left with half a pension, half a house, and ten grand in cash. I tell her to take it all out, divide half into bills and the other half into traveler's checks.

"Why on earth do you need traveler's checks?" my business manager asks, very curious indeed.

I think for a moment, and then I know exactly how to answer her. "I've decided to take the boys to Ireland for the summer."

Mother was thrilled when I told her about the trip but did not suggest that I visit the ambassador in Dublin. "Her schedule is very full, and Jean's a stickler for routine. But you should meet my friend Tim Hagan, who will be visiting Jean in Dublin at exactly the time you'll be there."

"We're not going to Dublin, Mother," I said. "We're flying to Shannon and heading straight for Dingle."

"Oh, too bad," she responded, "because Tim is terrific. A wonderful friend, a good guy, I know you'd love him."

"Oh, Mother, for God's sake—" But she cut me off, insisting that he was strictly friendship material.

"You'd never go for him in a million years," Mother declared.

"He's a politician from *Cleveland,* for God's sake," I interrupted, "and besides, didn't you imply that he's otherwise engaged? Not to mention his allegiance to the Honorable Jean Smith."

"Nothing of the kind, Kitten. Not everyone is consumed with lust, you know."

"No," I said, "but you'd agree that most interesting people have outsized libidos, wouldn't you?"

Mother paused. "Well, *all* interesting men have impossible

sex drives, but the really intriguing women simply know how to play the game. Should I give him your number?"

"Who?"

"Tim Hagan, for heaven's sake! A drink won't kill you."

My father, when visiting Ireland in the early seventies, stumbled into a pub in Dingle and discovered a woman there, tall and handsome, with a wide red mouth and a rich laugh, who poured him a whiskey and told him her name was Kate Ashe and that her husband was the publican. He fell in love on the spot and sent out an SOS to me and my brothers Tom and Joe to come to Ireland and judge for ourselves if we'd ever seen anyone so fair. We met in Dingle and convened in that pub, my brothers and I, and all of us were captivated by Kate's charm, her vivacity, her curtain of thick black hair, the style with which she poured a pint of Guinness, and the elegant generosity of her spirit. We understood that the James Ashe pub on Main Street was to be our local when we visited Dingle, and that there would be none other.

Now, twenty years later, we pushed open the door of the pub, the boys and I, to get out of the rain, and were warmly greeted by Kate, who stood, as she always did, behind the bar, dispensing pints and wisdom with equal dexterity, a cigarette never far from her lips. On any other woman, it would have been unbecoming, the constant fag going to and from that too-red mouth, accompanied by the abrupt pulling of the Guinness handle, the quick and sometimes sloppy pouring of the whiskey, all choreographed over a sink of dirty glasses, but on Kate it was a natural and even glamorous fit. Her eyes lit up with mischief when she saw the boys, and she was already teasing them, telling them there was to be no turf fire in the cozy back room, there were no more bottles of orangeade to be had, and certainly not a bag of crisps to be found in all of Dingle. These things she reported while popping the caps off bottles of orangeade, pulling bags of crisps from the rack over the bar, and leading the boys into the anteroom, where a turf fire glowed in the belly of the hearth and a dartboard hung like a round and hungry face on the wall. She handled the children easily, without artifice, and as a result they adored her.

I found a stool at the bar, and when Kate reemerged, I ordered a gin and bitter lemon.

"With the merest suggestion of ice," Kate said, to which I replied, "Correct, madam, and many thanks."

The usual suspects were gathered at the bar, as well as one or two tourists, who were easy to spot because of their eager, earnest faces and carefully nursed pints of beer. The regulars had their assigned seats, and I greeted them by name and asked how they were holding up.

"Pissing rain it is," said the confirmed bachelor three stools down, whose tweed hat never left his head, whose wellies were always wet and spattered with mud, and who, as he glanced at me, clutched his pint with unnecessary intensity. He'd have a cigarette soon, then another pint, and then he'd be up and off his barstool with a sureness of purpose so abrupt as to seem almost comical. He'd had his pint, and now it was home to the farm. Like clockwork, it went. These were men of habit, who honored and respected habit, and were seeking nothing but the solace of a daily ritual in a warm, familiar pub with faces they knew and trusted. They spoke sparingly, smiled wryly, and systematically avoided intimacy of any kind. Wild and vivid daydreams of lust and longing could be dancing in their heads, and no one would ever know as they stubbed out their cigarettes, drained the last from their pint glass, and placed their coins on the bar. "I'm off," they'd say, perhaps touching the bill of their caps, and then they'd be out the door, striding into the rain.

The phone rang in the room beyond the bar, a private room where Kate prepared the evening tea for her family. She disappeared down the three steps into her living room and reappeared moments later, a smile teasing the corners of her mouth.

"It's for you," she said, "a gentleman who says he's a friend of your mother's. Tim Hagan?"

I laughed, so unexpected was this phone call, on this day, at this hour.

I had spoken to the man before I'd left Los Angeles two weeks earlier, had liked the sound of his deep, rich voice, and so had told him where he could find me, if finding me was in the cards.

"You know, I love your mother," he'd said, which had delighted me. Not many people had said that to me about my mother and meant it. She was not the sort of person who inspired this kind of sentiment.

"And do you also love the ambassador?"

A pause on the other end. "Yes, I'm full of love for the entire human race," he replied, and we had laughed.

I picked up the phone in Kate's living room. "Am I speaking to the man who loves my mother?"

"You're speaking to the man who just arrived in Shannon and doesn't know whether to go east to Dublin or to see if my dear friend's daughter would like to meet and have a drink with me first."

This presented a few problems. I couldn't very well leave the boys to wreak havoc in the pub, Shannon was certainly too great a distance to travel for a drink with a stranger about whom I knew next to nothing, the car was low on gas, and it was raining.

"Excuse me for a moment, Tim," I said, and holding my hand over the receiver shouted to Kate in the adjoining room, "What's a good meeting point between here and Shannon? Anybody have an idea?"

Back like a shot came Kate's voice. "Tell him to meet you at the Hotel Tralee in two hours!"

"Did you hear that?" I asked, into the phone.

"I heard it, and so did half the people in the airport. I'll see you there in two hours. Meet me in the bar," said Tim Hagan, with authority. And then he hung up.

I gathered Ian and Alec, called good-bye to Kate, found the lovely boy Owen with the sweet smile and sandy hair who lived down the lane, and asked him to take the boys fishing; it was marvelous to fish in the rain, and on rainy days in particular, I promised my sons, the dolphin Fungie could be seen leaping from the sea, and afterward, when they were wet and tired, they could all come back to the pub for fish and chips in front of a warm fire, and I would be there to meet them. This seemed to assuage the anxieties that I knew were percolating in my sons' small but precocious brains.

I ran to the flat, traded my mac for a long and rather chic raincoat, wrapped a sheer scarf around my head, and jumped into the car. The rain had abated, and now it was only drizzling. I didn't know why I felt compelled to step on the gas, but I zipped across Kerry like a deranged swallow and arrived in Tralee an hour later. I parked the car, glanced at myself in the mirror, and adjusted the scarf so that it covered my head, which made me feel like a cross between Tippi Hedren and Peter Sellers.

Inside, it was dark, cool, very quiet. I walked down the main corridor, sure-footed but silent on the path to the hotel pub. Ahead of me, I could see the shuttered windows of the bar, and I realized with a start that it was off hours and the pub would not open until two p.m. I stopped just short of the bar, and as I stood there wondering where this stranger might have taken himself, I suddenly heard a voice, rich and deep, calling, "Kate?" I turned, and there, sitting in a corner banquette, the *Irish*

Times spread out around him, was a broad-shouldered man with a warm, crooked smile.

"Tim?" I asked, whereupon he rose from his seat and extended his hand. When I walked toward him, he would tell me later, he had said to himself, Ah, there really is a God.

After a brief volley of complaints about the bar not being open, we decided to have tea. I poured. When I passed him his cup, sweetened with sugar and softened with milk, just as I took mine, he chuckled and made a disparaging remark about the size of his hands. "Cement mixer's hands," he said, but they didn't seem so to me. A cement mixer would not have taken such care. His hands were large and strong, the nails trimmed and neat. He wore khaki trousers, a crisp white shirt, and a navy jacket. It was difficult to look at him for sustained periods of time, because whenever our eyes met, we burst into laughter. His face, were I to draw a face from some primitive memory, was exactly right. Feature by feature, it was irregular, a Cubist painting, but in composition it was almost perfect. For my taste, the face was perfect. And in that moment, over that absurd tea tray, my taste was all that mattered. The brown eyes, dancing, the broad high cheekbones, the smashed but noble nose, the crooked mouth, the warmth of the skin, where the sun had settled the day he was born, all of this evoked a response in me that I had never known before, and somehow understood I would never know again.

We spoke at the same time, laughing at the collision of words. Our thoughts rolled one over the other as we lobbied to express ideas, experiences. We both wanted to talk about my mother.

"You say you love my mother. Why?" I demanded, over the cooling tea in the increasingly busy lobby.

"One day we were on a plane to Taiwan, where we were visiting Jean," Tim explained, "and we were having an animated discussion about Bertrand Russell, whom we were both reading at the time. Suddenly, out of nowhere, we got caught in a terrible storm, and the plane began to buck and plummet, glasses flying, women screaming, it was very dramatic, and I looked over at your mother, who looked back at me, shrugged, and said, 'More drinks. Now, what do you know about Russell's private life?'"

I knew this was true, not because I'd heard it from my mother, but because it was so typical of her behavior.

The tea was cold, the boys would soon be expecting me, and so I said, "Speaking of drinks."

He agreed. "Yes, let's get the hell out of here and find a pub."

"I have a car," I said, "but don't you need to get to Dublin? I'm going west, to Dingle."

He was helping me on with my coat, and I couldn't find the sleeve; again and again I missed, we started to laugh, and he said, "Let's head toward Dingle, stop at the first pub. One drink."

At the first pub, we sat outside and drank Jameson and Harp. Tim told me to prove to him that I was an experienced and accomplished actress.

"Okay," I responded. "You know the *Godfather* trilogy?"

"Of course. Who doesn't?"

"And the Corleone family?"

"Yes, yes, of course!"

"But"—I stopped him, index finger in the air—"what you *don't* know is that the Corleone family loves Ireland and, in fact, is vacationing in the west country as we speak."

For the next hour, I improvised scenes between Don Corleone and his sons, Michael and Sonny, then switched and sat still and grave with my whiskey glass in my hand, eyes lowered, until Tim shouted, "The consigliere, Tom Hagan!" Bees began to swarm around us, drawn to the heat, the whiskey, and the animation. We jumped up, swatting and cursing, and when a bee alighted on my sleeve, I smashed it with my purse and watched as it fell to its death on the picnic table beneath us.

"You could have been somebody," I said to the dead bee, "instead of a bum, which is what you are."

We were high on the whiskey, the sudden sunshine, the bees, the honey, and the tears of laughter running down our cheeks, when I heard Tim say, "I'll keep you company to Dingle."

"What about the ambassador? You don't want to piss her off," I warned, playing coy.

"I won't be missed," Tim replied, but he seemed unsure.

"That's right, you won't be missed—you'll be whacked!"

"Then we better get the hell out of here!" he shouted, the two of us running to the car.

We stopped at a lake on the narrow, winding road to Dingle and got out of the car to investigate. Neither barbed-wire fences nor black-eyed bulls deterred us in our determination to reach that exquisite body of water. A deep blue pool, dancing in the sun, nestled like a sapphire in the cradle of a small valley. I approached the edge, Tim behind me, and decided to show off by nimbly hopscotching over a small lane of smooth-faced rocks until, suddenly, there were no more stones, and I slipped, knee-deep in the icy water. Tim, laughing, extended his hand to help me, but when he pulled me to him, everything stopped. It was an instant, nothing more, and I almost spoke, almost snipped it clean with a sharp scissors, but something stopped me. A tightening in my throat, a tension.

Then Hagan said, "You're intrepid on the rocks." The mirth again, bubbling up between us.

"A born rock hopper, a natural stone skipper, and a slippery little devil, that's me," I retorted.

The boys glowered at us when Tim and I at last came through the door of the pub and immediately began complaining about their day. They didn't see the dolphin, they didn't catch any fish, Owen was a drag, they were hungry, they were thirsty, I was late, I was always late, I was not a good mother. I should not have left them alone for so long. They were right, of course, and so I did what I always did when I felt particularly guilty. I bought them fish and chips, I bought them ice cream, I bought them books and games and fishing caps and took them to pub after pub, listening to music, listening to craic, stealing moments with Hagan in dark corners while my sons amused themselves for five minutes at a time. I wanted them to be well amused because I was drawn to that dark corner, again and again, a corner where tales were being spun and information doled out in small, sweet cups.

"I have two children myself," Hagan offered. "Daughters. I understand the need here. I get it."

Even when Ian ran up to the table and demanded another drink, another minute, my eyes on him, my attention full and focused, even then Hagan looked at me and smiled crookedly, teasingly, the father who knew that behind these demands there was only one need, and that was to be loved.

The boys were exhausted by eleven; it was time to take them home, and to bed. As we walked down the cobblestone street to the flat, with the mist rising from the earth, spun like silver mesh from the clouds above, enveloping us, we could hear the sounds of the boys shouting and arguing ahead of us, but they were invisible to us, and it was then that Hagan stopped, took my chin in his hand, and lifted my face to his. It was the briefest of kisses, his lips barely brushed mine, but it was enough, and I knew it was enough because he said, "I'd like to meet the man who marries you." He turned and walked away from me, then, disappearing into the fog.

The next day, we took the boys with us, and there was much merriment in the car. Ian was inordinately fond of Jim Carrey during this period and compulsively shouted, "All righty then!" in response to everything, which was followed by gales of hysterical laughter. Jim Carrey accompanied us to Slea Head, where we fished in a deep and mysterious mountain lake, and to Inch, where we ran on the strand and where Alec and Hagan ate ham sandwiches hunched over a picnic table like two old cronies, and to the ocean, where on a bet the boys and I rented wet suits and jumped into the glacial Atlantic, screaming, the cold and the crash of the waves and the pink faces of my brave boys as they howled with delight at the thrill of it, and the beauty of it, and the secret, profound knowledge that no one else in their world had ever done this before.

We drove back as night fell, the boys fast asleep in the backseat.

Hagan helped me carry them up the stairs to the flat, remove their clothes, and put them into bed. I covered them with extra duvets, kissed their hot, sun-kissed cheeks, smoothed the salty hair from their foreheads, and closed the bedroom door behind me. Then I turned to Hagan and asked him if he'd like to stay for a drink. In the darkness, I felt him smile. I poured two glasses of whiskey, and we drew close together on the window-sill, in the far corner of the living room, where the window opened onto a courtyard, and where the muted moon irradiated the sky. Hagan pulled a pack of cigarettes from his coat pocket, which provoked a small symphony of moans from both of us, now regretting that we had simultaneously reached for cigarettes a girl had been passing on a silver tray in the pub the night before, lit them and inhaled, whereupon I'd hung my head in shame and told him I hadn't had a cigarette in over a year. "A year?!" Hagan scoffed. "I haven't had a cigarette in *ten* years, and guess what? It tastes pretty. Damn. Good."

We talked all night long. We drank, and smoked, and we talked, and there was not enough time, that was all I knew. Not nearly enough time for the telling of all that needed to be told. He grew up in Youngstown, Ohio, the son of an Italian mother named Ada and an Irish father who fancied himself a comedian, although neither the circuit he played nor the copy he created brought home enough money to provide the family with financial security. Tim went to work when he was very young, as did most of his thirteen brothers and sisters, and when they gathered around the table for meals the conversation was lively: political and provocative. Liberal Democrats, the lot of them, with an outspoken, civic-minded, egotistical father and a diminutive, dark-eyed, darling mother with a quick wit and a posse of children, all of whom felt their mother loved each of them in a unique, special way. That was her great gift, said Hagan. When he moved to Cleveland, he pursued political office with focus and ambition, winning the seat of Cayahoga County commissioner at the tender age of thirty. This office had remained his, uncontested, for sixteen years. He had married a woman of considerable standing in the community, but the match had proved volatile and unhappy.

"There's no one. With the exception of my girls, of course," Tim said, "who mean everything to me."

"And you to them, I'm sure," I replied, sensing the seriousness in his tone.

"No doubt about that. They need me and I will see to it that they are brought to independence."

I half smiled. "With love?"

"Of course, with love. The love will bring them to independence." This Tim declared definitively, almost with an edge, as if it was a well-practiced and long-exercised mantra.

I reached for another cigarette and said, "I have a child who I will never bring to independence. Or to school or to parties or to anything else, for that matter. I gave her up for adoption."

There was a gentle silence. Tim asked me to tell him what had happened, and when I was finished, he looked at me and said, very softly, "You were very brave. That must have been agony for you."

How odd, to hear these words from the mouth of a near stranger and to know that they sprang from something deeply authentic. Neither my father nor any of my brothers nor, certainly, any man before or since had responded with such simplicity, such goodness. Hagan did not shift in his seat, his silence was not awkward, he was not shaken or unsettled, but I felt his empathy as keenly and surely as I felt the absence of my daughter, and this alone was enough to fill me with a solace I hadn't felt since the very hour she was born. Hagan reached for me, and I went into his arms as naturally as if it had been written. Oh, but it had, I thought to myself as I lifted my face to his, it had been written on the wall of some primitive cave in the savanna, millions of years ago. It had just taken a little time to find its way. Then Tim Hagan tossed his cigarette out the window and pulled me to him, putting every kiss I'd ever known to shame.

In the morning, I woke to a soft rain and Alec at my elbow, begging me for breakfast.

"Let your brother sleep," I cautioned him, "and we'll go over to the hotel and have breakfast with Tim. How's that?" A thumbs-up from Number Two, always gladdened by the prospect of an adventure.

"Have you considered changing your clothes in this lifetime?" I asked him as we skipped down the stairs.

"Nope! Gotta fly!" he called to me, running ahead, perfectly content to be the dirty, cheeky little devil he was.

At Benner's Hotel on Main Street, Alec and I waited in the lobby until we saw Hagan coming smartly down the stairs, fresh from a shower, carelessly tucking in his crisp white shirt. He beamed when he saw Alec, and Alec smiled mischievously, as if to suggest that it wasn't Tim's company he hankered for so much as a good breakfast and an adventure that didn't include his brother. We trooped into the hotel dining room and were seated at a bright, white table already laden with teacups, cream, and sugar. No sooner had we ordered our breakfast than a man entered the restaurant carrying an armful of wildflowers wrapped in cellophane and tied with a purple ribbon. Tim gestured to him, and when the man approached our table, he rose and pulled out his wallet.

The deliveryman, middle aged and absolutely delighted to have been sent on such a mission, placed the flowers in my arms with the same tenderness he would have used had he been handing me a newborn.

"Madam," he said with a beautiful formality, "your flowers."

I looked at Tim, looked at Alec, looked at the flowers, and then, of course, I knew. Hagan was leaving.

"The ambassador is at the end of her patience," he explained. "I've been gone a bit too long."

"When do you leave?" I asked.

I whispered it, couldn't find my voice.

"My flight leaves from the Kerry Airport in three hours. Could you give me a lift?"

I nodded, said, "Of course, but I need to see about someone to look after the boys."

"*No!*" shouted Alec. "I'm coming with you! I am coming with you and I'll be with you driving back! Get someone to babysit Ian—he *likes* Owen!"

Hagan and I looked at each other over our cups, and our glance spoke volumes. Our chaperone had spoken.

At the airport, Hagan gave Alec a handful of coins to play the game machines, which provided us with about ten minutes of uninterrupted privacy. But it was impossible to touch, impossible to speak, impossible to think clearly.

"If you change your mind and come to Dublin, I'll be there for a week," Hagan said, leaning forward. "I'll hold a couple of rooms for you at the Westbury, just in case."

Alec had almost finished his game of Pac-Man; I could sense that our time was almost up. "Do you remember what you said to me yesterday on the sea walk?" I asked. We had walked the ring around the bay, just the two of us, in a light rain, and just as we'd approached the remnants of an ancient castle that sat atop a hill overlooking Dingle, Hagan had turned me to him and said, "I'd love to see what you look like when you're eighty."

Now, however, he only nodded, and his smile was wistful. At that moment, boarding for his flight was announced, and we both jumped to our feet, eager to put an end to the terrible tension. I walked him out to the tarmac, the propellers started up with a roar, he leaned forward, and, avoiding my lips for Alec's sake, he kissed me gently on the cheek and whispered into my ear, "I think I'm in love with you." He was wearing aviator sunglasses, his Irish mac slung over his shoulder.

The door to the plane closed, and Alec pulled on my hand. "Come on, Mom, let's go!" he shouted.

Once in the car, my son chattered nonstop all the way back to Dingle, for which I was grateful.

I waited five days, and then made a decision. We were going to Dublin.

Irish Mist

It was late when we pulled into the quiet village of Adare. We were irritable and hungry. Mercifully, the large, family-style hotel had a room available with two double beds, onto which the boys immediately threw themselves, complaining of the cold, complaining of the damp, complaining of primitive Irish customs. No room service, no bar after eleven, no vending machines bursting with crap. I pulled a few tired ham sandwiches and a couple of apples from my bag.

"This is the best I can do," I said tightly. "Now, eat your sandwich, take a shower, and go to sleep. We're on the road at the crack of dawn."

They groaned in unison, a response I was accustomed to, having spoiled them well from the moment they were born. But this time I snapped. "Okay, that's it, lights out! I've had it, guys. You've pushed me to the limit." This silenced them sufficiently to get them under covers, clutching soggy sandwiches and pouting fiercely in the darkness. Very soon, however, their frustration gave way to sleep, and within minutes the room was as quiet as a chapel.

I sat on the windowsill, cranked open the window, and lit a cigarette. My head was pounding, my throat was raw, I was filled with anxiety. I swung my legs over the windowsill and dropped to the ground below, careful not to wake the children. Why hadn't Hagan called, as he said he would? What was he thinking? Could it possibly have been a ruse? Was I so dense as to have mistaken a mere diversion for the real thing?

In the lobby, I stared at the pay phone and pondered my dilemma. I had never willingly called a man before in my life. Only emergencies or a change of plans necessitated a phone call to a man. "If you ever call a man on the telephone," my mother had told me when I was ten, "you will get cancer of the hand." I looked at the piece of paper in my as-yet-nonmalignant hand, looked at the phone, dropped in the coins, and dialed.

A woman answered. "Ambassador Smith's residence, who's calling, please?"

I was ready. "This is Kate Mulgrew, I'm calling for Mr. Hagan, actually, he's a guest of Mrs. Smith's."

Tidy, the voice on the other end was, and officious. "Mr. Hagan is out for the evening. Would you care to leave a message?"

"I would," I replied, falling into the rhythm of her stiffness. "Would you kindly tell Mr. Hagan that Kate Mulgrew will be at the Westbury Hotel tomorrow night?"

"I will, indeed."

"Thank you."

"Not at all, madam. Good night."

I hung up and thought that approaching my own execution could not have been more agonizing.

*   *   *

The next day, Hagan didn't come. Not by cocktail hour, not by dinnertime, not by bedtime. Nor did he call. I ordered room service for the boys, bathed them, and got them into bed. The bathroom looked like a war zone. I didn't care. I waited until they were fast asleep, then opened the door to the adjoining room and curled up on the vast, beautifully made bed, wide awake. No man was worth this much effort, I said to myself. I have children to look after, I have things to do, I'm an actress, a woman of substance. Enough! I'll take a bath, open a split of wine, and shake off the humiliation.

I sank into the hot tub, luxuriating in the comfort and still-ness of this overpriced and magnificent hotel bathroom. At that moment, the phone on the wall next to the toilet rang. My eyes sprang open and my heart stopped as I lunged for the phone.

"Hello?" I was low voiced, sleepy sounding, ever so slightly dismissive.

"Kate, this is Tim."

"Well, well, what a remarkable surprise. Don't tell me: you're in the lobby and want to take me out on the town," I said, splashing about so as to make it clear that I was bathing and indisposed.

"As a matter of fact," Hagan replied, "I *am* in the lobby, and I know it's late, but I would like to see you, if I could."

I took a deep breath, tried to quell the rising anger.

"Tim, it's almost midnight. My children are asleep in the next room. Are you insane?"

"That's a possibility," he responded, "but I would still like to see you. We'll get one of the women at reception to keep an eye on the boys."

I hesitated, and then asked him bluntly, "Would you do that if they were *your* children?"

Hagan paused, but not for long. "Probably not," he answered, "but I'm hoping you will."

I did.

Hagan took me to a nightclub just down the street from the hotel.

Sitting at a table, waiting for us, were Kim Smith and her husband, Dylan. Kim was Jean Smith's daughter; she had fallen in love with this hardscrabble Irishman and had thrown in her lot with his. We drank and listened to music, and I pretended to chat with Kim when all the while there was a burning sensation in the pit of my stomach. I felt Hagan's leg brush against mine. I felt his eyes, the effort he made to appear relaxed. An hour ticked by, and with every passing moment my anxiety increased.

"I need to go. I'm worried about the children," I whispered to Hagan.

"Yes, of course. All right. I'll walk you back," he said, and rose from his chair.

We said our good-nights, and I could feel Kim Smith's curious eyes on my back as we made our way through the room and out into the cool, misty Dublin night.

We didn't say much, walking toward the hotel. It was as if it was too painful to make small talk. When we arrived at the hotel, it was well after two in the morning. We stood facing each other, just outside the lobby door. A minute passed in silence.

"Would you like to come up for a nightcap?" I asked, fixing a brave, cavalier smile on my face.

Hagan looked at his shoes, which I immediately interpreted as a rejection. Then he surprised me. "Yes, I would like to come up." This response was unexpected.

I giggled and, as I disapprove of giggling in others, said quickly, "But I won't be interfered with."

"Too bad."

"And what about the ambassador—won't she be upset?"

"Frankly, my dear, I don't give a damn," Hagan said, opening wide the hotel door and ushering me into the lobby.

Upstairs, the room was even more welcoming than I'd remembered. Everything in it was comfortable, clean, and plush. The lighting was soft, the lampshades a dusky rose. Two perfect chocolates sat on the pillows. "Thank God someone thought of dinner," Hagan said, scooping one into his mouth. I poured the wine—a lovely red—and we drank. He sat on the bed; I sat next to him. I asked why he hadn't called me in Dingle, why he hadn't made the reservation at the Westbury as he'd said he would, why he hadn't come for me until almost midnight. His discomfort was evident in the reddening of his cheeks.

He was embarrassed and explained that Jean Smith brooked no disloyalty and that when he was expected to escort her to a dinner, it went without saying that he was to be available to her for the entire night, until she ordained that the evening was over and that she was going to retire.

"How tiresome," I said, "and dictatorial. Is there any fun in it for you?"

"Oh, sure," Hagan replied. "Jean's terrific company, and she's full of mischief. She and your mother have that in common. She knows a lot of fascinating people. Jim Sheridan, Seamus Heaney, Daniel Day-Lewis. I've had some great all-nighters. The Irish are captivating talkers."

He paused, and then went on. "You know, it was Jean's husband who was my friend. Steve Smith. I promised him, before he died, that I'd keep an eye on Jean and see to it that she never lacked for an escort."

"Kind of you, but evidently there's a price to pay."

"A very small price," Tim corrected me. "Jean is a generous, smart, sophisticated woman, and she treats her friends very well. Besides, if it hadn't been for Jean, I wouldn't have met you."

"In which case"—I lifted my glass—"here's to the ambassador!" We clinked, looking into each other's eyes. "Why *did* we meet, do you think?" I persisted, and then Hagan had had enough.

The night unfolded as all mysteries do, with unexpected shocks to the system, suspense-filled silences, embraces stopping just short of danger, kisses portending unknowable depths. Between moments of almost excruciating desire, there was muted conversation, whispered, hurried, important.

"Are you really not otherwise engaged?" I wanted to know.

"No," he replied. "That's over. And you? I doubt you can convince me that you don't have a lover."

"I don't anymore," I said, and I meant it.

We talked about our families, the size of them, the endless sense of responsibility, the feeling that we were old well before our time. "At five, I understood the importance of time," Hagan said, with a wry smile. "I was in charge of the younger ones. I was accountable." He sighed then, and I understood that he was weary of the baggage of life, of the hand he had drawn, of the very goodness of his character, which prevented him from seeking his own happiness. In turn, he questioned me about the baby I had given up for adoption. How had I managed the sadness, all of this time? Where did I put it?

"In my work, I suppose," I answered, quietly. "Not very original, but there you have it. The work has saved me."

He looked at me, propped himself up on an elbow.

"Ah," he said, as if uncovering a secret, "that's it, then. Your work is what you love most."

"And my children, of course," I said.

"Yes, you love your children, but you can't *live* without your work."

This unsettled me, and I found myself growing defensive.

"I certainly couldn't live without my children, either, so it's an absurd argument."

"Ah, but it's not an argument at all." Hagan looked at me carefully. "No one is arguing your right to happiness, particularly after what you've been through."

"And what about you? Do your daughters define you?" Now I wanted some answers.

"Of course they don't define me, but they need me, and I have made a commitment to their well-being." He was grave, something had shifted.

"And that's the most important thing," I challenged him, "above and beyond all else."

Hagan lit a cigarette, and then replied so softly I could barely make out the words. "I'm afraid so," he whispered. "I'm afraid so."

It was almost dawn, and I knew he needed to get back to the Residence before he could be found out. We were neither lovers nor friends. We hung on the moment of separation as if it was very possible we would never see each other again. An extraordinary strength of will kept me from saying anything more. Hagan slipped into his jacket and ran a hand through his thick black hair. He shook his head, and chuckled.

"This was a wonderful night," he said.

"Yes, it was," I agreed, "but we were wise not to—"

"Absolutely," Hagan interrupted, "because what if it isn't real? What if it's only Irish mist?"

I smoothed his collar and put my hand to his cheek. "Time will tell," I said. He nodded, opened the door, and walked into the corridor.

I moved quickly to the window, which opened onto the lane, where I knew he would soon appear. Such an unbearable suspension of time, before I saw his figure under the streetlamp. Not particularly tall, not particularly burly, not particularly

anything, but indisputably and singularly Tim Hagan. Just as
he reached the end of the lane, he turned and, seeing me in the
window, lifted his hand in farewell. I waved and kept my hand
in midair, a salute. The dawn had crept in on little cat's feet,
and now here she was, whispering with light, lifting the mist.

A week later, I found myself lying like a corpse in a tiny bed
in a bad hotel in Piccadilly. The boys were safely ensconced in a
slightly larger box down the hall and were now fast asleep,
after having been to the Tower of London, the London Zoo,
and Madame Tussauds. It was two in the morning, and I was
wide awake, anticipating the hand-off that would take place the
following day. Robert Egan had arrived in London and would
take the boys for the last two weeks of the summer holiday. I
was imagining how I would feel in the moment of seeing Egan
and delivering the children into his hands. The politeness I
would assume, the veneer of congeniality, the strain—at this
moment, the phone rang, startling me. I reached for the receiver
and whispered, "Hello?" as if the tiny room had been bugged
by the CIA. A pause, very slight, on the other end, and then a
voice, rich and deep, said my name.

"Kate."

"Tim," I replied. "How on earth did you find me?"

"Well, I'm afraid I had to disturb your dear mother to get
the details, but she gave them to me."

"Was she surprised to hear from you?" I asked.

"No, not surprised to hear from me, but surprised as hell to
hear that I was looking for her daughter in London."

Even with happiness flooding through me, I was smart
enough this time to make him do all the talking. "I just wanted
you to know"—he paused, clearly nervous, before continuing—"I
wanted you to know that I don't think it was Irish mist, after
all." He said, "I'd like to see you again."

Softly, I asked, "And when would you like to see me again?"

"As soon as possible" was Hagan's response, his voice gathering confidence. I looked out the postage stamp–sized window and, listening to the cacophonous sounds of early morning Piccadilly Circus, understood that it was up to me to walk to the cliff's edge.

"I could meet you in New York next week. I'll be visiting my good friend Nancy Addison. Come in for the weekend."

Thousands of miles separated us, but I could envision him sitting in his favorite chair in the living room of his house in Cleveland, his mind turning, weighing the odds. We lived in different cities, we were both raising young children, I was thirty-nine, he was forty-eight, and we were passionate about our careers. The stakes were very high, and we both knew it.

"I'll be there a week from Friday."

"Four twenty-five West End Avenue, apartment twelve-A."

"Got it. See you." Hagan hung up.

I flipped on the light by my bedside, got out of bed, and went directly to my suitcase. Searching wildly, my hand finally found what I was looking for at the very bottom of the suitcase, impeccably packed in white tissue paper.

The perfect little black dress.

We Begin

Nancy Addison's apartment was like an oversized hothouse orchid. Everything in it was meant to look exquisite, but to me it was preposterous. No item of furniture was authentically functional, so my sleeping quarters were confined to a corner of the diminutive dining room, where Nancy had contrived to convert an air mattress into an eighteenth-century bed, replete with expensive linens, satin neck rolls, and at least six pillows of various sizes, none of which were practical. (I do not risk offending my dear friend, because she has been dead now for many years. Besides, had I given voice to this opinion then, she would merely have rolled her eyes and said, dismissively, "Oy, and the shiksa from Iowa should talk.")

This was Friday, and the shiksa from Iowa was in a state. It was pissing rain, and although this was the designated day for our rendezvous, I had not heard a word from Hagan, and I had an audition in Times Square at two p.m. I dressed informally, in the same cotton frock I had worn when I'd first met Hagan at the Hotel Tralee. It was a commodious gray-green shift with little to recommend it, and why I thought it appropriate for the captain of a starship I'll never know. My mind was clearly on other things, and even when my manager spelled it out for me, I could not quite grasp what he was saying.

"The captain of a—what did you say?" I asked.

"The first female captain in the history of the *Star Trek* franchise," my manager responded, somewhat testily. "It's called *Star Trek: Voyager.* You would be playing the captain of a starship."

"For what? A movie?" I asked, still oblivious to what was being laid out for me.

"Now listen, Kate. You're an intelligent woman. This is a big deal. They are looking for an actress to play the first female captain in one of the most successful franchises television has ever known. *Star Trek*! You do know what *Star Trek* is, don't you?"

Not wanting to provoke him further, I mumbled, "Vaguely. They travel around in space wearing strange costumes, right?"

My manager counted to ten. "They travel around in space making billions of dollars, that's what they do! William Shatner, Patrick Stewart, and now—a woman. They want to put you on tape today at two p.m. Be prepared."

"Oh, Alan." I sighed, impatiently. "When am I ever *not* prepared?"

I caught a taxi on the corner of Eighty-Second Street and West End, which was a minor miracle, given the stormy conditions. Sheets of rain pelted the taxi as we staggered through Midtown traffic, finally arriving at Forty-Fourth Street and Seventh Avenue just minutes before two p.m. I had looked over the additional pages, known as sides, but hadn't memorized them. On this day, in this state, I was incapable of memorizing a street sign.

A casting assistant greeted me when I got off the elevator and escorted me to a room at the end of the corridor. The hallway was lined with chairs, placed there for the comfort of the many actors who would be put on tape that day. A few faces looked up as I passed, assessing the competition, and none too pleased to see an actor being taken directly into the audition room, which indicated privileged status. I was jumping the line, and this was against the unspoken rule of fair play, but I allowed myself to be led into the room, accepted with pleasure a glass of cold water, and asked for five minutes in which to collect myself. "Of course, Miss Mulgrew," said the assistant casting director, "take your time."

I sipped the water and looked at the pages on my lap. I could make little sense out of the dialogue, it sounded so foreign. My mind, like a broken tape, returned again and again to Hagan and why I hadn't heard from him. My heart was racing, and not out of nervousness over the part, but because I was frantic that I had somehow confused the date on which we were to meet. Could I have missed him? In my eagerness to see him again, could I have made a mistake?

The casting assistant appeared at my side and asked, "Are you ready, Miss Mulgrew?"

I looked at her and smiled sheepishly. "As I'll ever be," I mumbled, and followed her into the room. I told them I'd had no time to memorize the pages and so would hold them for the audition and hoped that would be all right. A perfunctory nod from behind the camera suggested that it wasn't actually all right, that it lacked professionalism, but, under the circumstances, it would have to do. On action, I delivered an audition so devoid of meaning, so completely inauthentic, stilted, and false, that on several occasions I had to bite my lip to keep myself from laughing. When I finished the scene, I held up my hand to let the casting director know I was not yet finished.

"I'd like to apologize to those of you watching this audition," I said into the camera, "it is not good work by any stretch of the imagination, but you see I've fallen in love and I can't concentrate and I'm meeting him today and I'm very sorry for having wasted your time. Thank you."

The camera clicked off, and I heard the casting director say, "Well, that was interesting."

It took what felt like hours to get back to Nancy's place. The day had unfolded badly, and hope was draining from me with every passing hour. I was sodden and miserable by the time I opened Nan's front door, and I could tell immediately by the look on my friend's face that Hagan had not called. It was devastating to have once again fallen for his charm and to once again have been proven so terribly wrong. What was it about the guy that made me so wholeheartedly believe in him? Severe disappointment brought tears to my eyes, whereupon Nancy pounced.

"Forget about it! Let's go out! And you never know, shit happens. Life isn't black and white—"

I stopped her right there. "You know, Nanny, life *is* in fact black and white when it comes to men. There are good men, and there are bad men."

"Oh, for God's sake, don't launch into a lecture," Nancy warned. "Get out of those wet things and take a shower. Danny had to go out of town, so we can sleep in the same bed tonight."

This was meant to cheer me up, and it did provide comfort, of a kind. At least I knew I'd be spending the night soul searching with someone I loved.

Just as I turned to go into the bedroom, the doorbell rang. I froze. Nancy froze. My eyes widened in disbelief. Nancy looked at me, took one step to the door, and opened it. Hagan stood there, wearing a trench coat, blue jeans, and loafers.

"Sorry I'm late," he said as I stepped forward, barefoot and disheveled, completely at a loss, and asked, "Are you late?"

Hagan laughed. "Well, I'm sure as hell not early!"

Nancy ushered him into the living room, divested him of his raincoat, and disappeared into the kitchen to get a bottle of wine and glasses. We stood looking at each other like school-children but with considerably less bravado.

"I didn't really know what was going on, when to expect you, we didn't exactly plan this very well, did we?" I asked breath-lessly, feeling awkward, euphoric, and idiotic, all at once.

Nancy looked at me and said pointedly, "Don't you want to change your clothes? You look like a dead rat."

"I don't think that's quite the expression," I protested.

"Maybe not, but it works, I see what she means," Hagan said, putting an end to any further discussion about rats. I excused myself and went into the small master bedroom, closing the door behind me.

Ten minutes later, I reemerged wearing the little black dress, simple black heels, a touch of mascara, and the merest sugges-tion of pink gloss on my lips. My legs were bare, my long hair had been brushed, and my cheeks were flushed. A woman can count on one hand the number of times in her life when she actually felt beautiful. This was one of them. I saw it reflected in Hagan's eyes, and I was pleased.

We sipped champagne and discussed where we should go for dinner. "I'm not tagging along!" Nancy declared, but it was a losing battle. Tim and I were adamant that she join us. She knew of a good Italian place just down the street, got up to grab a sweater, leaving the two of us alone for the first time.

"It's good to see you," I said to him.

"Yes," he answered, "it's very good. Hard, expensive, com-plicated, and very good."

Nanny breezed into the room, ready to go, and Hagan and I jumped to our feet.

The lights in the Italian restaurant were low, the red wine was mellow and full-bodied, and we three sat and talked for two hours. Hagan was very interested in Nancy's career, in her hus-band Danny's work as a journalist, in her views and interests and politics. He was articulate. He was irreverent. He was utterly charming. Hagan and Nancy laughed together as if they'd known each other for years. When Hagan excused himself to go to the bathroom, Nancy leaned over, grasped my hand, and whispered fiercely, "If you screw this up, I'll never forgive you."

Out on the street, Hagan attempted to flag a taxi. Nancy whispered hurriedly in an aside to me, "Go with him."

"I'm scared," I whispered back. And I was. As a taxi approached and Hagan moved forward to open the door, Nancy put her arms around me and said, "It's all right. You can trust him."

Hagan helped her into the cab and turning to me said, "How about a nightcap? I'm at the Mayflower." I nodded in dumb acquiescence, but as Nancy's cab pulled away from the curb I desperately wanted to call after it, to stop whatever it was that had started before it was too late.

But then, it was too late, and a taxi was whisking us off to the Mayflower, where we entered the lobby and hesitated, helpless, looking around like two newly arrived tourists.

"I would like to have a nightcap in the bar," I said stiffly, to which Hagan immediately responded, "Great idea. This way."

The bar was dark, illuminated by the streetlights that stood sentinel on Central Park West. We pulled out stools and waited for the bartender to take our order. I was freezing. In my eagerness to impress Tim with my good looks, I'd decided against a wrap, and now I sat in the air-conditioned bar in a thin cotton summer dress, having spent a good part of the day in a cold and unforgiving rain, and I was trembling. Tim ordered two whiskeys, and when I reached for mine, I saw that my hand was shaking. Hagan noticed it, too, and asked if I was all right.

"I'm afraid of you," I said to him.

He laughed and said, "And I'm afraid of you, so we're even."

"You're joking, but I'm not," I told him. "Even in Ireland, I could sense that for you everything is light, amusing. Everything's a kind of entertainment, and then it's forgotten. You move on to the next."

"And you don't?" Hagan asked and, although his eyes were merry, his tone was anything but, so I decided to tell him the truth.

"I'm not officially divorced yet, and I don't want to tell you what I went through to get out of that marriage. It was difficult and heartbreaking—we even tried divorce therapy! I did it, but only to appease my husband, who is fantastically stubborn. And throughout, I was less than honest, which I couldn't stand, so I can only imagine how he felt. But I didn't care. I just wanted out, and I was prepared to do whatever was necessary to expedite the process. That's why I took the boys to Ireland—so we could lick our wounds. If it had been just Robert and me duking it out, it would have been wrapped up in a matter of weeks, but the kids are what draw it out. You can't bear to hurt them, and so, by trying to keep the canoe afloat, you plunge everyone into treacherous waters. It was horrible, and I'm still recovering."

Hagan gestured to the bartender. Two more.

"So what's your story?" I asked him, lighting a cigarette. "Your *true* story, please," I added, emboldened by the whiskey.

Hagan hesitated. Clearly, this was not easy for him, and whereas I felt a moment's compunction for having forced his hand, I was not about to let him off the hook. He cleared his throat, looked down at the glass in his hand.

"I've tried to do right," he began, "but I've made mistakes, and now I'm paying for them. I loved my wife and was prepared to do anything to salvage the marriage. And, believe me," he continued, shaking his head, "I tried damn near *everything*, but in the end I just couldn't cope. I also knew the sooner I acted, the less my daughters would suffer. And that, I believe, is true. They're only three and five, so as far as they're concerned, they're living a normal life."

"Ah," I responded, "you're probably right. Had I left my husband earlier, there may not have been such turmoil. Boys aged nine and ten are so impressionable, they see and feel it all, and what's worse, they're too young to really understand what's happening, and so they're full of a kind of free-floating anxiety. They don't know who to blame, so after they've finished lashing out at the parents, they punish themselves."

My eyes filled with tears, which often happened when I considered the divorce and what it had cost my children.

"But the fact is," I continued, "that despite their sadness, and despite my guilt, and despite Egan's anger, I went ahead and did what I needed to do for myself. In the end, it's selfish."

Hagan interrupted me.

"I think you're wrong there. It feels selfish at the time, because the pain is excruciating, but there is no nobility in hanging on to something that is miserable and false. We have to fight for our happiness in life." My hand was next to his on the counter. It looked pale and small; his looked warm and strong.

"How do you know what will make you happy?" I asked, not looking at him.

"I don't know. It's a crapshoot. But I'd say I'm pretty happy right now," he said, and my heart pitched.

Then he put his hand over mine. "We don't have to go upstairs, if you don't want to," he said, "but I'm praying to Jesus that you want to."

"I thought you were a confirmed agnostic."

"It's conditional," Hagan responded.

I laughed, but my heart was in my throat. This was the ultimate crapshoot, and I knew that never before in my life had I encountered such high stakes. I looked into his eyes and said in my softest voice, "And I'm praying to Jesus that there's a minibar in your room."

He put the key in the lock and opened the door to his suite.

I followed, taking the heavy bag from my shoulder and throwing it on the sofa. The *Star Trek: Voyager* script I had been lugging around all day and that now resembled nothing more than a soggy pile of detritus spilled out onto the floor.

Hagan moved quickly to retrieve it and, his curiosity piqued, asked, "What's this, then?"

"Oh, nothing," I replied, "some science fiction series. They're looking for a captain of a starship, but it doesn't matter because my audition was appalling."

He flipped through the pages of the script, pausing here and there to read bits of dialogue, which I found irritating given the circumstances, so I grabbed the script out of his hand and threw it in the wastebasket. Hagan studied me for a moment and, before pulling me into a kiss that would last all night, said, "You're going to get that part."

In the morning, having slept not a wink, I watched as the first light crept through the window. My back was to Hagan and, as I started to turn, I heard him say, "Don't move."

"Why not?" I asked.

"Because this is perfect happiness, and I want to remember it."

On Sunday, we dressed for brunch. This was the third consecutive day I'd worn the little black dress, but Hagan didn't mind. He told me he thought it was a very pretty dress. He said nothing about my face or my figure, nothing about the way I walked or the way I danced (which we did late into the night on Saturday, to golden oldies on the radio in the hotel room). He was a man of few words when it came to flattery. He wasn't raised that way; it was false to him. That was fine with me.

We took a last walk through the park, and once, when I stumbled, he took my hand and tucked it in his arm. Past the baseball fields we walked, past Sheep Meadow, past the Tavern on the Green. Neither of us spoke. People sat on the wooden benches that lined the sidewalk leading to Central Park West, and just as we were about to reach the street, an elderly woman sitting with her husband pointed at me and said, "I vote you the prettiest woman in the park today." Hagan laughed and said, "You just made her day." But I could see that he was pleased.

We picked up Hagan's duffel bag at the hotel and crossed to the opposite side of the street, where he would have a better chance of flagging a taxi to the airport, where he would board a plane back to Cleveland. I stood there in my little black dress, unable to speak. When Hagan raised his arm, I could hardly bear it. It took every ounce of self-control and willpower I possessed to do nothing. A taxi screeched to a halt in front of us. Hagan threw his bag in the backseat of the cab, then turned to me. "Thank you for the most wonderful weekend of my life," he said, and I believed him. He kissed me then, fast and hard, jumped in the taxi, and was soon swallowed up in the maelstrom of New York Sunday-afternoon traffic.

Three days later, the phone rang in my bedroom in Los Angeles. "Kate, this is Tim." He announced himself on the telephone in much the way the captain of an airplane will say, "Well, ladies and gentlemen, looks like we're in for a little chop, so I'm going to turn on the seatbelt sign." That level tone of voice, betraying nothing, maintaining power.

"How are you?" I asked, searching for the right tone.

"Well, that's what I'm calling about. I'm not sure how I am. I'd like to see you again."

"That's called missing me," I said.

"Semantics," he replied. A strange pause ensued, during which both of us sought a foothold, sensing that this vulnerability might be dangerous.

"I miss you, too," I said at last, and this was the handle he was waiting for.

"I called your mother, just to see how she's doing," Hagan went on, "and she told me she's having an art show in two weeks, and a reception at Derby Grange afterward. She invited me to come." He was waiting for me to react before he would continue. It wasn't cat and mouse, but it was close.

"You'll never believe it, but I'm invited, too," I said, as if it were an extraordinary coincidence. "What would you think about meeting me in Chicago and driving to Dubuque together?"

"I think that would be terrific," Hagan replied, a lift in his voice. We were agreed. It was settled. We would see each other again, soon.

He was waiting for me as I came off the jet bridge. Leaning against a pillar, white collared shirt, blue jeans, the ubiquitous navy jacket slung over his shoulder. He was brown from the sun, his eyes were sparkling, and he was attempting a mischievous grin that immediately upon seeing me transmuted into tenderness. I went directly into his arms and would have stayed there had he not patted me on the back and said, "Now, now, that's enough, no public displays of affection."

"You're a dinosaur, aren't you?" I laughed. "Because we certainly are fond of those *private* displays of affection."

Hagan relieved me of my overnight bag and, as we started down the concourse, said, "What kind of car should we rent?"

"Silly question, on a beautiful August night in the Midwest," I responded. "A convertible, of course."

Driving through the Iowa countryside, I thought I had never seen it look so beautiful. An early harvest moon illuminated the sky. We drove down winding roads, past countless cornfields, through small towns and gentle valleys, my hair whipping in the wind, Hagan behind the wheel. I looked up into the perfect star-studded sky and admonished myself to pay attention, that this was a moment to be fully present to. Don't throw it away on what could be, I cautioned myself, just concentrate on what is. I threw my arms in the air and shouted, "This is *my* country!" Hagan smiled at me, and put on the gas.

When we drove through the old stone gates of Derby Grange, the house was lit from within, every room aglow, and in the front yard, a bonfire blazed. Hagan was duly impressed. "What a beautiful place."

I jumped out of the car, pulled my overnight bag from the backseat, and called, "Come on!" as I turned and headed up the brick path to the front porch. I stopped just short of the steps, staring in astonishment at my old friend Claire Labine, who was sitting on a picnic bench next to my father.

"Claire!" I cried, running forward to embrace her. "I didn't know you'd be here."

"Neither did I," she replied, "but I'm awfully glad I came. Don't know how I'm getting back to New York, however, because I'm completely broke."

With my arms around her neck, I said, "How many paintings did you buy?"

"Oh, sweetheart." Claire laughed. "You don't want to know."

My father, having sat and observed this reunion in silence, now spoke.

"Hi there, sugar. Nice to see you again. I believe I'm your father." I went to my father, kissed him soundly on the cheek, then turned to Hagan and said, "Daddy, Claire, this is Tim Hagan. I met him in Ireland and he's been stalking me ever since."

Claire hooted and said, "Ireland has that effect on perfectly normal people. I understand."

My father rose from his seat, extended his hand, and said, "Hagan, how the hell are you? And what are you drinking?"

Hagan was smiling broadly, when suddenly the front door opened and my mother ran out, shouting, "Kitten Kat Feathers of Joy! You're here! And with Tim!" She went up to Hagan and gave him a kiss.

I started inside, stopping to whisper into my mother's ear, "Wait until I tell you," to which my mother responded, "Oh, dear."

Inside, bodies came at me furiously. With each recognition, there was a scream of joy. My sister Jenny flew into my arms; my brother Sam, deep in conversation with a tipsy priest, saw me and shouted, "Hooray!" I was pulled from room to room, until I came across my dangerously handsome brother Joe in the kitchen, surrounded by a gaggle of pretty girls.

"Nothing changes," I said, announcing my presence, whereupon Joe came forward and, giving me a big hug, declared for all to hear, "I have to maintain some order, you know, or they'd be on me like mosquitoes." Laughter carried me into the living room, where I encountered old friends and, with Jenny at my side, out to the front porch, where I introduced her to Hagan and said, "He's my ride."

Jenny looked from me to Hagan and back again before lifting her glass and remarking drily, "I'll bet he is."

We made our way down to the bonfire, where at least ten of my fourteen nieces and nephews were gathered. A lot of the kids were singing and dancing, my nephew Rory's face shone in the firelight, and we smiled tenderly at each other. He was fourteen years old, Joe's oldest son, and ever since he was born, I'd had a special fondness for him and saw to it that he accompanied me and my boys on as many adventures as possible. I went over and kissed him, then nudged him and gestured toward Hagan. "Go meet Tim Hagan," I said.

"Who he is, Aunt Kate?"

"He's a special friend, darling, now go shake his hand." An hour later, the singing was more subdued, and the fire had taken ahold of us, as it always did, mesmerizing us into silence. I scanned the familiar circle of faces until my eye fell on Hagan and Rory, exactly where I'd left them an hour ago, standing side by side, completely at peace, gazing into the fire.

In the wee hours of the morning, when the house was finally still, I stole out of bed and made my way to the maid's room, where Hagan had been temporarily ensconced. The door creaked when I opened it, and Hagan whispered, "Shhh, they'll hear us." I could barely suppress laughter, knowing, as I did, that not only this room but many other rooms in this house, and very likely at this very moment, were experiencing the creaking of doors and of mattresses, too.

I climbed in beside him and asked, "Well, what do you think?"

Hagan put his hands behind his head and said, "Terrific. Wacky, eccentric, and probably dangerous, but terrific."

"This is how I grew up. Now you know." I know I sounded proud, and a little defiant.

"There's a lot of drinking, which I'm not accustomed to," Hagan observed, "but there's a lot of joy, too, and great creative energy. As for your father and your siblings, it's parry and thrust all the way, but they're good-hearted and full of laughter. Your mother almost seems out of place."

"If she didn't paint and play the piano and dance on the lawn, if she weren't completely eccentric, I might agree with you. And she is wildly eccentric. Do you know she set me up with a friend of hers in Ireland? Old enough to be my—" But Hagan stopped my mouth, and we spent the next few hours creaking our way to bliss.

As dawn broke, and we were weary, spent, and perfectly happy, Hagan, nearly asleep, murmured, "Who will do the cleaning up downstairs? It's a disaster area."

"Oh, generally we just leave it. Mother gets up early and makes a halfhearted pass at it," I said.

"Well, not this morning, she doesn't," Hagan declared, suddenly up on an elbow. "Now get your ass out of bed and I'll meet you in the kitchen in five minutes."

The kitchen at Derby Grange hardly knew what to make of itself by the time we were finished. We scoured the walls, the floor, the counters, the windows. Every glass and every dish was recovered from the front yard, the living room, the dining room, the porch, and washed and dried until they sparkled. Beer cans were collected and put in crates, old food was thrown out and carefully tied in garbage bags, a pot of coffee was brewed, and a bowl of fruit was assembled prettily in a bowl and placed in the center of the kitchen table. It was a complete transformation.

Finally, we sat at the table, coffee in hand, and I turned to Hagan. "Just wait," I said, "the acid test."

I heard Jenny first, from the bottom of the front stairs. "Who cleaned up the house? My God, it doesn't look like itself!"

"You mean, without the feral cats foraging for that one cube of fossilized cheese," Sam said.

"Oh, shit, don't tell me the *cheese* is gone!" Jenny screeched. The two of them sauntered into the kitchen, slightly bleary eyed. My sister stood stock-still, astonished. "Oh my God, did you two do this?" she cried.

"Saints. Veritable saints," Sam declared. "Now get the hell out of my way so I can have a cup a coffee." Everyone laughed. Mother came through the dining room, humming, and entered the kitchen as if it always looked like this after she'd thrown a party for two hundred people. In fact, she went immediately to the sink and began to wash the single coffee cup that sat in the basin, which sent us all howling.

"Very nice," Mother hummed, "very, very nice."

Next, my father walked slowly into the kitchen. He was showered and hungover, and it was anybody's guess which way the wind would blow. The room fell silent as he made his way across the floor, opened the cupboard to retrieve his favorite cup, then slowly proceeded to the coffeepot, where he felt it necessary to rest for a moment before lifting the pot and pouring the coffee into his cup. This he did, laboriously, but successfully. Then he turned to the group of us gathered around the kitchen table, took a sip, looked at Hagan, and said, "Still here?"

As the day unfolded, everyone slowly dispersed. Mother disappeared into her studio, and I asked if she were going to paint. "Are you nuts?" she called as she pulled the door closed. "I'm counting my loot." It was understood that everyone would reconvene for dinner, and it went without saying that I, who loved to cook for my siblings, would prepare the meal. In the meantime, the day was ours. Oh, the whole day was ours, to do with as we wished.

"Come on," I said to Hagan, "let's take a walk." Hagan looked at me skeptically, as if walking through the woods and valleys might be less than idyllic, but I assured him he would see unimaginable beauty. "And every manner of wild creature," I whispered.

"I know," Hagan replied, "I'm walking with one of them."

We went through the green glen, past Pee River, into the timberland.

"Pee River?" Hagan asked.

"Tom named it that when we were very young," I explained. "He was a dazzler with words and a born cartographer."

Through the thicket we went, under the barbed-wire fence, and into a clearing, where rolling hills sloped to a winding creek. Real Iowa farmland. Again, I experienced a sudden, unexpected surge of pride. Hagan observed this and said, "It's pretty here."

"Oh, Tim, it's not pretty, it's beautiful," I said and, when I put my arms around him, said again, "It's beautiful and you *know* it's beautiful."

We kissed for a long time, and lovemaking seemed imminent when we suddenly heard the low but distinctive bellow of a bull.

"Jesus," Hagan said, jumping up, "did that thing follow us from Ireland?"

"Yes, he did, and they become very aroused when they see humans making love." I lay on the ground, arms outstretched.

"Let's get the hell out of here!" Hagan was pulling me up, and I was laughing so hard I nearly stumbled and fell, but I shouted to him, "Run for it, Tim, here he comes! He's full of fury, he's aroused, and he will follow the scent of the male of the species!"

We clambered up the hill, slipping and shouting, made it under the barbed-wire fence, and were crashing through the timberland, when Hagan suddenly fell on his ass. Down he went, like a great tree. I doubled over with laughter, gasping, "No time for rest, that bull knows a thing or two about a measly barbed-wire fence."

"Oh, knock it off, you nut job," Hagan said, pulling me to him.

When we came through the door, red cheeked, disheveled, and covered with pine needles, no one said a word. It was a rare display of familial solidarity and indicated to me not only that Tim was well liked but that he had been accepted. Jenny and Sam were sharing a beer with Mother, who looked at the two of us and said, "That was a nice long walk."

"Loooooong walk," Jenny chimed in.

Then Sam, my beloved brother and keeper of the peace, came to the rescue. "We're starving, what's for dinner?"

As I assembled the ingredients for the pesto sauce, Jenny pulled out a chair for Hagan and asked him if he'd like a drink.

"I don't really drink," Hagan told her.

There was a collective gasp. And Sam followed this with "Ever?"

To which Jenny responded, "Are you on medication?"

Hagan held up his hands and said, "Well, I do occasionally like a screwdriver."

"Atta boy!" Sam slapped him on the back, adding, "Without the orange juice, however. Orange juice is persona non grata in this house."

Dinner was delicious, wine was served, and the conversation swelled. Hagan was a born raconteur, but, more important, he listened with his whole being, thus inviting all manner of subjects to be explored. It wasn't long before Mother, Sam, and Hagan found their way into an argument about metaphysics. I'd seldom seen my brother so animated, or my mother so engaged.

"So, that's why I abandoned the Church and became agnostic. Self-exile," Hagan said.

"Self-examination, really," Sam interjected, "which often leads us into dark places."

"More interesting, the shadow side," Mother offered. "More honest, somehow. Although I do think, like Spinoza, that God is Everythingness."

Everyone mumbled in agreement, as if it went without saying that God was Everythingness, and then Jenny said, "Speaking of the shadow side—doesn't anyone want to talk about sex?"

At this moment, my father opened the back door. "We're talking about sex," I called to him, "so pull up a chair!"

He studied us for a moment, shook his head, and said, to no one in particular, "Jesus. H. Christ."

That night, I again crept into Hagan's bedroom, but this time there was no resistance. He pulled back the sheet and took me in his arms. The moonlight filled the little room, just as it had twenty-one years ago when Tessie had wept about the injustice of her disease. "I'm the good one," she had said. The little room, full of secrets, grew still.

The next day, we prepared to leave. Many things were said to me, many whispered asides, many bright eyes met mine, and it was clear that they all understood that I was truly in love. Even as we pulled away in the little red convertible, Mother stood in the lane, watching until we disappeared around the bend.

"I always cry when I say good-bye to Mother, isn't that silly?" I asked, wiping my eyes.

"No," Hagan answered. "That's love."

At O'Hare Airport, we returned the car to the rental agency and took a shuttle bus to the concourse. We had about an hour before his flight was scheduled to leave. Mine was an hour later. We found a nondescript airport bar and drank Coke out of paper cups. I glanced at the clock on the wall. Forty-five minutes to go. I so much wanted to talk to him, because talking to him was such a pleasure, his listening such a gift, but I found myself at a complete loss for words. I felt a low-grade nausea stealing over me. As the clock ticked, my nausea intensified, until it was impossible not to say, "I'm afraid I have to find a bathroom."

Hagan immediately stood up and said, "Of course, of course. I'll walk you to the ladies' room and then be on my way."

No, no, I wanted to shout, that's not what I meant! We still have twenty minutes! Instead, I nodded, and we made our way out into the concourse where, of course, because Murphy's Law is the law of sadness, there was a women's bathroom immediately to our right.

"I love you," Hagan said. "I'll call you." Then he turned abruptly and walked away, without a backward glance.

The Audition

Iowa changed me. An infatuation was transformed into love. I was possessed with an energy and sense of purpose I'd never known before, and I was confident that I was among the few to have found that elusive thing called true love. I knew that in Hagan I had found my soul mate. The part of me that had searched for this, longed for this, hoped for this, could finally rest. My happiness was complete. And somehow, this happiness hardened my resolve to work as hard as I could and to raise my children well. To prepare for a new life. Back in Los Angeles, I called my manager and my agents and told them in no uncertain terms that I was on the warpath and to be prepared for bloodshed. My manager found my new attitude refreshing and told me that just that week the French Canadian actress

Genevieve Bujold, who had been hired to play the captain in the new *Star Trek* series, had quit.

"Evidently," Alan told me, "she lasted a day and a half before she realized that eighteen-hour days, pages of technobabble, endless press, and seven years of being away from her only child was not her thing, so she called the producers to her trailer and gave them her walking papers. Now they're in a real fix because shooting has started, but they don't have their star, without whom the show, as they say, cannot go on. So they're scrambling, to say the least."

"Listen, Alan," I replied, "I know I blew the audition on tape in New York, but I want you to get me back in that room. Just get me in the room, and leave the rest up to me. If there is any hesitation on their part, tell them to look at my track record. Long hours and difficult dialogue are what I do best. Get on it."

The next morning, Alan called and told me an audition had been arranged for the following day. Paramount would be messengering a script, sides, and details of where and when the audition would be held within the hour.

"You're going directly to network, which in this case means that anybody and everybody could be in the room. Rick Berman, Jeri Taylor, and Michael Piller are the executive producers. They carry the patent for Gene Roddenberry and this is their baby, but UPN will be the fledgling network working with Paramount to make this show a hit. It's a seven-year franchise, about as solid as it gets in this industry. Only a handful of women are being called in, some of them have been seen before, and they may already have a particular interest in one of them, which is why you need to go in and knock the ball out of the park."

I took a deep breath.

"Thank you, Alan, for what could be interpreted as a little

too much information, but I'm grateful for the warning. You just make sure the script is at my house within the hour."

I went into the kitchen and found Lucy at her favorite station, assembling the ingredients for fajitas. The boys and some of their friends were outside in the pool, performing cannonballs and devising games that required excessive noise, near-death penalties, and an abandon known only to those who have no understanding of time.

"Luce, I need you to help me out," I said to the woman who had heard this supplication so often that it actually evoked a chuckle.

"I know, señora," Lucy responded. "You got to work and you need quiet. Gimme some money and I take the boys to the movies."

I cocked my head, none too coyly. "And a pizza afterward?" I asked.

"What kinda pizza you mean—until bedtime pizza or short pizza?"

"This is important," I said, "so I'm going to encourage you to have a really good time. I need at least four hours."

Lucy wiped her hands on a kitchen towel, removed her apron, and said, "You got it, señora."

"Oh, Luce, what would I do without you?"

"*Ay, Dios mio, señora.*" Lucy sighed. "What I do without *you*? Anyway, you know I like the movies."

She walked briskly out of the kitchen and, even before I could make it to the stairs leading to my bedroom, I heard her calling outside, "Okay, pies, we go to the movies! All righty then! Now, hurry up!" In Lucy's singular approach to the English language, she had decided to do away with the "sweetie" in "sweetie pie" and had shortened that endearment to "pie," which, as far as I could tell, everyone preferred.

The children were gone and the house was quiet when the

messenger arrived bearing the much-anticipated manila envelope. I took it upstairs to my bedroom, which was my haven. Iced coffee at hand, I curled up on my chaise for a good, long read and was almost immediately aware of unfamiliar roadblocks. Many words made no sense to me; it was a particular kind of language, highly stylized, while at the same time much of the dialogue between officers seemed informal, even casual. What was at once evident was Captain Janeway's love of science, her unusual friendship with the Vulcan Tuvok, her need for adventure, and her mettle. In the pilot script, her name was Elizabeth Janeway, and although I knew I had my work cut out for me, I felt an instant and natural affinity with this woman. I liked her style.

The next morning, I woke early and went downstairs, script in hand. The audition was scheduled for two o'clock that afternoon, and I needed coffee. A lot of coffee. Overnight, I had developed a cold and a low-grade fever, which was very unusual for me. I was constitutionally as strong as a bull, and this sudden malaise unsettled me.

Accompanying the script were sides, and this additional copy constituted the audition material. I would need to perform two scenes; one with Tuvok and the other a monologue, explaining to my crew that we were lost in a part of the galaxy called the Delta Quadrant. Neither scene demanded a grasp of the technobabble that dominated so much of the pilot, and this went a long way toward putting me at ease. Clearly, the executives wanted to see what qualities we, as personalities, would organically bring to the role. It occurred to me that they would be in no mood to work with us on the text, as is sometimes the case. Instead, my instincts told me that it was going to be all or nothing at all in that room, that the decision would be based almost entirely on intuition. There was no time for anything else. They needed a captain, and they needed her now.

Three hours later, I pulled up to the gates of Paramount Studios and submitted my name to the guard. The guard smiled at me and said, "Good luck, Captain." Incredible. How could he possibly have known that I was here to audition for the part of the captain on a new *Star Trek* series? Studio buzz, undoubtedly, and all the gossip that went with it.

These studios were miniature worlds unto themselves: self-contained, well-regulated, financial gold mines. The original actress's defection must have gone through every soundstage and production office like wildfire.

An assistant greeted me when I pulled open the door to Rick Berman's office. "Good afternoon, Miss Mulgrew, please come with me," she said, leading the way through a maze of rooms. I passed what looked like a conference room and saw two actresses sitting there, one of whom I recognized, the other I'd never seen before.

The assistant ushered me into a private room and said, "We're going to put you in here by yourself, you'll be more comfortable that way. Would you like something? Coffee? A glass of water?"

I smiled in gratitude and said, "A glass of water would be terrific. Have they started yet?"

"Oh, yes," the young woman replied. "Two actresses have already done their first scene. It won't be long before you're called."

I have always had nerves of steel, but when it comes to the last step on the high dive, something else takes over. The fight-or-flight syndrome, some might call it, but in no way was I inclined to flee. In fact, as the adrenaline flooded through me, a peculiar calm came over me, intense and empowering. I was aware that I had a cold and was slightly feverish, but none of this bothered me in the least. It didn't even occur to me to powder my nose. I was ready, and I wanted in.

There was a knock on the door, and the amiable young assistant poked her head in and said, "They're ready for you, Miss Mulgrew." Those words. As many times as I'd heard them in my career, they still gave me a jolt. I braced myself for the last stop on the line, stood up and said, "And I'm ready for them."

I walked into a large room full of unsmiling and not particularly welcoming people. Three long tables sat against the back wall, and in every seat sat a person who would weigh in for the final decision. I didn't recognize any of the faces, which was a tremendous relief. I didn't want to know who was judging me. I would approach this audition exactly as I would an audition in the theater. The people watching constituted the audience, that was all, and it was in my nature to embrace this dynamic, to play with the audience, just as the audience would play with me.

"Which scene would you like first?" I asked, addressing a man who was leaning forward, chin in hand, exuding indifference.

"As you wish," he replied, and I thought, Oh dear, they're tired, unimpressed, this process has not gone as well as they'd hoped.

"I'll do the scene with Tuvok, then, my Vulcan friend." I smiled and, turning to a young man sitting next to the door, asked, "Are you reading with me?"

"Yes, I am."

"Okay, hang on to your hat," I said to him, which elicited a few chuckles.

It is a wonderful thing to know and understand friendship. It is a gift, without question. I have been blessed with a handful of the most extraordinary friends, whose allegiance and devotion have, again and again in my life, lifted me up. Now, in this stiff room full of important people, I showed them Janeway's capacity for friendship. I laughed with Tuvok, I teased him, and then suddenly turned and found myself utterly vulnerable in his presence, seeking his counsel, needing his guidance. In the end, I embraced him, and put my hand to his cheek.

The scene had ended, and the man with the wry expression said, "Would you mind doing the next scene? The monologue? Or do you need more time?"

I looked him in the eye and retorted, "If there's one thing an actress doesn't need more of, it's time."

He chuckled, looked down, and said, "Then please begin when you're ready."

There were two ways to approach the monologue. I could give it to the reader, seat him closer to the table, or I could address the executives themselves, as if they were my crew. I chose the latter. Standing alone in the middle of the room, I looked at each of them, in turn, as I explained that we were lost in an uncharted part of the galaxy, that we would have to find a way to work together if we were to survive, that we must triumph over old rivalries and embrace new friendships, that we must face each unexpected challenge with courage and audacity and hope and that, above all, and despite seemingly insurmountable odds, I would find a way to get them home. Somehow, I promised them, someday, I would set a course... for home.

There was silence in the room. No one smiled. A few studied me with curiosity, and then the man with the first indifferent, and now bemused, expression said to me, "Thank you very much. Please wait outside."

This time, I walked into an open room where the other candidates were seated. Collectively, they looked at me, as if searching for a lost compass. I simply shrugged my shoulders and said, "That was fun." One of the actresses groaned, as if my idea of fun was her idea of a root canal.

After no more than five minutes, the assistant came into the room and, smiling, said, "Well, thank you, ladies. You've all been dismissed. Please sign out as you leave."

We all looked at one another with open-faced surprise, having fully expected a second round of auditions to follow the first. This was most unusual, and none of us knew what it portended.

We gathered our things, our handbags and our script bags, our garment bags and our makeup bags, and slowly made our way down the stairs and toward the parking lot. A more disparate-looking group of women you would be hard-pressed to find. I searched for the commonality, and came up empty. Certainly, no one would consider us uniformly beautiful. One woman was short and comely with long blond hair and startling blue eyes, another quite tall with a dark bob, black eyes, and an air of cockiness, and yet a third was similar to me physically, but somehow softer and more vulnerable. When we reached the parking lot, we paused briefly as if to consider how best to part—rivals or comrades? No one had yet thrown down the gauntlet, so I assumed we would part ways amicably, perhaps with an easy joke, wishing one another the best of luck and carefully concealing our nerves, which had just been put through the ringer. The dark-haired actress looked directly at me and said, "I have two kids and I really need this job. Maybe some of you don't feel as strongly as I do, in which case..." But here she trailed off, because there was nothing further to say. We all knew, and knew that she knew, that it was utterly out of our hands. It struck me almost like a prayer, so I pressed her hand and said, "If it's meant to be, it's yours. Good luck, one and all." I climbed into my jeep and headed home to my boys for a night of wrestling with postaudition angst, and perhaps, to alleviate this suffering, there would be a phone call from Tim.

The audition had fallen just a few days before the Jewish

High Holiday of Yom Kippur, but I was not as aware of this as I should have been and therefore interpreted the silence from my manager, as well as my agents, as a definitive dismissal of my audition for Captain Janeway. I did what I always did in the face of rejection—I wallowed in self-pity for about two hours, then jumped into the pool and swam sixty laps. It stung, this rejection, and it lingered, but that's the way it was, and there was absolutely nothing I could do about it.

It was important to put on a brave face for the children, who were inordinately sensitive to my moods, particularly where work was involved. I wanted to teach them that rejection, and the sadness that attended it, were an integral part of loving something passionately and therefore nothing to be ashamed of. Still, young boys think in a linear fashion, and I know it was difficult for them to grasp the notion that, despite having done well in the audition, I failed to get the part. After all, in their world, a payoff was immediate and almost always gratifying. Alec's primitive painting of a campfire garnered an A-plus, and in the top-right-hand corner of Ian's rather dark interpretation of the "The Twelve Days of Halloween," the teacher had written: "This is truly frightening, Ian. Keep up the good work."

After exhausting myself in the pool, I told Lucy I was going to the market and to set the table outside; we were going to grill steaks. The market was always a pleasant diversion. I could escape within the aisles of the air-conditioned and impeccably appointed San Vicente Market, and I could leave feeling a sense of satisfaction and anticipation, despite having spent enough to have sustained a small Mexican pueblo for a month. I packed the red-and-white-striped grocery bags into the back of my jeep and drove home.

When I pulled into the driveway, I was greeted by what could only be interpreted as an alarming sight. Lucy, Ian, and

Alec were standing on the front porch, waving their arms and shouting at me to get out of the car and come quickly. I thought, Oh, no, the dog is dead, and then amended that to Oh, good, I hope the dog is dead, she's such a miserable creature. That, then, had to be corrected for reasons of absolution before I jumped out of the car and heard Lucy reprimanding me.

"Señora, you got to get in the kitchen and listen to the phone. Why you never listen to those messages, señora, huh?"

And now I was thinking, Oh my God, someone I love is dying—not dead. This I could glean from the look in my boys' eyes, which simply said: *Listen to your bleeping messages, Mother!*

I reached into the backseat to gather a few grocery bags, but Ian interrupted me with a sharp, "Mom, get out of the car, do that later, go into the kitchen! Go!" I did as I was told and went into the kitchen, where I pressed the button to replay the messages on my answering machine.

There was only one, and it said, "Kate Mulgrew, this is Rick Berman, the executive producer of *Star Trek: Voyager,* and I simply wanted to say welcome aboard, Captain. I'll see you on the bridge Monday morning."

The boys were suddenly screaming, Lucy was screaming, and I was screaming, but all of this came to an abrupt halt when I held up my hand and said, "On your knees, everybody, and let us thank God for His wonderful and mysterious ways." They did as instructed, we clasped our hands in prayer, and then I turned to Lucy and said, "Now get over to that refrigerator and pull out that bottle of champagne, because tonight we are going to celebrate *all night long!*" And while everyone scrambled for glasses and the mad cheering of my children rang out from the kitchen, I stepped into the quiet of the bathroom, looked at myself in the mirror, and said out loud, "Now, *this* is happiness."

That night, my time-honored resolve vanished into thin air

as I picked up the phone to call Tim in Cleveland. His voice was hushed and distant when he answered.

"Hello?"

"I just wanted you to know that you were right," I said, barely able to contain my excitement. "I *did* get the part of the *Star Trek* captain. How could you possibly have foreseen that?"

There was an odd, protracted pause, before Hagan replied in a low voice, "Because you deserve it, because you're a natural commander."

"Tim," I asked, "why are you whispering?"

"My girls are asleep next to me, and I don't want to wake them. Can I call you later?"

A small letdown, but perfectly understandable. His children were sleeping. "Of course," I replied. "Good night."

"See you," Hagan said, and hung up.

Now, *Voyager*

It was as if I were shot out of a cannon, life changed so quickly and so dramatically. One night, I was celebrating my good fortune with family and friends, and the next, I no longer knew who I was or what was happening to me. The phone did not stop ringing. My agents were busy negotiating the final deal, UPN was busy launching its network with *Star Trek: Voyager* as its flagship show, Paramount was busy announcing its new captain and the immediate resumption of shooting, and Rick Berman was saying to me, "Your life is about to change in ways you can't begin to imagine."

This gave me pause, as it would any thinking human being. "By which you mean, it will it be exciting?" I asked.

"By which I mean, it will be . . . phenomenal," Berman said.

"Now come to the studio immediately, we need to do costume and makeup tests."

Incredibly enough, the same guard greeted me when I arrived at the Paramount gate that afternoon. "What did I tell you, Captain?" He beamed, as the gates lifted.

"You must be psychic." I laughed, to which he immediately responded, "No, ma'am, just smart."

I parked in what was referred to as "the Tank" and found my way to Stage 8, navigating between speeding golf carts, down dark alleys, and past huge hangars known as soundstages. As I approached Stage 8 a young man, clearly on the lookout for a captain, walked briskly toward me.

"Kate?" he asked, already pulling his walkie-talkie from his belt. I nodded.

"I'm Mike," he said, "the second AD. Pleased to meet you, everyone's very excited. I'll be taking you through the process today."

Beep. "Stage."

Crackle. "Kate Mulgrew has arrived, I'm going to start her in hair."

Beep. "Roger that," came the disembodied response. "Then take her to costumes, makeup is last. Test on the bridge at two o'clock. I'll call the office."

"Check."

The friendly and unassuming assistant to the assistant director named Mike could not have known at the time that it was he who placed me squarely in the one-man luge, supine and feet first, and gave me the push that started me down a chute so fast moving and perilous that, for the seven years that followed, I felt as if I were competing against a timer so precisely calibrated that often a thousandth of a second could make a difference. It was immediate, breathtaking, and completely immersive.

Once in the hair trailer, I was introduced to the head of the hair department, Josée Normand, a stout, good-natured, and very tough French-Canadian woman whom I liked immediately. She sat me in a chair, placed an apron around me, and turned me slowly to get a look at what it was she had to sculpt to perfection within the next hour. We considered every conceivable hairstyle until the door to the trailer was pulled open and two men and a woman entered, filling the confined space with a sense of importance so great that Josée immediately stopped what she was doing and stepped back.

"Kate, Rick Berman," said a tall, nice-looking man, as he stepped forward and shook my hand.

I laughed and said, "Ah, you're the man who seemed to find me amusing at the audition. I felt like winking at you."

"Probably wise you didn't," he responded, with a slight smile. "Not very captainly of you."

"One captain to another, as it turns out," I said, standing to shake the hands of the other executive producers, Michael Piller and Jeri Taylor. All three were professional and composed, but Berman alone struck me as someone who hid beneath the surface of these qualities, a man who might be concealing the more genuine aspects of who he was. I was aware, for the first time in my career, that I was facing the old guard, a conservative and successful group of producers who had worked for a long-established cause, known as the *Star Trek* franchise. There was a discipline in place, an unshakeable order, and a principle of such significance that this initial meeting was almost entirely lacking in bonhomie. Even the woman, Jeri Taylor, who, because of her gender, might have expressed a certain solidarity, did just the opposite. She was polite but detached. Berman was the alpha, no question about it, which probably explains why I was so quickly attracted to him. Indeed, within minutes he had issued instructions to Josée and her team about how to style Captain Janeway's hair.

"We'll test it a couple of ways, but let's take a look at it up first."

"Up in a chignon, a French twist, or a bun?" Josée inquired. Berman studied me.

"Keep the front of her natural hairline, and pull it up with another piece into a bun. You're probably going to go through a lot of changes in the next few weeks, so fasten your seatbelt."

"Isn't outer space more advanced than that?" I joked.

"Not much," Berman said drily, "but you'll find that out for yourself soon enough."

Jeri Taylor stopped at the door and turned to me.

"Oh, by the way, you should know that we can't, after all, use Elizabeth as Janeway's first name, there happens to be a living author with that name, so we've decided to call her Kathryn. We thought that would please you."

"Very much," I responded. "How do you spell it?"

"K-a-t-h-r-y-n. Do you like it?" Jeri Taylor asked.

I swallowed, on the verge of suggesting the spelling of my own name, Katherine, which I considered the more classic version, but I caught myself and said, "It's lovely. How nice."

The triumvirate of producers, no doubt in a hurry to complete my deal and get on with the show, offered their congratulations, their best wishes for a successful seven years, and their collective assurance that should I need anything at any time, I need only say the word. No sooner had they stepped out of the trailer than I was spun around in the chair and a coven of hairdressers wielding scissors, pins, and hairpieces went to work, furiously converting my head into that of a futuristic captain who might exude an effortless command but who was, nonetheless, a lady.

I was then ushered from one trailer to another, delivered from one set of hands to the next, all of them pushing, plucking, kneading, tightening, snipping, zipping, and snapping. When I walked onto the bridge for the first time to undergo a series of tests, I felt completely transformed and admitted as much as I introduced myself to the director of photography, Marvin Rush.

Unsmiling but not unkind, he said, "Nose to the grindstone, eye on the prize."

Then he said, "Turn around, please, slowly."

"Hey," I joked, "this is a family show!"

Neither Marvin Rush, the camera operator, the focus puller, the gaffer, nor the best boy broke a smile. The heat was on, and standing there in my handmade Italian boots with four-inch heels, I could feel it from the tips of my toes to the top of my bun-enhanced head.

On Monday, my makeup call was four fifteen a.m., which necessitated a three a.m. wake-up at home. I needn't have set the alarm; I'd been lying in bed, wide awake, since two. Now I jumped out of bed and began the ritual that would serve me well for the next seven years. My work clothes were laid out on the back of my desk chair; I had showered the night before, so I had only to wash my face, brush my teeth, and pull my hair back into a ponytail. On the way out of my bedroom, I grabbed my script bag, a light jacket, and my purse before heading down to the kitchen, where Lucy had prepared the coffee the night before. I pressed the auto button, opened my script, and spent the following ten minutes sipping my coffee and going over my lines. This was my first day, and the first scene on the call sheet was scheduled to shoot on the bridge. Janeway enters from her office, which on the USS *Voyager* was called the captain's ready room, and walks slowly through the bridge, greeting each officer in turn.

I was about to meet my comrades-in-arms, and I was excited. Curious. How would I react to these actors, with whom I would be spending the next seven years of my life? And more important, how would they react to me? Having already experienced the confusion and disappointment of Genevieve Bujold's defection, they were unlikely to be in any mood for fun. We were down to the wire, and now it remained to be seen whether or not I could control the set, and command the bridge.

It took nearly three hours that first day to get me camera-ready, a process that, over the next months, I would whittle down to an hour and a half. I was to become the bane of Josée Normand's existence, in her ongoing effort to achieve a coiffure that would suit not only Janeway but all of the Paramount executives, as well. Obviously, this had not been a concern during the production of *Star Trek: The Next Generation*, and without having even met the man, I envied Patrick Stewart his freedom from this kind of attention. For the extra sleep it allowed him, if nothing else.

While I was being helped into my captain's uniform, there was a knock at my trailer door.

"Come in!" I called out, realizing that there would be no such thing as standing on ceremony.

The door opened, and a voice inquired, "May I come in?"

"Yes, yes, come in and close the door behind you!" I shouted.

A young man bounded into the small space and filled it immediately with his vitality, his charm, and the completely unaffected way in which he greeted me.

"I'm Kevin Brockman, publicity for UPN, and I'll be looking after you personally for the next few months. We're going to have some fun."

He laughed, and I laughed with him. His handsome face was lit by something else, something more than beauty, more than charm. He struck me as essentially incorruptible, and I instinctively knew that I could trust him.

I took his hand and said, "Help me, will you?"

"Oh yes, ma'am, that I will do, but some of this ain't going to be easy, especially initially," Kevin explained. "You're going to be pulled in every possible direction over the next months, it will be very demanding, but I'll be there to guide you."

"Just don't let go of my hand, whatever you do," I said.

Kevin Brockman smiled broadly, looked me dead in the eye, and replied, "I promise that I will never let go of your hand."

A pause, during which we sized each other up.

"As long as you do everything I ask of you," he quipped, slamming the trailer door behind him.

Mike, the second AD, knocked on the door and informed me they were ready on the set. These were words that I would come to respond to with Pavlovian discipline. As I walked through the door of Stage 8, I was greeted by several strangers, crew members, day players, technicians, all of whom stood sharply to attention and said, "Good morning, Captain!" Mike led the way to a group of people huddled in conversation around a monitor. The *Star Trek* triumvirate was present, of course, and there were a number of Paramount personnel present, as well, come to see the goods for themselves.

A trim man with an intelligent, handsome face approached me and, extending his hand, said, in a slight German accent, "I'm Rick Kolbe, the director. It is a great pleasure to meet you, and rumor has it that you are not only ready to work but willing and able to boot."

"Yes, sir," I assured him, "that's what I'm here for, so let's get going."

Kolbe laughed and, taking my arm, led me onto the bridge, where the other officers had gathered for introductions.

The first to greet me was Robbie McNeill, who jumped up from his post at the helm and said, "Welcome aboard, Captain! I cannot tell you how happy I am to meet you!" His handsome Celtic face shone with mischief, and I felt the first gladdening of a spontaneous friendship.

"Is that a book you're reading, Lieutenant Paris?"

Robbie hid the book behind his back, looked at me sheepishly, and said, "Yes, ma'am, I'm afraid it is. Will I be punished?"

"Depends on what it is," I replied.

"Russell Banks, ma'am. I find him difficult to put down."

"Then carry on, Mr. Paris, but don't read and drive." We laughed, and although my nervousness was growing with every passing minute, I maintained a poise I thought becoming to an officer of my rank and gender.

Ensign Harry Kim stepped out from behind his station at operations, took my hand in a formal and extremely gracious manner, and said, "I'm Garrett Wang, and this is where you will always find me. Unless, of course, I'm promoted."

"Easy does it, Ensign," Kolbe interrupted. "Let's get through the pilot before we start promoting people. For all you know, you'll be dead."

Garrett blanched, and we all laughed again as the first AD called out, "Okay, ladies and gentlemen, find your marks! Get ready to roll on scene four, episode one, 'The Caretaker'!"

Rick Kolbe showed me to my ready room and, pulling me aside, said, "This is your home, and the bridge is your living room. You own it; it's yours. You should feel completely at ease, and in total command."

I entered the bridge from my ready room, assured Harry Kim that it wasn't "crunch time" yet, acknowledged another actor who was playing my first officer but who would soon be dead (Chakotay and Tuvok were still on the renegade Maquis ship, and we had not yet joined ranks), sat in the captain's chair, nodded to Mr. Paris, and said, "Engage."

When Kolbe called "Cut!" I looked out into the near darkness from my vantage point on the bridge and regarded the row of faces before me. Paramount brass, *Star Trek* brass, UPN brass, all there to keep the make-believe brass on the bridge in line. And if they weren't exactly beaming with unmitigated joy, they appeared to be satisfied with my delivery of that most excellent Starfleet directive: *Engage!*

As we prepared for the next scene, the long, intimidating line of executive personnel had, as they say, left the building.

Kevin Brockman was true to his word, and never did let go of my hand. When I wasn't actually filming a scene on set, he'd be waiting for me, and I would be whisked to a distant part of the soundstage, where an altogether-different crew would be lying in wait, shrouded in black cloth, ready to video my initial reactions to having become the first female captain in the history of the Star Trek franchise. An unending stream of journalists and photographers came through the doors of Stages 8 and 9, and this lasted for many months. The interviews were well organized, Brockman was nothing if not completely efficient, but the unremitting pattern of work and press began to take its toll, and within the first three months of playing Captain Janeway, I lost close to fifteen pounds. No one commented on this weight loss, except perhaps Rick Kolbe, whose job it was to train a high-intensity lens on me, and who watched my every movement from the moment I arrived on set until we wrapped, some twelve to eighteen hours later. It was an unspoken rule on *Voyager* that no day should be shorter than twelve hours, and often, in those beginning months, I would leave home in pitch darkness only to return in pitch darkness. Alec later confessed to me that he would lie in bed and wait for the headlights of my car to illuminate his room, and only then would he fall asleep.

Life was at full gallop, and I had almost no time to myself. Hagan was constantly on my mind, but when I arrived home at midnight, anticipating a message on the answering machine, there was none. This concerned me, but I assumed he was giving me my space, generously allowing me the time he knew it would take to adjust to this new and all-consuming way of life.

Three weeks into filming *Voyager*, a long white box was delivered to my home on a Saturday afternoon. I assumed it was a gift from either the studio, the network, or my agency. Carelessly, I pulled off the white ribbon and lifted the lid. Inside, an array of exquisite red roses. I caught my breath. Red roses could mean only one thing. My heart was racing as I plucked the card from the arrangement and opened it. "Dear Kate, Thank you for the best forty-nine days of my life. Love, Tim."

Again and again, I read that card, trying to discern a deeper meaning, a meaning other than the one so clearly in evidence. What did he mean, "Thank you for the best forty-nine days of my life"? And here's to the remaining seventy-three hundred? Surely, then, a phone call would follow, filled with the usual affectionate teasing, until Hagan would no longer be able to control himself and would say, *Well, did you get the damn roses or not?* A curious way of saying I love you, but I understood it. It was his way.

The phone call never came. For that unbearably long weekend, I made sure I was within earshot of a telephone, and when it rang I jumped and my heart soared. But it was a friend, just checking in, or an AD sending revisions, or Brockman with yet another press request. As the clock ticked inexorably to ten o'clock on Sunday night, I understood, at last, that the phone call would never come. That the roses were Hagan's way of saying good-bye, that he had chosen to leave me because he thought that a life together was impossible. His daughters. My sons. And most important, though unstated, my career. He wouldn't want to get in the way of my brilliant career.

After the first wave of insupportable sadness, another followed, and this one was more devastating than the first. It was a wave of fury and unspeakable disappointment. Hagan was, after all, nothing but a coward. He didn't have the guts to call me himself, to face the music, to end with dignity and courage what he knew would break my heart. And so he hid behind a box of roses and disappeared from my life.

On Monday morning, as the dawn broke over Paramount Studios and I made my way to Stage 8, it was impossible to check myself. I wept uncontrollably, barely escaping the watchful eyes of Mike DeMeritt, intrepid AD, as I slipped into my trailer and closed the door behind me. I was still weeping when there was a knock on the door.

"Yes?" I called, not wanting to see anyone, least of all an impatient AD.

"Kate, it's Jeri Taylor, may I come in?"

I couldn't very well say no to the executive producer of my show, so I hastily wiped my eyes and opened the door for her. She took one at me and immediately apologized.

"I didn't mean to disturb you. Is something wrong?"

Then, to a woman I hardly knew, I poured out my heart. How quickly our emotions reveal themselves, and how cavalierly we share them! It didn't take long before she'd heard the story of my romance with Tim Hagan, my conviction that this was the only man for me, and the forty-nine roses he had sent signifying the end.

To her credit, Jeri Taylor was empathetic and kind. I knew she had come on a professional errand, but she sat and listened to me as I staggered through the story of the forty-nine days that constituted my epic love affair. When I finished, she smiled as women do when there is nothing left to say, sadly and softly, and handed me a script.

"This might help a little. The next episode. I thought you might want to take a look. I think it's particularly strong."

We embraced quickly, I thanked Jeri for listening, and she

left. Within minutes, I was sitting in the hair trailer, and an hour later, I was on the bridge, issuing orders as if it were just another day in the bizarre and wonderful world of make-believe, as if my heart had not been broken into a million pieces, as if this were all possible to endure. Kolbe peered at me through the hard and clinical lens of the camera, then he shouted, "Cut! Print! Moving on!"

Grief moves through the system much as love does. It seeks expression. So I put my grief where it naturally belonged, in the company of an old and experienced wound. I gathered my feelings, shattered, scattered, and wild, and locked them in the same place where I kept my feelings about my daughter.

Weeks passed. The atmosphere on set became increasingly relaxed as my costars and I got to know one another. *Voyager* had taken on the crew of the Maquis, a terrorist group that had lost its ship in battle and now had no other option but to seek shelter on our starship. The leader of this group, Chakotay, was played by Robert Beltran. Strikingly good-looking, he was a curious combination of come hither and go away. He exuded an easy charm, but I often thought Robert was in a world of his own, dreaming of Shakespeare or women, anything but being lost in the Delta Quadrant. There was no question about his sex appeal, however, or his virility. Captain Janeway didn't hesitate before promoting him to first officer on her ship, which was met with a raised eyebrow by Tim Russ, who seamlessly inhabited the role of Tuvok, our resident Vulcan and tactical officer. He had been sent to spy on the Maquis and kept his opinion about Chakotay and his crew to himself, particularly when B'Elanna Torres, played by Roxann Dawson, exploded in one of the temper tantrums so endemic to her race, the Klingon. The other half of her, the human half, was disciplined, intelligent, and brave and soon became very important to Janeway, who quickly promoted Torres to chief engineer.

I was fond of my cast, and I was pretty sure it worked both ways, especially when long nights turned into mornings on the bridge, when we were all exhausted and slaphappy. It took next to nothing to send us into gales of uncontrollable laughter, and the boys knew exactly how to push my buttons. It was bad enough when Beltran, McNeill, and Wang stood in a chorus line, crooning oldies and high kicking in their skintight twenty-fourth-century uniforms. Sometimes, on a whim, Beltran would stand up and do his spot-on impersonation of Burt Lancaster. This often occurred only seconds before my close-up, which was, invariably, the last close-up of the shooting day. Production somehow understood that I would find a way to fix my face into a perfect mask of composure for that final ECU, despite being surrounded by a bunch of madmen. And if Ethan Phillips happened to be present, or if the doors to the turbo lift opened and Bob Picardo made a sudden, unexpected appearance, order could unravel within seconds, leaving me doubled over, gasping for breath, begging them to stop, which, of course, only whipped them into a lather of lunacy, because they were men and it was Friday and the camera was on me, the only female, and this was their biological imperative, to reduce me to tears of helpless, hysterical laughter.

One night, I noticed that Patrick Stewart had stopped by our set and was helping himself to a cup of coffee at craft service. Between takes, I strolled over and introduced myself, very curious indeed to meet my predecessor. We leaned against the table, coffee cups in hand, and I asked him how he had managed it so successfully for seven years. The demanding, sometimes grueling hours, the diabolically challenging technobabble, the lack of a private life, and the expectation that, as captain, we were not only meant to set the tone on the set but to perform at a high level of professionalism while doing so. It went without saying that we were to leave our personal concerns at the stage door. Stewart looked around the soundstage, taking it in, then suddenly broke into a sly smile.

"If you show up and do the work to the best of your ability, and keep your eye on the sparrow, then I promise you that when the next seven years are up, you will be very proud of what you have accomplished. Very proud, indeed," he said, and winked at me. "Now, hadn't you better resume command before all hell breaks loose?"

The work did not let me down, and neither did the part. When Mulgrew suffered, Janeway picked her up. And when Janeway felt like giving up, Mulgrew slapped her into shape. I was put to good use in every way, and this saved me. Tim had hurt me, but that was his choice, not mine. For me, it was best to shake Patrick Stewart's hand, down the last of my coffee, and bound onto the bridge. Where I belonged.

Rubik's Cube

Paramount held a special screening for the premiere of *Star Trek: Voyager*. The lobby of the Paramount Theatre was crawling with press when I arrived with my sons in tow. I wanted Alec and Ian, now ten and eleven respectively, to understand this achievement and to celebrate it with me. I somehow thought it would shed light on why I was so often absent, why whole days drifted into late nights, why I wasn't present to tuck them in and kiss them good night, to cheer them on at their soccer games, to applaud their accomplishments. In my naïveté as a mother and my egocentricity as an actress, I honestly thought that seeing me on the screen would make my children proud. If nothing else, I rationalized, they would have to appreciate the effort involved, for surely the effort deserved to be acknowledged. Finally, I thought, my sons would see for themselves how hard I worked and, however grudgingly, would be forced to admit that their mother was a disciplined and passionate actress, someone clearly devoted to her craft.

No sooner had the lights dimmed than the nightmare began. Ian pulled the straw from his soft drink and, turning his head, put the paper covering protecting the straw into his mouth and started to chew. His brother followed suit and, before the opening credit sequence had ended, my sons were doing their level best to pelt the screen with spitballs. Mortified, I turned to Ian and whispered fiercely into his ear, "Stop that right now, Ian! What in God's name are you doing? You're embarrassing me! I am telling you to knock it off. Right now." Incredibly, a small, devious smile of victory tugged at the corners of his mouth, while on my other side Alec prepared to load his straw and fire. "Alec, please don't do what your brother is doing—you're hurting my feelings. This is my *premiere!* Come on, darling, don't humiliate me in front of all these people." Mercifully, we were far enough from the screen to ensure that the spitballs fell short of their mark, but I'm sure that several of my colleagues were aware of my children's outrageous behavior and, in an attempt to conceal their amazement, pretended to ignore what was going on. The night unfolded in agony, with my sons threatening mutiny at every turn, and their mother, the star, barely maintaining composure, surrounded on all sides by curious onlookers.

When, at last, the lights came up, I took my children by the their hands, which they tried unsuccessfully to pry loose, and dragged them out through a side exit, across the parking lot, and into the waiting limousine. Once we exited the Paramount gates, both boys erupted in glee. They shouted and screamed victoriously as the car moved slowly up Melrose Avenue, as if they had masterminded a brilliant coup d'état.

For a long time, I was unable to speak, I was so rigid with fury. My sons had undermined me in public and on purpose, but, most disturbingly, they were behaving as if they'd done something brave, something necessary. When at last they settled down, it was into a hard silence, each looking out his window with cold, indifferent eyes. They were not afraid of me, they were furious with me, and they had decided, secretly and perhaps even unwittingly, that this would be the perfect night to demonstrate their hatred of my work and everything it represented.

The boys went to bed, sullen and without apology, and I made my way to my sanctuary upstairs. On the deck outside my bedroom, I lay on a chaise under the cool January sky and lit a cigarette. I replayed the evening in my mind with a growing sense of desperation. Why would my children behave in such a manner? Was something wrong with them? Was I a derelict mother?

At midnight, I stole downstairs and went to look in on each of the boys in turn. Alec lay curled on his side, dead to the world. I looked at his hand as it lay open and vulnerable on the duvet and thought, He doesn't hate my work, he hates that I am gone. He misses the security of my daily presence, and he hasn't yet absorbed the full impact of the divorce. He blames me for going to work, even work that I love. Perhaps more than anything, he resents that I love it. I bent and kissed the freckle on his nose, kissed his little running elephants of eyebrows.

Ian was a different story, lying on top of his bed with nothing on but a pair of shorts. He lay quite still, his hands clasped over his chest, like an old man taking a Sunday siesta. I peered at him closely.

Lately, he'd been having nosebleeds, and this worried me, made me wonder if something serious might be causing them. When this happened, I'd prop Ian up to a sitting position and attempt to put a damp cloth to his nose, but invariably he'd push me roughly away as if I'd rudely interrupted his sleep.

"Jeez, Mom, let me sleep! It's okay!" Now he lay quietly and looked so beautiful in repose it was hard to believe that he was capable of hurting me as deeply as he had. And yet, I had seen him take aim with my own eyes. It was deliberate, and menacing. He, too, was furious with me, but somehow it went even deeper than it did with Alec. He wanted me to pay a price for all of it: the divorce, the work, the celebrity. Everything.

I sat in the blue armchair in Ian's bedroom and studied him. Who could blame him? The initial promise, the one that takes place at birth, had been one of unconditional love. He had internalized that as an infant and now, as an eleven-year-old, could not understand why the rules had changed so dramatically. Surely, if the mother deliberately upsets the apple cart, then that must mean that she has lost her love for the child.

Actresses. What a bunch of sad saps we are, I thought. Madly in love with the child. Madly in love with the craft. Trying desperately to forge an alliance between the two, and constantly failing. If I were a man, I said to myself, none of this would be in question. My children would respect me, my wife would honor me, and everyone would exalt the work. But turn the knife just slightly to the left, and what you have is a harried woman sneaking out before dawn, cracking the whip for sixteen hours on a soundstage, creeping back home under cover of night, forever explaining, forever apologizing, forever in conflict. Picasso wasn't in conflict, you can bet your bottom dollar on that. He said, *Scram! I need to work,* and his mistresses and their spawn ran for the hills. Dickens wasn't in conflict. He had ten children and wrote as many novels in almost as many years, because it was both understood and appreciated that he was gifted, famous, and rich. The male artist has always been respected.

For the actress, there is no resolution. Read the life of Eleanora Duse, read the life of Sarah Bernhardt. Conflict and toil, occasionally leavened by illicit romance. Duse, arguably the greatest actress who ever lived, sent her only daughter to a convent so as not to expose her to the tawdry perils of life in the theater. Shortly after giving birth to an illegitimate son, Maurice, Bernhardt resumed her lucrative career as a courtesan. It wasn't until she clawed her way back to her rightful place on the stage that she bought the famous "coffin" in which she was photographed, eyes closed. Maurice must have had mixed feelings about nap time.

I played Captain Janeway in an era that had not resolved the conflicts surrounding mothers and work. The major studios were still struggling to present their actresses as superwomen. No one wanted to hear about the difficulties of raising children. Not really. It was only acceptable to talk about rising above these difficulties and managing to do everything well, to contribute to the great myth: women are master multitaskers, who fly through space spouting technobabble at warp 9.9, who then beam themselves home in time for dinner, prepared by hand on a four-burner Viking stove, tuck their tired but happy children into their lavender-scented beds, learn ten pages of dialogue to perfection while soaking luxuriously in a bubble bath, and, finally, reluctantly, turning out the light because, by God, she still has energy to burn!

I sighed and got up from the chair. I dropped a light kiss on Ian's brow and then, as an afterthought, gently stroked his hair. Such beautiful hair, such a beautiful boy. I turned out the hall light and looked in on Alec before I headed upstairs. The hand outstretched, relaxed, beckoning. I tiptoed to his bedside, knelt down, and kissed those fingertips, one by one. He didn't stir. Then I climbed the stairs to my bedroom, where I would forgo a bath, run a toothbrush across my teeth, remove my fancy premiere makeup, force myself to study my pages for tomorrow's work, set the alarm for a 3:45 a.m. wake-up, and switch off the lamp.

Multitasking, indeed.

Catalyst

My friend Nancy Addison was going to die, but we didn't know that then. We knew only that she had been diagnosed with a malignancy in her adrenal glands, that she would need to undergo chemotherapy, and that she was going to fight like hell.

"In fact," she said, "we're going to have a party!"

"A party, Nanny? Are you sure?" I asked, calling long distance from my trailer at Paramount.

"Of course, a party. In honor of my charity and, evidently, in honor of me. I would like you to cohost it and to present me with a lifetime achievement award. Do you think you can do that with a straight face?"

"I don't know, darling, who's writing the material?"

"Rosie O'Donnell! Isn't that terrific? You two can riff on

Ryan's Hope all night long, for all I care—just give me that statuette!"

The Copacabana had never looked so good. With her intuitive sense of whimsy, Nancy and her committee had transformed the ballroom into something unexpected. A huge silver-and-red motorcycle sat directly in the middle of the room, red balloons rising from its handlebars. Elegant silver and white streamers hung from the ceiling, loveseats in black and white were scattered throughout the room, pots of white and pink roses adorned every available surface, champagne was passed on silver trays, and everyone was in black tie, according to his or her unique code of formality. The crowd that had assembled in the main room consisted of doctors, philanthropists, actors, politicians, and priests. It was an eclectic and lively mix. When I presented Nancy with the Lifetime Achievement Award for her accomplishments not only as an actress but also for the tireless work she'd done on behalf of the Incarnation Children's Center in Harlem, I could not keep my emotions in check. Tears were streaming down my cheeks when Nancy stepped onto the stage to deliver her eloquent and very moving acceptance speech, in which she referred to me as her soul mate, then added, "And you're very lucky if you find one in this life."

Rosie O'Donnell came up, embraced Nancy, then turned to the crowd and said, "Okay, time for deep pockets, ladles and germs! Who wants to buy a 1998 Red Hot custom Harley Davidson Sportster and send that check *directly* to Incarnation Children's Center? Do I have a bid?" Laughter. "With you driving at breakneck speed and Kate Mulgrew wrapped around your six-pack, *Do I have a bid?!*"

The place erupted into cheers and, in the midst of this mayhem, I made my escape to the dining room, where the food and drinks were being served.

A young woman in a dark suit approached me as I stood waiting for a glass of wine at the bar and said, "Miss Mulgrew, there's someone here who would like a word with you. Please come with me." I followed her to an enclosed area at the back of the room, concealed by a dark wood-paneled screen. A figure emerged from the shadows and stood looking at me. Tall, erect, hair cut short but still more black than gray, and eyes that I would recognize anywhere, in shadow or in light. Eyes trained to withhold mercy, eyes that knew how to cut away at the first sign of tears, eyes that betrayed nothing. And there was the silver cross, her sole adornment, hanging simply and yet prominently around her neck. The jewel of her status. She stepped forward and smiled.

"Kate," said Sister Una McCormack, "what a surprise to see you here." The executive director of the Catholic Home Bureau, lieutenant to Terence Cardinal Cooke, and holder of the sacred keys of the kingdom of adoption extended her hand, and I took it.

"I was so pleased to hear of your support of Incarnation Children's Center," the nun continued, "and of your friendship with Nancy."

Sister Una's hand still rested in mine, and now I grasped it tightly and pulled the woman toward me, just a little, not so as to frighten her but to bring her closer. I wanted no strain, no confusion, and no possibility of escape.

"Sister," I began, "over the years I have reached out to you, and you have always had an excuse as to why I could have no information regarding my daughter. Not a document, not a photograph."

Sister Una was silent, her eyes on mine.

"I found out through a private investigator that my daughter had been moved out of state and adopted by a family in Watertown, Massachusetts, because Cardinal Cooke had a relative who knew someone that wanted a baby. At the last minute, the couple I had chosen was told not to bother coming into the city. There had been a mistake, there would be no baby, after all. Then you told me there had been a fire and all of my files had been destroyed, so there could be no possible way of communicating with my daughter. All of this may or may not have been true, but what I do know is that you were a woman doing her job, that Catholic Charities had you on a very tight leash, and that I am no longer afraid."

I paused, gauging her response. Her gaze was steady, unflinching.

"My daughter is now twenty years old," I continued, "and I know that you have the power, and the means, to reach her. I am not going to beg you. That's over. I've done the best I could with what I've been given, which is next to nothing, and now I want more. I want you to tell my daughter that I am looking for her and that, if she chooses, I would like to write a letter to her or, perhaps, even speak to her. I wrote a letter to her when she was born — did you give it to her adoptive mother?"

I then perceived the first chink in the armor, as Sister Una withdrew her hand and said, "I gave it to her adoptive mother, but there can be no guarantee that she gave it to your daughter."

"I understand very well that there are no guarantees of any kind," I said, "but this time I want you to promise that you will let my daughter know that I am looking for her, and how to find me if she chooses to do so."

A silence between us, a pause, and then a shift occurred. The professional woman, bearing the burden of years of secrets, suddenly stepped across the divide and did what she knew might jeopardize her position, as well as her reputation. She didn't seem to care. Her expression was clear and open. She had made up her mind.

"Go back to your hotel," Sister Una said quietly, "and in the morning I will send you documents from the International Soundex Reunion Registry. Fill them out and put them in the mail. I will have the same documents sent to your daughter. I cannot promise that she will respond, but I can promise that she will receive them. More than this, I simply cannot do."

So it was true, then. My instincts had been right all along. Sister Una knew where my daughter was. She had always known.

Still, there was to be no verdict. Pontius Pilate had spoken. Not good, not bad. She had washed her hands, certain that her own God would determine the best outcome.

"What time will the documents arrive at the hotel?" I wanted to know.

"Long before you're awake," Sister Una replied, with authority.

But Sister Una was wrong. I was dressed and waiting at the front desk of the Mark Hotel when the first post arrived, at five thirty in the morning.

You Can See the Moon, but the Moon Can't See You

Nancy's party at the Copacabana kicked off the beginning of *Voyager*'s fifth season hiatus, which was our annual four-week break from shooting. Robert had decided to take the boys on a fishing trip, and I, unwilling to let even a day of the precious holiday go by unobserved, called my mother and said, "Hold on to your hat and pack your bag. I'm taking you to Istanbul to visit the Blue Mosque and to stand on a spot overlooking the Bosporus where you can see three continents at once, after which we will slowly sail up the Aegean Sea on a vessel famous for its ostentation, with ports of call at silk-producing factories where young girls slowly go blind in the daily extraction of the silk thread from the reluctant worm, and, finally, we will fly to London to visit your youngest daughter, who is presently with child and wandering around Kensington unchaperoned while her money-mad husband spends his days converting yen into gold bullion. What do you say?"

No pause.

"I say, Kitten Kat girl," Mother sang into the phone, "that *now* you are speaking my lingo!"

And so it was that we found ourselves ensconced in a deluxe cabin aboard the Seabourne Cruise liner, elegant and sleek and chock-full of people with little to do but hurl money at the map. Rich people. Strangely, the cabin had only one bed, but it was so large, so satin sheeted, tasseled, and fringed, that it was borderline vulgar.

"For a sultan?" I asked my mother.

"A sheikh," she responded perfunctorily, "and one of his harem. Maybe his entire harem."

We considered this in silence.

"But this I do know, Kitten," Mother continued, "I do not sleep in beds with my daughters, nor do I walk three abreast, so let's get the world's most expensive rollaway in here and I will sleep on it."

"Absolutely not, Mother," I countered. "You are my mother and you shall have the bed."

"Au contraire," Mother protested. "*You* are the big shot and *you* are paying all the bills, so *you* will sleep in what has to be the most boorish Moorish bed I have ever seen."

That night, we were invited to dine at the captain's table, a tantalizing prospect because Mother and I assumed that the table would be populated with interesting and extremely sophisticated people, some of whom would inevitably end up inviting us to their villa in the south of France and that, despite severe time constraints, we would be compelled out of politeness to accept.

Before we left the cabin, we had a cocktail on the small deck overlooking the Aegean Sea. Two fingers of Jameson with one cube of ice, each. Staring at the Turkish moon, which hung in the sky like a vast and astonishingly beautiful Japanese lantern, Mother and I slowly sipped our drinks.

Suddenly, eyes heavenward, Mother said, "Do you want to know how special you are? You can see the moon, but the moon can't see you."

Then, quite unexpectedly, she asked, "Kitten, what has been the greatest sorrow in your life? Aside from the baby."

I took my time. I deliberated. I understood that she wanted me to go deep, and not to present her with the obvious. She wanted a mysterious response, something that would surprise and perhaps shock her. Something unrelated to the misfortunes that had befallen me, misfortunes that she had witnessed with her own eyes, misfortunes with which she was altogether too familiar.

"Well, you should know, since you alone are responsible for it," I said at last. "Tim Hagan. The only man I ever truly loved. I found him, and then he disappeared, and it's all your doing. If you hadn't set up the meeting in Ireland, I never would have known the difference between great love and mediocre love, and now I have to live with it for the rest of my life."

I watched her, then tipped the rest of my glass into the sea and said, "Tim Hagan is my greatest sorrow. "

Mother looked at me.

"Really?" she asked. "Is that true?"

"As true as the moon that can't see me," I replied, and opened the cabin door to escort my mother to the dining room.

At the captain's table, we were surrounded by a group of very well-dressed, very polished people. I was seated next to the captain, and Mother had been strategically placed at the opposite end of the table, where she immediately engaged the man to her right by telling him about a visit she and Jean Smith had once made to a sheikh's elaborate Bedouin tent and that inside they had been served a silver tureen of raw sheep's eyes, which were considered a great delicacy and therefore could not be rejected by the guest.

"And so, following Jean's example, I just popped one in and downed my tea, and you know what? It wasn't bad!"

Her voice rose to a high pitch and carried across the long table, so that the captain was forced to clink his glass in an effort to draw everyone's attention and make his welcoming toast. This he did with a gracious if slightly resigned manner, whereupon I made the mistake of asking him how he'd begun his nautical career, what had inspired him to go to sea, and what experience would he single out as his most death defying. His face lit up as if I'd suggested a midnight skinny-dip in the ship's pool, and he launched into the story of his early life as a Scandinavian ne'er-do-well with a penchant for uncharted waters and high seas.

About ten minutes into his dissertation, I heard someone yawn so loudly that it almost masqueraded as a guffaw, an unspeakable gaffe at such a time, and at such a table. I looked up sharply, my eyes rapidly traveling the length of the table until they fell, with horror, upon the image of my own mother, sitting back in her chair, wineglass in hand, mouth wide open, yawning not only with sound effects, but with evident abandon. She caught my eye and I mouthed "Mother!" and quickly shook my head, trying all the while not to draw attention to this exchange. Mother stared at me down the long, linen-covered, crystal-appointed, candlelit table and declared, with perfect clarity, "But he's so *boring!*"

To his credit, and that of his dinner companions, the captain pretended to ignore what my mother had said and, turning to the infatuated middle-aged woman on his left, continued his story without a hitch. Meanwhile, my mother had risen from her seat and excused herself from the table and was now skipping hastily through the dining room. I watched in disbelief as she sped through the room, and then, in an instant, I understood the cause of her agitation. As she tripped along, a stream of urine flowed from the hem of her black silk evening pants and trailed onto the polished parquet floor, as vivid as blood. I leaped up from my chair and ran after her, all the way through the labyrinthine corridors of the ship, until we had found the way to our cabin, where I pulled open the door and led Mother inside, saying, "My God, Mother, what happened to you? You've wet your pants! Here, let me help you off with these things. Are you all right?" As I forced my mother to sit and began to take off her pants, I noticed, with a chill, that she was humming to herself.

When I looked up, I saw that my mother was half smiling as she hummed, and when she caught my eye, she patted my head and said, dismissively, "Oh, Kitten, leave me alone, it's nothing! Let's go and see the moon and bring some you-know-what."

With that, my mother pulled open the doors to the deck and stood there, her hands on the rail, looking at the sky. She was wearing only her bra, the Mikimoto strand of pearls my father had given her, and her urine-saturated underpants. She appeared to be entirely unconcerned with both her modesty and her discomfort and showed not a hint of embarrassment. I stood and observed her for a long time, until she turned abruptly and called out, "Kitten Kat! The moon needs a nightcap!"

In London, my little sister greeted us with an extravagant display of emotion. Jenny was eight months pregnant with her first child, living in a foreign land with a husband who worked in finance, and no one near to call her own. She threw her arms around me and cried, "You need to stay and *live* here! London is better than New York! In fact, New York sucks, and all hugely pregnant ex-pats know it."

I kissed her on both cheeks and asked, "What about Mother?"

From across the lobby of the Kensington Royal Garden Hotel, Mother called out, "Fine with me! Call your father! But don't call him collect!"

We did all things English. The Victoria and Albert Museum, high tea at Claridge's, the National Portrait Gallery, fish and chips at Jenny's local, the Churchill Arms, and a play in the West End, which nobody could understand. Mother collected every feather she could find and tucked them in the sleeve of her cashmere cardigan, to be placed on her drawing table when she got home and used as articles in the shadow boxes she loved to make. Strolling toward our hotel one afternoon, Jenny suggested we take the more scenic route through Kensington Park.

"Why would I want to walk through a park? I *live* in a park!" Mother exclaimed.

Two days before we were to leave, I woke early in my hotel room and looked at the clock. Six thirty a.m. Mother and I had adjoining suites, designed like a small apartment. My room was long and elegant and contained a queen-size bed, with steps leading down to Mother's room, which was equally long and rather narrow, with two twin beds against one wall and an armchair, table, and ottoman against the other. She preferred a twin bed, she had said, looking at me sideways. "I went to a convent school," she stated, by way of clarification.

In the gray morning light, I stood on the landing that preceded the steps that led to Mother's room, and from this vantage point I could see everything. Mother was sitting straight-backed on the edge of her bed, fully dressed in her traveling costume, wearing her Burberry raincoat, holding her purse on her lap, and her passport in her right hand. Her suitcase rested on the floor in front of her, packed, zipped, and brightly beribboned. She was humming. I watched as she sat there, looking for all the world like a very young, very well-mannered schoolgirl. Something in her posture broke my heart. She lightly drummed her fingers on her handbag and continued to hum, as if she were simply biding her time.

I walked very quietly down the stairs, and when she acknowledged me, I asked, "Mother, why are you up so early?"

Mother looked at me with big eyes through her magnifying glasses. She blinked.

"Well, we're leaving, and I'm waiting for my daughter to come and say good-bye."

I sat next to her on the small bed.

"Which daughter?" I asked, taking her hand.

Mother smiled and, tapping my forehead with her fingers, said, "You don't fool me. You know the one."

She couldn't find the name; she didn't know the day. The room crystalized into a tiny space with just the two of us in it, barely able to breathe.

"But Mums, we're not leaving today, and Jenny won't be over until later."

I waited then, for the moment of recognition, for the sliding out of one place into another, for a sudden, clear illumination, but instead my mother dropped her hands to her lap and said, a little sadly, "Hmmm. She's a funny one."

"Well, the good news is, we have another three days in London, so let's unpack this suitcase and order breakfast—what do you think, Mums?"

My mother looked at me curiously, as if perhaps I might be teasing her or saying something I didn't mean. She cocked her head, unsmiling, and smoothed the duvet on the bed. I sensed that she was trying to work something out, a new and difficult puzzle, as yet still hidden. I took her hand and lifted it to my lips. "Really, Mummy, we're going to have a wonderful time. I promise."

She looked directly into my eyes. I saw there something I had never seen before, and it unnerved me. My mother was bewildered and terrified. For the first time in our relationship, the earth shifted, and I understood that a chasm, however incipient, had begun to form between us. I somehow understood, looking at her as the day beckoned through the window, that this would be our last adventure. There would still be time to catch my mother's eye, to tease her into confidences, to share the long, family dinners that inevitably ended in wild, irreverent laughter, to watch her hands as they brought life to the piano, the casserole, the canvas. The feather. There would still be time but, as it turned out, not nearly enough.

Reclamation

Four a.m. I walked into the kitchen where the coffee, on an automatic timer, was ready to be poured. It was dark, and very quiet. The house would not come to life for another three hours. As was my habit, I spread out my script on the kitchen counter and looked over the scenes I was to shoot that day. I'd learned the lines the night before, but always brushed up in the morning, particularly when the technobabble was unusually challenging, as it was today. We were going to be spending the entire day in engineering, and despite the fact that Stage 9 was exactly the same size as Stage 8, it somehow felt more cramped to me and more confining. I anticipated a good sixteen hours of shouting, running, climbing up and down the stairs in engineering, because the warp core was misbehaving again, and B'Elanna Torres, our chief of engineering, would be at her most exasperated. God have mercy on me, I mumbled to myself as I packed my script away, put my cup in the sink, and, finally, looked in on Alec, who lay sleeping as teenagers do, as if in a dark, remote cave with velvet-covered walls and a stream of perfumed oxygen filling their lungs with an endless capacity for more sleep.

The drive to Paramount was uneventful and, five years into my *Star Trek* career, I could have done it with one eye closed. I flew down Sunset like a seasoned race-car driver, zipped across Melrose, and was waved through the studio gate by my favorite guard, Doug, who always reserved for me an expression that was equal parts respect and sympathy. The Captain Look, I called it, pulling into the Tank and turning off the ignition. And now, my favorite part of the whole day was upon me.

I had found a shortcut to my trailer, one filled with eerily lit offices and dark alleys, where delivery boys on bicycles sped past me with breakfast orders, and golf carts carrying writers rolled smoothly along. I opened the door to the rear entrance of Stage 8, one few actors knew about, and made my way through the pitch-black sets, the mess hall, the galley, past the captain's quarters, and through a small corridor of tiny offices, all brightly illuminated and busy with the activities that stood outside the filming itself but were nonetheless imperative to it. The assistant sound engineer was labeling mikes, and I thought, Oh, damn, we're going to have to be body miked for engineering, such a to-do with our skintight uniforms. The mike was always strapped to the inside of my narrow thigh and as the day progressed began its inexorable journey to my ankle. I passed a young PA, whose name I could never remember (and thus invariably mumbled something that could be interpreted as any one of a variety of common monikers), carrying sheaves of revisions to deliver to every actor working that day. Finally, as I crossed in front of the bridge, Johnny Craft Service looked up at me from the feast he had laid in preparation for arrival of cast and crew. Johnny knew my habits well. "Coffee, white?" he asked. I nodded, gratefully accepted the Styrofoam cup, and made my way through the heavy doors that led to the alley outside, where my trailer sat, brooding.

Up the two metal steps, through the door (already unlocked by the PA, who also knew my habits), lights switched on, coffee placed on the desk, script pulled from the script bag and placed next to the coffee, open to the first working scene, uh-oh, a tricky line, new to engineering vernacular, I'd have to nail that before going in for rehearsal, otherwise it would continue to nag at me, let's find the key word and work around it—suddenly, the phone rang and I jumped. Who in God's name would be calling me in my trailer at five a.m. on a Tuesday? The kids, I thought, and my heart skipped a beat.

I reached for the receiver and said, "Hello? Lucy?"

There was a slight pause, and then I heard a woman's voice on the other line, a gentle voice, unfamiliar to me.

"Is this Katherine Mulgrew?" the voice asked.

I hesitated, momentarily thrown by the formality of her question, then answered, "Yes, it is, but I'm afraid I'm about to go into work, so what can I do for you?"

Then the woman actually said, "Miss Mulgrew, I think you should sit down."

An invisible hand cut me hard under the knees, and I sat abruptly in the desk chair.

"Miss Mulgrew, this is Anne Lowry from the International Soundex Reunion Registry, and I would like to ask you a few questions. Are you available to answer these questions now or would you prefer it if I called later?"

I breathed in; I breathed out.

"I am available now, of course," I said as a bolt of anxiety was screwed into my spine, because it was time for makeup, and the PA would be knocking any second, any second.

"Please go on," I said, tethering the urgency in my voice, slapping it into submission.

"Miss Mulgrew, is your full name Katherine Kiernan Mulgrew and were you born on April twenty-ninth, 1955, and did you give birth to a baby girl on May third, 1977, at New York University Hospital, and did you give her the birth name of Phoebe Colomba Mulgrew?"

My heart had stopped, I couldn't feel it beating, and all I could provide was the weakest of emanations and I whispered, "Yes, yes, that was me, I gave birth to that child, yes, that's me, that's right, that's her, yes, yes."

The briefest of pauses, during which I understood that my life was about to end, that the truth was near and that it was catastrophic, hopeless. Anne Lowry seemed to catch her breath on the other end, there was a sound of—what? Discomfort? Uncertainty? Disappointment?

Then she spoke clearly and this is what she said: "Katherine Mulgrew, we have received documents from your birth daughter, and it is my pleasure to tell you that we believe we have a match."

Oh, Father in heaven, oh glory be to God, oh forgive me my sins—knock, knock!

"Kate, it's time! Makeup!"

Cupping the receiver, I said in a tone so contained, so utterly foreign to my own, that I knew I had fashioned it to save my life, "Miss Lowry, please hang on for exactly one moment, will you do that for me?"

Knock, knock!

"Yes, of course," Anne Lowry said.

Covering the receiver with my hand, I wrenched open the door, and, grasping the collar of the second AD, Mike DeMeritt, I pulled him to me and whispered with a ferocity unknown to past whisperers, "Now listen to me, Mike, and listen carefully. I need to take this phone call and it may take fifteen minutes, it may take longer, but I am not to be disturbed while this door is closed, do you understand? Tell them to start on someone else, tell them it's urgent, and tell them that if I am disturbed before I open this door myself, I will leave this lot and not come back, and tell them that I mean it. Do you understand?"

Poor Mike DeMeritt, so well intentioned, so professional, so kind, didn't know what to do with himself, and simply muttered, "Yes, Kate, okay. Okay."

I closed the door and locked it, brought the phone to my mouth, and said, "Miss Lowry, forgive the interruption, I'm at work—"

"Yes, Miss Mulgrew," Anne broke in, "we know you're at work, but we felt it was important to share this with you as soon as possible. Do you have a few more minutes?"

"Oh, yes," I assured her, "I've just spoken to production and they told me to take all the time I need."

"Well, then, Miss Mulgrew, if you will just sit tight, I believe your daughter will be calling you in the next few minutes."

"Calling me? Here? She will call me, or I will call her?"

It made no sense, it was senseless, it was time out of time, I was lost, I was found, and Anne said, "Miss Mulgrew, your daughter will call *you*, if you will just be patient and wait at this number."

"I am patient," I replied. "I am very patient. I will wait until she calls. I will wait right here. I should wait, right?"

Anne Lowry, at last, made a sound I understood. It was laughter. And then, this angel whom I would never know, said, "You must wait and I *promise* you that your daughter will call you shortly. Now, please, hang up, so we can facilitate that phone call."

"Thank you, Anne," I whispered. "I'm hanging up now. Good-bye."

"Good-bye."

Good-bye? Anne Lowry said good-bye. Not hang on, not sit tight, not just a minute, but good-bye. Oh, did she know something I didn't know? How would I reach her again? Was this a dream? I stood up, I paced, I listened to the early morning studio sounds that I suddenly loathed beyond expression. I wanted to throw open the door and scream at everyone to go away, get a life, leave me alone! This is a television series, it isn't real, *this* is real! Oh please dear God in heaven, make everyone go away! If Mike DeMeritt knocks one more time, I will slap him in the face, I will slap him so hard and fast he won't know what hit him, oh but that's wrong to think that, wrong and unkind and unjust, but what if—the phone rang! It rang again! I looked at it, I saw it not as a phone but as an angel and in slow motion my hand reached for the receiver. As I brought it to my ear, I noted the dust motes dancing around the venetian blinds hanging in the window, and I put the receiver to my mouth and said, "Hello? This is Kate Mulgrew."

A muffled sound, unintelligible, and then, "Hello, Kate? This is Danielle. Danielle Gaudette."

Her voice. At last. A voice so unexpected, so light, so sweet, from a place I could not recognize. But what name was this? How could this be?

I tightened my resolve, I breathed deeply, and I replied, "Hello, Danielle. My name is Kate Mulgrew, and I believe I am your biological mother."

There was a sharp intake of breath.

"Oh, yes, they told me. They told me I am your birth daughter."

"Who told you?" I asked, would have asked anything, anything, to keep her on the line.

"The people from Soundex, they sent the documents. We filled them out, but my father mailed them."

"Danielle, I don't have any idea what you know or don't know about me, but I'm an actress and I'm at work and pretty soon they're going to start worrying about me and then they're going to come for me, so I want to ask you something right away, before that happens," I explained, and waited for an affirmation.

"Yes?" she asked, so lightly, like a little bird.

I could feel Paramount Studios encroaching, I could hear them all in a heated conclave, *Go get her, We have to start shooting, Enough is enough, Someone knock on that door, Goddammit, we're losing money!*

"Danielle, I know this may sound pushy and maybe it's too soon, but I would like to meet you, if that's possible. Do you think that's possible?"

Silence.

"Well, um, I'll have to ask my parents first," she replied. Her parents.

Whom she loved. She would need their permission.

"Yes, of course, you should ask your parents. Are they there with you? Can I hang on while you ask them?"

I heard a shuffling, muted voices in the background, a brief negotiation. Then that voice, my daughter's voice.

"They said it would be all right," Danielle whispered, probably in an attempt to protect their feelings.

"Oh, how lovely of them, they must be wonderful people to have helped you find me," I asserted, and then, before she had an opportunity to change her mind, or slip away, or ask for another phone call at another time, I asked, "Do you think I could come and see you this weekend? Would that be possible?"

I sensed, now, through the line and far across the country, a slight hardening, a recognition of fear, of a possibility too large to handle, and she again said, "I'll have to ask my parents. Do you want to wait?"

"Yes, yes, of course, I'll hold on, I'll wait," I almost cried and almost but not quite added, I've waited twenty years, what's a few seconds more? Soon she came back, and I could hear in her voice a rising up of feeling, an expectation, and she said, "My parents said that would be all right." I leaped, then, into the sea.

"Well, then, I will come to you this weekend. This Saturday. Is that okay with you? Can you meet me this Saturday?"

"Yes," my daughter replied, "I don't have work this Saturday."

Suddenly, I was struck by an awkward realization, oddly painful to reveal.

"But I don't know where you live, Danielle. Where do you live?"

There was a letting down inside of me, the beginning of the unfolding of twenty years.

"I live in Watertown, but we can meet in Boston. There aren't really any good hotels in Watertown." Watertown, Massachusetts. I understood, in that moment, that there was nothing to do but go to her. Go, and see. My daughter had something to say.

"You could stay at the Charles Hotel in Cambridge, that's easy for me to get to." But she didn't live in Cambridge. She lived in Watertown.

"That's perfect," I responded. "I will meet you in the lobby of the Charles Hotel this Saturday at noon. Is that good?"

My daughter hesitated and then she, too, jumped into the sea.

"Um, yes, that's good. Okay, then, I'll see you Saturday."

"I'll see you Saturday," I repeated. "At noon. In the lobby of the Charles Hotel."

Danielle giggled. It sounded like a giggle, but could have been relief that the phone call was finally coming to an end. "I'll know who you are," she said. "See you then."

My daughter hung up, and I went to work.

*   *   *

The Charles Hotel is designed for people who have money. Not pretentious money, not fast money, but money as old as time itself. The people who stayed at this hotel had attended Harvard, and their children, in turn, had attended Harvard, and their grandchildren, if all went according to plan, would attend Harvard. The colors of the interior of the hotel were blue and white, the rooms were nautically themed, also blue and white. Nothing fancy, nothing suggesting luxury, but all meeting in a place of perfect comfort and serenity. A bowl of apples sat on the foyer table. The beds were low, the pillows ample, the reading lights superb. I had taken a late flight the night before and arrived at Logan Airport at midnight. I had unpacked, taken a bath, and slipped into bed, but not before calling the front desk for a wake-up call as well as setting the alarm clock next to the bed. "It is imperative that you wake me at eight o'clock," I told the operator. The operator assured me that she understood.

I wanted to be left alone, to think, and to reflect. I wanted to dwell on the past, the birth of my daughter, the years that followed, and what exactly it was that had led me here. I thought of David, of his blue-black hair and his beautiful mouth, of Beth riding with me in the taxi to the hospital, of the very kind young nurse who had let me look at my daughter through the nursery window. My daughter, whose name was Danielle, who lived in Watertown, Massachusetts, and whom I would meet in just a few hours. My mind turned over restlessly, like a colicky child. Then, like the vigilant mother she is, Nature switched off her lamp and put me to sleep.

At five forty-five, defeated and anxious, I rose. I had had very little sleep, but was hyperalert. I steadied myself with a long shower, ordered coffee, and slowly dressed. I had chosen the outfit carefully and hoped that when my daughter first laid eyes on me she would feel neither threatened nor dismayed by my appearance. So absurd, this business of thinking I needed to look one way or another. I looked like a reasonably attractive, reasonably prosperous, reasonably nice woman in her midforties, I assured myself as I assessed the reflection in the mirror. I wore a white silk blouse with covered buttons over long cream silk pants. My only concession to glamour was the Tiffany pearls and matching earrings that Richard Cushing had given me many years before, which I wore because in the moment that Richard had presented these jewels to me, his own eyes had sparkled like sapphires, and he had said, "Tell me you'll wear these forever," and I had promised that I would.

At nine a.m. I was in the lobby of the Charles Hotel on a reconnaissance mission. Where could I situate myself so as to maximize my viewing ability? I decided on a brown leather sofa that sat off to the right as one entered through the revolving doors. The concierge was to my left, and running the length of the far wall was the reception desk. The lobby was long and deep, revolving doors stood in the center, and at the opposite end a staircase rose, leading to the bar and restaurant. I saw that the hotel had laid out coffee and muffins on a sideboard. After I had poured my coffee, I resumed my vigil on the brown leather sofa. It was 9:15 a.m. I knew this was preposterous, three hours before the designated meeting time, that waiting in a state of suspension and acute anticipation for 180 minutes made no sense.

And yet, I waited, and I watched, and I learned something about human nature.

I learned that longing has no reason. The mind switches off, almost willfully, and closets itself in another place, away from the moment of waiting. The focus is absolute, ardent.

A young boy rushed through the doors, carrying a skateboard, which he immediately flipped to the ground and, jumping on top of it, skated off through the lobby. This was my daughter.

An old woman with her Latina aide came through the doors at the other end and made their slow journey to the coffee table. The aide was my daughter.

A handsome middle-aged couple descended the center stairs, and I thought, Oh, she must have gone upstairs to look for me, because the woman was my daughter and the man was her father.

Once, an eight-year-old girl skipped up to me and my heart stopped, because, of course, this was at last my daughter, here she was, so young, but then the little girl leaned forward and snatched an apple from the bowl on the coffee table and, glancing at me mischievously, merrily skipped away.

A young couple, good-looking and laughing, came through the center revolving doors and stood there, as if looking for someone. Something hit my solar plexus when I saw the girl's dancing brown eyes, and in the moment that I willed myself to rise, the girl suddenly dashed forward and threw her arms around an older woman who was coming down the stairs.

I sat again, carefully. I smoothed my blouse. I fingered my pearls. I waited. Time ticked by with punitive stealth, and I welcomed the punishment.

At twelve o'clock, the Harvard bells rang out. I looked from one set of revolving doors to the other, frantic that I would somehow miss her, that she would sneak a look at me and run out through the side exit, sure that this had been a mistake, disappearing from my life forever.

And then, I saw her, and I knew. A girl in a light brown sundress, carrying a backpack, walking across Harvard Square. Her magnificent long hair tied back with a blue kerchief. I tried to rise, failed. This girl came through the revolving doors and, finding me immediately, smiled. "Kate?" she asked, from a distance away, in that voice new to me, so light, so sweet. She was unmistakably my daughter. Tall and straight she stood, with a cloud of inky-black curls framing a face that could have been my face, were it not for the deep-brown eyes, her father's eyes, looking at me with something between curiosity and kindness. I rose to my feet and started toward her, and at the same time she moved toward me, and when we met we simply stood there for a moment and looked at each other, she with a fixed smile on her face, me in open awe, and then we embraced and I whispered into her ear, "I believe I am your biological mother" and she whispered back, "Yes, I believe you are."

She took my arm and helped me up the stairs, where we found a quiet table in the bar and ordered drinks. She had chamomile tea; I ordered white wine. She told me she had always known she was adopted, but that the documents from Soundex had only just arrived a few weeks before. In fact, she had just arrived home from college and had asked her father if anything had come for her in the mail. Absentmindedly, he had said, "Oh, yes, I think an envelope did come for you—over there, in that pile." She had found it, filled it out, and her father had offered to put it in the mailbox on his way to work.

"That was good of him," I said, and Danielle looked down at the drink in her hand. "What about your mother?" I asked.

Danielle shook her head and offered a small, wry smile.

"Mom's a little shaky about all this. She's very sensitive to everything, so this, well..." Her voice trailed off, and I finished her thought, saying, "So this, well, it could be extremely unsettling for her. Will she agree to meet me?"

Her face lit up and she answered, "Oh, yes, they'd like to have breakfast with you tomorrow. We'll come here, there's a nice brunch buffet in the restaurant."

Suddenly, I understood that it had been discussed, this meeting, carefully and at length. I imagined the three of them sitting around a kitchen table, a family conclave, negotiating the fine points, alternately spiking into emotion, then dissolving into tears, and, finally, settling uncomfortably into resolution. Danielle had signed the documents, and so had I, and the International Soundex Reunion Registry said we were a match. The rest was now inevitable.

As I studied her, I marveled at how completely she had bridged the genetic gap. She was a beautiful hybrid, this girl with her wild Sephardic hair, her rich-brown eyes, her chiseled Irish bones and delicate Celtic nose, dusted with freckles. She had a wonderful laugh, genuine and infectious. Periodically, she hooted. This, I suspected, was a trait she had developed growing up. No one in my family hooted. In a moment, she could turn from lively to grave, and this, I knew, she had inherited from her biological father. As the afternoon unfolded, I sensed her strength, her dimension, her courage. I was astounded when she told me that she attended the University of Iowa and had taken her junior year abroad in Ireland.

"My family lives in Iowa, and we go to Ireland all the time!" I cried, but she only nodded and said, a little shyly, "How strange."

"I know you must be exhausted," I said, "but there's something I have to ask you."

Danielle looked at me with interest. "Yes?"

"I promised your biological father, David Bernstein, that if this day ever came, and if you were so inclined, that we would call him. Do you think that is something you'd like to do?"

Danielle needed no time to consider.

"Yes," she said decisively, "I would like to do that."

"Let's go to my room, then," I responded. "We'll have privacy up there."

David Bernstein was caught off guard, to say the least. He concealed his surprise beneath a veneer of polite wariness, but when I told him where I was, and with whom, his emotional pulse quickened.

"Danielle Gaudette is her name, she is very lovely, and she would like to say hello to you."

David paused.

"Now?" he asked, incredulous. Twenty years had passed, during which we had never once spoken, and now here it was, that voice that had caused him so much turmoil, so much pain, a voice he was sure he would never hear again, asking if he didn't want to say hello to his biological daughter.

He measured himself, as he always had, and judged it best to lean into the inevitable. "Yes, of course," he said. "I would like to speak to her."

Their conversation was brief, formalities were exchanged, and then, quite unexpectedly, I heard Danielle say, "Well, I could come down to Wilmington sometime and see you, would that be okay?" She laughed softly, then, said good-bye, hung up, and turning to me said, "He sounds nice."

We sat side by side on the blue-and-white bed, and although I longed to take her hand, I demurred and instead looked into her beautiful, sparkling brown eyes and said, "Yes, he was—he was nice when we were young." She looked at me expectantly, and looked suddenly so young, that I added, "Tall, dark, and handsome, too."

The next morning, I watched as their daughter escorted Beverly and Bob Gaudette up the center stairs of the Charles Hotel, where I stood waiting for them on the landing. I went first to Beverly, who pulled me into a fierce embrace and whispered, through tears, "I knew this day would come, I just knew this day would come." Then we separated, and I greeted Danielle's father, Bob, who struck me as steady as a rock, and infinitely kind. They were hungry, so we moved into the restaurant. Bob and Danielle excused themselves to go to the buffet, leaving Beverly and me alone. She was Italian, she told me, working-class Italian.

"Manzelli? Is that Italian enough for you?"

I studied her as only an actress would, stealthily, dissecting every word, every glance, every emotional turn. I was surprised to see that she had multiple piercings in her ears, each one filled with a different-colored jewel. Beverly's green eyes had been carefully and dramatically made up to enhance their beauty, her nose was prominent, and her lips, painted a fuchsia pink, were full and sensual. This was an extremely sensitive woman who wielded great power over her husband and whose children were bound to her by a fierce allegiance. It was very brief, our time alone together, but within those few minutes we were able to get what we needed from each other. I wanted her to approve of my relationship with Danielle and to endorse its future. In turn, she elicited from me the unspoken promise that I would never do anything to take her daughter from her. It is extraordinary what two women, complete strangers to each other, can negotiate over coffee and buttered toast. Within minutes, we had accomplished our respective missions.

Before brunch was over, the Gaudettes had very graciously agreed to my hosting a dinner that evening, to which the entire extended family was invited. We decided on Jimmy's Harborside, a local seafood restaurant, and it was there, at seven in the evening, that the Manzelli family convened to lay eyes on the woman who had, after twenty years, materialized out of nowhere, claiming to be Danielle's birth mother. They all knew who I was, of course, but the reality of my actual presence seemed to fill them all with a kind of amorphous horror. Grandmother Manzelli howled like a wounded animal when I was introduced to her, whereupon Danielle immediately went to her and sat in her lap. Beverly wept, cousin Carly wept, Uncle Frankie wept. Only Danielle's sister Renee and Grandfather Manzelli remained dry eyed and silent. Grandfather Manzelli sat apart, scowling in his seat of honor, regarding the wine before him with open disdain. It was like the wedding at Cana—no sooner had the wine been consumed, but another bottle appeared, as if by magic. When I reproached the waiter for being a little too easy-handed, he said, "It's not me, Miss Mulgrew, it's that guy over there," he said, and pointed to a table in the corner. That "guy" was a top UPN executive, in town on business, and wanted to impress Captain Janeway with his generosity, as well as showing off to his dinner companion our working camaraderie. I went over, thanked him for his kindness, and when he asked what we were celebrating, I replied, without thinking, "I've just met my daughter, after twenty years." The two network executives looked at me as if I had, in fact, beamed myself in from the Delta Quadrant, but, as businessmen so typically and adroitly do, their expressions betrayed nothing.

That evening, when dinner had come to an end and we had all gathered outside to say our good-byes, I took special care to tell Beverly and Bob that they had raised a magnificent girl, smart and funny and brave.

"And talented!" cried Beverly. "She's a wonderful writer!"

Danielle lowered her head and said, softly, "Oh, Ma."

A light rain was falling and there was a fine mist in the air when Danielle and I finally sought each other out to make our farewells. Her parents were already in the car, waiting for her, but they gave me a great gift when they allowed me an opportunity to be alone with my daughter for what might be the last time in a very long time.

I stared into her eyes and said, "I'm afraid I'm shaking. There are so many things I want to tell you, so much I have to say, and so much I want to *hear*, and now there's no more time."

Danielle smiled and responded, "Well, I *do* go to school in Iowa City, you know."

I laughed with her, the sheer coincidence of it, the serendipity. Then I took her hand and said, "You have two half brothers who would love to meet you, whenever you're ready. If you feel—"

Danielle interrupted me, nearly shouting, "Oh, yeah, I want to meet those guys! Maybe I'll come out at the end of the summer."

Breathless, I asked, "You will come? You will?"

And again, she giggled, uncomfortable, and said, "Sure, if I can bring my boyfriend."

I put my hand to her cheek, fresh with the rain, looked into her father's deep-brown and very beautiful eyes and said, "Bring two."

You Can See the Moon

I had yet to unpack from my trip to Boston and was lying on my bed in a gentle stupor, when the phone rang. Production, no doubt, giving me my shooting call for the next day, eager to remind me that my idyll had come to an end and that it was time to get back to work. I picked up the receiver and said sharply, "Yes."

Someone chuckled on the other end and said, "Well, and hello to you, too."

Of all the voices in all the world, his was the one I least expected to hear. I breathed deeply before speaking.

"Tim Hagan," I said, "what a surprise. I haven't heard from you in five years."

"Five years, more or less," Tim countered, although his voice was gentle and his manner reserved.

"Exactly five years," I replied, "so I'm very interested to know what it is you're calling me about. And why."

"I got a phone call from your mother a couple of weeks ago," Tim explained, "in which she made it clear that she thought I should call you."

"Why? What on earth did she say?" I demanded.

"She simply said, 'Tim, this is Joan. Are you married?' And I said, 'No, Joan, I'm not,' to which she replied, 'Well, neither is Katy. You should call her.' And then she hung up."

Oh, Mother, I said to myself, you didn't. Oh, my little mother, you did, didn't you? And I thought of the night under the Turkish moon and her question, so unexpected. What, she had wanted to know, had been my greatest sorrow.

My Greatest Sorrow now spoke, and he said, "Kate, I know it's been a long time, and I'm fully aware that I am culpable and that there can be no excuses for my behavior, but I would very much appreciate it if you'd give me a chance to explain why I behaved the way I did. I want you to understand it from my perspective."

Five years I'd waited, and not a day had passed without my thinking of him. I would squander no more time.

"I'm very busy these days, shooting a series, and my time off is extremely limited, but I'm looking at the advance schedule and I see that I will be released early this Friday."

He said nothing. I allowed the sensation of regret to fill the space between us, and then I made up my mind.

"I'll be in the Bar at the Bel-Air Hotel this Friday at one o'clock," and without giving myself the chance to unbutton the past, I hung up the phone.

I finished my scenes by noon on Friday and went into my trailer to change into an exquisite white linen dress with matching jacket and a broad-brimmed straw hat graced with a black ribbon. I wore Richard Cushing's pearls.

The valet at the Bel-Air jumped to open the car door, and I

walked swiftly inside, where the maître d'hôtel was waiting for me. I could not think why he would be waiting for me, but it was clear, by the way he held himself, that he was.

"Miss Mulgrew," he said, with a sleek formality and just the hint of a smile, "Mr. Hagan has already arrived. He is waiting for you in the Bar."

Without a word, he took my overnight bag from me and opened the door that led directly to the Bar.

I crossed the terra-cotta-tiled path and wondered at my own ability to walk forward, for I knew very well what lay behind that door, and everything I had of grace and courage conspired to bring me to the entrance of that bar where the world was suddenly dark and cool and mysterious, where from the deep recesses of a corner table I half made out the silhouette of a familiar figure, rising out of his seat, unable to maneuver himself from behind the heavy table, and so it was I who moved first, stepping lightly out of the harsh sunlight, closing the door behind me.

Acknowledgments

In the beginning, my dear friend Laura Ross encouraged me to meet her best friend, Christopher Schelling, a literary agent. He urged me to send him some pages of what I might consider memoir-worthy and, when I had done so, asked if he could send those pages to several publishing houses, after which it seemed to take on a life of its own. My deepest thanks to Christopher and Laura.

I interviewed each of my siblings in turn, and they were remarkably helpful. First, I must thank my brother Joe, who is not only a fount of information but has the retention and mind of a world-class historian. His photograph graces the cover of this book. My gratitude to my older brother Tom, my younger brother Sam, and my sister Laura for their support and allegiance. And, finally, I am beholden to my sister Jenny for the important role she has played in this book and for her unconditional love.

Lucila Ledezma came to the beach and took me back in time. She will never know how deeply I value her friendship, her honesty, and her goodness.

My readers were my closest friends. Love does not lie. So my gratitude to Laura Ross, Augusten Burroughs, Saul Rubinek, Samantha Eggar, Kevin Brockman, Mary Kay Norseng, and Vicky Jenkins. Thanks to my dear friends Annie and Kevin Stapleton, who, over the years, have been extraordinarily generous and true. Fittingly, I wrote the last chapters at my best friend's cabin on Lake Champlain and, as always, she met me there. My love and gratitude to Beth Danon.

Many thanks to my manager, Lisa Loosemore, for appreciating and affirming the significance of this undertaking and to my assistant, Sarah Levithan, who organized and steadied me along the way.

I have been very lucky in my team at Little, Brown and knew they were for me the minute I entered Reagan Arthur's office and shook the hands of Nicole Dewey, Heather Fain, and Judy Clain. Reagan Arthur is exactly the kind of editor a first-time writer yearns for—the kind that inspires trust, truth, good taste, and, most important, another book.

A special thanks to Bennett Zier, who recognized the journey and saw to it that I made it back to shore, in time for dinner.

Deep thanks to my sons, Alec and Ian Egan.

Finally, it is impossible to express the size of my gratitude to my daughter, Danielle Gaudette, whose spirit guided this book and who has shown me what grace means.

About the Author

Kate Mulgrew is an American actress noted for her roles as Captain Kathryn Janeway on *Star Trek: Voyager*, Mary Ryan on *Ryan's Hope*, and, most recently, Galina "Red" Reznikov on *Orange Is the New Black*. She has performed in numerous television shows, theater productions, and movies. She is the winner of a Golden Satellite Award, a Saturn Award, and an Obie Award and has been nominated for a Golden Globe and an Emmy.